The Business Analyst's Handbook for Data Mastery: Translating Business Strategy into Powerful Data Solutions

Ikwe Gideon

Published by Ikwe Gideon, 2024.

While every precaution has been taken in the preparation of this book, the publisher assumes no responsibility for errors or omissions, or for damages resulting from the use of the information contained herein.

THE BUSINESS ANALYST'S HANDBOOK FOR DATA MASTERY: TRANSLATING BUSINESS STRATEGY INTO POWERFUL DATA SOLUTIONS

First edition. March 22, 2024.

Copyright © 2024 Ikwe Gideon.

Written by Ikwe Gideon.

Table of Contents

The Business Analyst's Handbook for Data Mastery: Translating Business Strategy into Powerful Data Solutions 1

Business Analysis in Data-Driven Projects 3

Role of a Business Analyst in Data-Centric Projects 6

Data Science Fundamentals 12

Data Analytics Essentials 30

Business Intelligence in Modern Business Analysis 51

Artificial Intelligence Basics 67

Business Analysis Basis-Requirements Elicitation and Analysis 81

Communication and Stakeholder Management 97

Data Modeling and Process Mapping 107

Process Mapping and Optimization 111

Data Governance and Compliance 131

Agile Business Analysis 141

Case Studies in Business Analysis for Data Projects 148

Navigating Data-Driven Project Challenges 171

Summary of Strategy, Techniques and Tools Use by BA in Data Driven Projects 184

Emerging Trends in Business Analysis and Data Technology 199

Further Reading 205

Introduction

The Business Analyst's Handbook for Data Mastery: Translating Business Strategy into Powerful Data Solutions

In an era where data unfurls across the digital expanse with unprecedented velocity, my journey through the terrains of tech, consulting, finance, and telecom over the last two decades has granted me a front-row seat to the monumental impact of data. This evolution has redefined business strategies, sparked innovation, and opened the floodgates to untapped opportunities. Today, as we navigate through this relentless data-driven vortex, the role of the Business Analyst (BA) emerges as a linchpin in the machinery of projects that are anchored in data analytics, data science, business intelligence (BI), and artificial intelligence (AI). It is within this context that "The Business Analyst's Handbook for Data Mastery: Translating Business Strategy into Powerful Data Solutions" was conceived — a tome crafted to empower BAs with the acumen and dexterity required to navigate and excel in these complex domains.

Imagine, by the year 2025, we stand on the brink of a data colossus, with the global digital universe expanding to an astounding 180 zettabytes of data. This forecast, outlined by Reinsel, Gantz, and Rydning (2020), isn't just a mere extrapolation; it serves as a beacon, illuminating the vast seas of opportunity and challenge that sprawl before us in a data-centric world. Such staggering growth underlines the infinite potential for businesses to harness data for strategic decision-making, innovation, and securing a competitive stronghold. Concurrently, it accentuates the critical demand for skilled professionals who can adeptly steer through the intricacies of data analysis, interpretation, and application.

This book is your compass in the tumultuous seas of data, offering a comprehensive arsenal of tools, techniques, and insights needed to unlock the true potential of data analytics, data science, business intelligence, and AI. From the foundational bedrock to the pinnacle of advanced methodologies, this guide aims to serve as a navigational chart for BAs to sail through the dynamic realms of data-driven projects.

What implications does this exponential data growth harbor for businesses and industries? How can enterprises leverage the colossal tide of data to steer strategic decision-making and fuel innovation? What essential skills and knowledge are imperative to thrive in the realm of data analytics, data science, business intelligence, and AI projects?

Poised at this pivotal juncture, "The Business Analyst's Handbook for Data Mastery" embarks on an enlightening voyage of discovery and mastery within the sphere of business analysis for data-driven projects. Together, we will unearth the foundational pillars, cutting-edge techniques, and real-world applications vital for triumph in the dynamic and evolving fields of data analytics, data science, business intelligence, and AI projects.

In the chapters that lie ahead, we traverse the expansive landscape of business analysis in data-driven projects. From an immersive exploration into the cores of data science, data analytics, and AI, to arming BAs with essential strategies for deciphering, analyzing, and transmuting business requirements into actionable blueprints, this book is sculpted to serve as a holistic manual for both aspiring and seasoned BAs.

Drawing from a reservoir of experience and expertise across business analysis, data analytics, and BI, I aim to infuse this guide with insights gleaned from a relentless pursuit of excellence. My odyssey, characterized by strategic data science initiatives and transformative process enhancements, stands as a testament to the formidable power of data when strategically harnessed. Armed with a Master of Science (MS) in Data Science and Analytics, a Bachelor of Science (B.Sc.) in Mathematics/Statistics, and professional certifications from Microsoft, my narrative is one of unwavering dedication to the domain of data analytics.

As we delve deeper into the intricacies of business analysis in data-driven undertakings, we will illuminate the significance of data governance, quality assurance, agile methodologies, and the art of storytelling through data, augmented by real-world case studies. This book transcends being a mere guide; it is a beacon for those poised to embrace the transformative potential of data.

It is with great anticipation that I invite you to journey through this guide, hopeful that it will not only enrich your understanding of the nuances of business analysis in data-driven projects but also inspire a continuum of learning and professional growth in the exhilarating realm of data analytics, BI, and AI.

Business Analysis in Data-Driven Projects

The Evolution of Business Analysis

Business analysis, in its essence, is the systematic exploration, evaluation, and transformation of a business domain. It encompasses the identification of business needs, the determination of solutions to business problems, and the implementation of changes, all to enable organizations to achieve their goals. The evolution of business analysis has been intricately linked to the changing landscape of technological advancements, economic shifts, and the ever-increasing importance of data-driven decision-making.

Earliest Origins:

The earliest origins of business analysis can be traced back to the emergence of commerce and trade in ancient civilizations. The need to assess market trends, forecast demand, and optimize resource allocation laid the foundation for rudimentary forms of business analysis. In ancient Mesopotamia, for instance, clay tablets containing records of transactions and inventory levels served as early indicators of the need for systematic business evaluation. This trend continued through the ages, with the evolution of business analysis closely mirroring the development of human civilization and economic systems.

Major Milestones: Chronological Sequence:

1. Industrial Revolution: The Industrial Revolution marked a significant milestone in the evolution of business analysis. With the proliferation of factories and mass production, businesses faced the challenge of optimizing processes, managing supply chains, and forecasting demand. This led to the emergence of early business analysis techniques focused on operational efficiency and resource allocation.

2. Rise of Management Science: The mid-20th century saw the rise of management science, bringing quantitative analysis and decision-making models into the business realm. Concepts such as operations research and linear programming revolutionized how businesses approached problem-solving and resource optimization.

3. Information Age: The advent of the Information Age brought about a paradigm shift in business analysis. The digitization of data and the emergence of computing technologies enabled businesses to gather, store, and analyze vast amounts of information, paving the way for more sophisticated analytical methods and decision support systems.

4. Integration of Data Analytics and Business Intelligence: The convergence of data analytics and business intelligence in the late 20th and early 21st centuries marked a pivotal moment in the evolution of business analysis. Businesses began leveraging data to gain insights into customer behavior, market trends, and operational performance, driving a shift towards a more data-centric approach to decision-making.

Highlight Cultural or Regional Variations:

The evolution of business analysis has not been uniform across different cultures and regions. While the fundamental principles of business analysis are universal, cultural and regional variations have influenced the specific approaches and methodologies adopted. For example, in some cultures, a more hierarchical approach to decision-making may have shaped the way business analysis is conducted, whereas in other regions, a more collaborative and consensus-driven approach may be prevalent.

Discuss Modern Interpretations or Adaptations:

In the modern era, business analysis has adapted to incorporate data analytics, data science, business intelligence, and AI, reflecting a broader shift towards a data-centric business environment. The integration of advanced analytical techniques, machine learning algorithms, and predictive modeling has empowered business analysts to extract deeper insights from data, enabling organizations to make more informed and strategic decisions.

Address Challenges, Controversies, or Turning Points:

The proliferation of data-driven technologies has presented both opportunities and challenges for business analysis. One of the key turning points has been the need to navigate ethical considerations and data privacy concerns in the era of big data. Additionally, the rapid pace of technological advancement has posed challenges in terms of skill acquisition and talent retention, as organizations seek to equip their business analysts with the necessary expertise to harness the potential of data-driven technologies.

As business analysis continues to evolve, it is imperative for professionals in this field to stay abreast of emerging trends, adapt to technological advancements, and leverage data-driven methodologies to drive organizational success. The journey of business analysis, from its earliest origins to its current state, reflects the dynamic interplay between human ingenuity, technological innovation, and the ever-changing demands of the business landscape.

Defining Business Analysis in a Data-Driven Context

Business analysis, when viewed through the lens of data analytics, data science, business intelligence, and AI, takes on a dimension that is deeply intertwined with the utilization of data to drive strategic decision-making. In this context, business analysis becomes the conduit through which organizations transform raw data into actionable insights, providing the foundation for informed business decisions and strategic planning.

Business analysis in a data-driven context can be defined as the systematic exploration, evaluation, and transformation of data into meaningful insights that drive business strategy, operational improvements, and innovation. It involves the identification of business needs, the interpretation of data patterns, and the communication of insights to stakeholders, enabling organizations to leverage data effectively for decision-making and goal attainment.

Key Elements of Business Analysis in a Data-Driven Context

1. Data Interpretation: At the core of business analysis in a data-driven context lies the ability to interpret and derive meaning from complex datasets. This process involves employing statistical methods, data visualization techniques, and predictive modeling to uncover patterns, trends, and relationships within the data.

2. Stakeholder Engagement: Business analysis in a data-driven context necessitates close collaboration with stakeholders across various functions and levels of the organization. Business analysts must understand the specific information needs of different stakeholders and effectively communicate data-driven insights to support decision-making processes.

3. Strategic Alignment: A critical element of business analysis in a data-driven context is the alignment of data insights with organizational goals and strategies. This entails translating data findings into actionable recommendations that contribute to the achievement of business objectives and competitive advantage.

The Evolution of Business Analysis in a Data-Driven Context

While the historical evolution of business analysis has been intricately linked to technological advancements and economic shifts, the advent of the digital age has propelled business analysis into a data-centric realm. The integration of data analytics, data science, business intelligence, and AI has redefined the role of business analysts, emphasizing the importance of leveraging data as a strategic asset for organizational success.

Business Analysis as a Strategic Imperative in a Data-Driven World

In a data-driven world, business analysis serves as a strategic imperative for organizations seeking to harness the full potential of their data assets. It operates within a broader framework that encompasses the seamless integration of data analytics, data science, business intelligence, and AI, enabling organizations to make data-informed decisions that drive performance, innovation, and growth.

Real-world Applications of Business Analysis in a Data-Driven Context

1. Customer Segmentation: Business analysts leverage data analytics to segment customers based on their purchasing behavior, demographics, and preferences. This enables organizations to tailor marketing strategies, product offerings, and customer experiences to specific segments, driving customer satisfaction and loyalty.

2. Predictive Maintenance: In industrial settings, business analysts utilize predictive modeling to forecast equipment failure and optimize maintenance schedules. This proactive approach reduces downtime, maintenance costs, and enhances operational efficiency.

3. Performance Analytics: Business intelligence tools enable business analysts to track key performance indicators (KPIs) and visualize performance trends across various business functions. This facilitates data-driven decision-making and continuous improvement efforts within the organization.

Dispelling Misconceptions about Business Analysis in a Data-Driven Context

One common misconception is that business analysis in a data-driven context solely revolves around generating reports and dashboards. While reporting is an essential component, the role of business analysis extends far beyond data visualization, encompassing the critical interpretation of data, stakeholder collaboration, and strategic alignment to drive business outcomes.

As organizations continue to navigate the complexities of a data-driven landscape, the role of business analysis will remain pivotal in leveraging data as a strategic asset. The evolving nature of business analysis in the context of data analytics, data science, business intelligence, and AI underscores the need for professionals in this field to cultivate expertise in data interpretation, stakeholder engagement, and strategic alignment, positioning them as key enablers of data-driven decision-making and organizational success.

Role of a Business Analyst in Data-Centric Projects

Responsibilities of a Business Analyst

As businesses increasingly rely on data to drive decision-making processes and gain a competitive edge, the role of a business analyst (BA) has become pivotal in ensuring the success of data-centric projects. BAs act as the bridge between the business and technical domains, playing a multifaceted role in gathering, analyzing, and communicating requirements to align with organizational goals and drive data-driven initiatives forward. In this chapter, we will delve into the key responsibilities of a business analyst in the context of data analytics, data science, business intelligence, and AI projects, exploring the intricacies of their role and the impact they have on project success.

Requirements Elicitation

One of the primary responsibilities of a business analyst in a data-centric project is the gathering and documentation of business requirements. This involves engaging with stakeholders to understand their needs and objectives, translating them into clear and comprehensive requirements that serve as the foundation for the project. BAs utilize various techniques such as interviews, workshops, and document analysis to elicit requirements, ensuring that they are aligned with the strategic direction of the organization and the desired outcomes of the project. By effectively gathering and documenting requirements, BAs set the stage for the successful execution of data projects, providing a clear roadmap for the technical teams to follow.

Data Analysis

In the realm of data-centric projects, BAs are required to leverage their analytical skills to derive insights and recommendations from the data. They work closely with data scientists and analysts to interpret the data, identify patterns, trends, and anomalies, and provide actionable insights that drive informed decision-making. Through data analysis, BAs facilitate the understanding of complex datasets, enabling stakeholders to make strategic and data-driven decisions that positively impact the business. Whether it's uncovering customer behavior patterns, forecasting market trends, or identifying operational inefficiencies, the ability of BAs to analyze and interpret data is instrumental in driving value for the organization.

Stakeholder Management

Effective communication and collaboration with stakeholders are paramount to the success of data-centric projects. BAs serve as the conduit between business stakeholders and technical teams, ensuring that there is a shared understanding of project objectives, requirements, and progress. They facilitate workshops, meetings, and presentations to convey complex technical concepts in business-friendly language, fostering alignment and buy-in from stakeholders. By cultivating strong relationships and managing expectations, BAs mitigate the risk of misalignment and ensure that the project remains on track to deliver value to the business.

Process Improvement

In the pursuit of leveraging data for business advantage, BAs are tasked with identifying opportunities for process optimization and efficiency gains through data-driven insights. They collaborate with business process owners to analyze existing workflows, identify bottlenecks, and recommend improvements that are supported by data. Whether it's streamlining supply chain operations, optimizing customer acquisition processes, or enhancing product development cycles, BAs drive process improvement initiatives that are underpinned by data analysis and business acumen.

Project Coordination

The oversight of the entire project lifecycle falls within the purview of the business analyst. From project inception to delivery, BAs are responsible for orchestrating and coordinating the various activities, resources, and stakeholders involved in the project. They create and maintain project plans, track progress against milestones, and ensure that the project is executed within scope, time, and budget constraints. By exercising strong project management skills, BAs mitigate the risk of project delays, scope creep, and budget overruns, thus contributing to the successful delivery of data-centric projects.

Change Management

As data-driven initiatives often entail organizational change, BAs play a crucial role in assessing the impact of these initiatives and implementing strategies to manage change effectively. They work with stakeholders to understand the implications of adopting new data-driven processes, technologies, and practices, and develop change management plans that mitigate resistance and facilitate smooth transitions. By addressing the human side of change, BAs contribute to the successful adoption and integration of data-driven solutions within the organization, ultimately driving business transformation and growth.

Data Governance

In an era of increasing data privacy concerns and regulatory requirements, BAs are entrusted with ensuring compliance with data governance policies and regulations. They work closely with data stewards, privacy officers, and legal teams to establish and enforce data governance frameworks that safeguard data integrity, privacy, and security. BAs play a critical role in promoting a culture of data governance within the organization, advocating for best practices, and educating stakeholders on the importance of data compliance. By championing data governance, BAs mitigate the risk of data breaches, regulatory non-compliance, and reputational damage, thereby fostering trust and accountability in the organization's data practices.

Skills Required for Success

Core Competencies of a Business Analyst

In order to excel in the dynamic and multifaceted fields of data analytics, data science, business intelligence, and AI, business analysts (BAs) must possess a diverse set of skills and competencies that enable them to navigate complex challenges and drive the success of data-centric projects. This chapter will delve into the essential skills and competencies required for business analysts to thrive in the rapidly evolving landscape of data-driven initiatives, emphasizing the critical role they play in driving value for organizations through their proficiency in analytical thinking, communication and stakeholder engagement, and technical skills and tools.

Analytical and Critical Thinking Skills

In the realm of business analysis for data centric projects, the ability to think analytically and critically is paramount. These skills enable a business analyst to dissect complex datasets, identify patterns, and extract meaningful insights that drive strategic decision-making. Analytical thinking involves the systematic examination of data to discern trends, correlations, and anomalies, while critical thinking entails evaluating the significance and implications of the findings within the context of the business environment.

To refine their analytical skills, business analysts need to be proficient in data manipulation and transformation techniques, statistical analysis, and data visualization tools. They should be adept at using programming languages such as Python or R to conduct advanced data analysis and modeling. Additionally, proficiency in using business intelligence platforms and visualization tools like Tableau or Power BI is essential for presenting insights in a compelling and actionable manner.

Cultivating critical thinking abilities involves honing the capacity to question assumptions, challenge prevailing thought processes, and evaluate the implications of data-driven insights within the broader business context. Business analysts must be able to discern the relevancy and potential impact of their findings on organizational goals, operational efficiency, and competitive positioning. This necessitates a deep understanding of the business domain, industry dynamics, and strategic objectives, enabling the business analyst to contextualize data-driven insights effectively.

In a real-world scenario, the application of analytical and critical thinking skills by a business analyst may involve conducting a thorough analysis of customer purchasing behavior to identify cross-selling opportunities, analyzing operational data to optimize supply chain efficiency, or evaluating market trends to support product development strategies. By leveraging these skills, business analysts play a pivotal role in guiding organizational decision-making processes and driving business performance through data-driven insights.

A key aspect of analytical and critical thinking for business analysts is the ability to formulate hypotheses based on data patterns and then rigorously test them to validate or invalidate assumptions. This iterative process of hypothesis formulation and testing forms the foundation for evidence-based decision-making, enabling organizations to make informed choices guided by empirical evidence rather than conjecture.

With the increasing integration of AI and machine learning in business analytics, the role of analytical and critical thinking extends to the understanding of algorithmic outputs, model validation, and the interpretation of AI-generated insights. Business analysts must possess the acumen to scrutinize and interpret the outputs of machine learning models, ensuring that the generated insights align with business objectives and ethical considerations.

In the landscape of business analysis for data-intensive projects, the cultivation of analytical and critical thinking skills is indispensable. These competencies empower business analysts to navigate complex data environments, extract actionable insights, and influence strategic decision-making, ultimately contributing to organizational success in the era of data-driven business.

Communication and Stakeholder Engagement

Effective communication and stakeholder engagement are fundamental competencies that distinguish exceptional business analysts. BAs operate at the intersection of business and technology, interacting with a diverse range of stakeholders, including business leaders, subject matter experts, data scientists, and IT professionals. Their ability to articulate complex technical concepts in clear and concise language, engage stakeholders in meaningful dialogues, and foster alignment and collaboration across cross-functional teams is instrumental in driving project success. Through active listening, persuasive communication, and diplomatic negotiation, BAs cultivate strong relationships and build consensus, ensuring that project requirements are accurately captured, understood, and endorsed by all parties. By championing effective communication and stakeholder engagement, BAs mitigate the risk of misinterpretation, misalignment, and resistance, thus fostering a shared commitment to project objectives and outcomes.

Technical Skills and Tools

In the rapidly evolving landscape of data analytics, data science, business intelligence, and AI, business analysts must possess a robust foundation of technical skills and familiarity with a diverse array of tools and technologies. Proficiency in data analysis, process modeling, data visualization, and database querying empowers BAs to extract, transform, and analyze data, uncovering actionable insights that drive informed decision-making. Furthermore, their familiarity with tools such as SQL, Python, R, Tableau, Power BI, and other data visualization and analytics platforms equips them to manipulate and visualize data, create interactive dashboards, and communicate insights effectively to stakeholders. As organizations increasingly embrace advanced analytics and AI technologies, BAs are encouraged to upskill in machine learning, predictive modeling, and natural language processing, enabling them to leverage emerging technologies to drive innovation and competitive advantage. Their technical acumen, coupled with a keen understanding of business needs, positions them as catalysts for the successful adoption and integration of data-driven solutions within the organization.

Domain Knowledge

In addition to analytical, communication, and technical competencies, business analysts are expected to possess domain knowledge that pertains to the industry, business functions, and organizational context in which they operate. A deep understanding of industry-specific trends, market dynamics, regulatory requirements, and business processes enables BAs to contextualize data insights, recognize business implications, and tailor solutions that are aligned with the strategic objectives of the organization. Whether it's healthcare, finance, retail, manufacturing, or any other industry vertical, BAs are entrusted with the responsibility of becoming subject matter experts, bridging the gap between data and domain expertise to drive value-driven outcomes. By immersing themselves in the intricacies of the business environment, understanding customer behaviors, and anticipating market shifts, BAs position themselves as trusted advisors who can guide the organization in leveraging data to gain a competitive edge and drive sustainable growth.

Continuous Learning and Adaptability

The dynamic nature of data analytics, data science, business intelligence, and AI necessitates that business analysts embrace a mindset of continuous learning and adaptability. As technology and methodologies evolve, BAs are required to stay abreast of industry trends, best practices, and emerging tools, continuously upskilling to remain relevant and effective in their roles. They demonstrate agility in adapting to new business requirements, technological advancements, and organizational changes, proactively seeking opportunities to enhance their knowledge and skills. By cultivating a growth mindset, embracing innovation, and embracing lifelong learning, BAs position themselves as agile and resilient professionals who are capable of navigating uncertainty and driving meaningful change within the organization.

Navigating the Data-Driven Landscape

In the ever-evolving landscape of data analytics, data science, business intelligence, and AI, the role of business analysts (BAs) in mastering the intricacies of data-driven projects is paramount. This session will delve into the multifaceted responsibilities of BAs, focusing on their pivotal role in understanding business needs and bridging the gap between business objectives and data-driven solutions.

Understanding Business Needs

The foundation of a successful data-driven initiative lies in the thorough understanding of business needs. Business analysts serve as catalysts in this process, leveraging their analytical prowess to help businesses define and refine their objectives in light of available data. This involves a deep dive into the intricacies of the business environment, including market dynamics, customer behaviors, and industry-specific trends. By immersing themselves in the organizational context, BAs gain a holistic understanding of the business landscape, allowing them to identify opportunities and challenges that can be addressed through data-driven insights.

Furthermore, BAs play a pivotal role in aligning data initiatives with strategic business objectives. They collaborate closely with business leaders and stakeholders to discern the key performance indicators (KPIs) and metrics that are instrumental in measuring the success of data-centric projects. By translating business objectives into quantifiable measures, BAs ensure that data-driven solutions are tailored to address the specific needs and priorities of the organization. This alignment of data initiatives with strategic goals not only enhances the relevance and impact of analytical insights but also fosters a culture of data-driven decision-making across the organization.

Bridging the Gap

The translation of business needs into actionable data-driven solutions and insights necessitates the expertise of BAs in bridging the gap between business and technology. This entails the seamless integration of business objectives, data analysis, and technological capabilities to deliver tangible value to the organization. BAs act as intermediaries, facilitating effective communication and collaboration between business stakeholders and data experts, ensuring that the insights derived from data analysis are aligned with the strategic imperatives of the organization.

Moreover, BAs are instrumental in guiding the translation of business requirements into technical specifications for data analytics, data science, business intelligence, and AI projects. They work closely with data scientists, data engineers, and other technical professionals to articulate the business needs in a language that resonates with the technical aspects of the project. This collaborative approach not only ensures that data-driven solutions are tailored to address specific business challenges but also mitigates the risk of misalignment between business objectives and technical implementations.

The proficiency of BAs in bridging the gap between business needs and data-driven solutions is further underscored by their ability to navigate the complexities of data governance, privacy, and ethical considerations. In an era where data privacy and ethical use of data are paramount, BAs assume the responsibility of ensuring that data-driven initiatives adhere to regulatory requirements and ethical standards. By fostering a culture of responsible data use and governance, BAs instill confidence in stakeholders and customers, positioning the organization as a responsible custodian of data assets.

In conclusion, the mastery of business analysis for translating business strategy into powerful data solutions necessitates a comprehensive understanding of business needs and a keen ability to bridge the gap between business objectives and data-driven solutions. Business analysts who embody these core competencies are poised to drive the success of data-centric initiatives, leveraging their proficiency in data-driven insights to shape the future of business through innovation and strategic advantage. As organizations continue to harness the power of data, the role of the business analyst will remain integral to driving value and fostering a culture of data-driven decision-making, positioning them as indispensable assets in the pursuit of organizational excellence and sustainable growth.

Data Science Fundamentals

Introduction to Data Science

Data science has emerged as a critical discipline within the realm of business analysis, playing a pivotal role in driving data-driven projects across various industries. This session serves as an introduction to the fundamental principles, methodologies, and tools that underpin the field of data science, with a specific focus on how business analysts collaborate with data scientists to extract actionable insights from data.

Principles of Data Science

Statistical Analysis:

At the core of data science lies the application of statistical methods to delve into data distributions, relationships, and trends. Through the use of statistical techniques, data scientists are able to uncover patterns and anomalies within datasets, thereby enabling informed decision-making and predictive modeling.

Machine Learning:

A cornerstone of data science, machine learning involves the utilization of algorithms and models to enable systems to learn from data, make predictions, and identify patterns without the need for explicit programming. This capability empowers organizations to leverage historical data to forecast future trends and outcomes, thereby enhancing strategic planning and resource allocation.

Data Visualization:

Visual representations, such as charts, graphs, and dashboards, play a crucial role in conveying complex insights in a comprehensible manner. Data scientists employ visualization tools to communicate findings effectively, enabling stakeholders to grasp the implications of the data and make informed decisions based on the presented information.

Big Data:

The proliferation of large and complex datasets has necessitated the development of specialized frameworks and technologies to handle and analyze such voluminous information efficiently. Distributed computing frameworks, including Hadoop and Spark, have become indispensable tools for data scientists in processing and gaining insights from big data.

Domain Expertise:

Understanding the specific domain or industry context is paramount for data scientists and business analysts alike. It is essential for framing meaningful questions, identifying relevant data sources, and interpreting results accurately within the context of the business environment.

Methodologies in Data Science

CRISP-DM:

The Cross-Industry Standard Process for Data Mining (CRISP-DM) outlines a structured approach comprising six phases: Business Understanding, Data Understanding, Data Preparation, Modeling, Evaluation, and Deployment.

This methodology provides a systematic framework for conducting data science projects, ensuring that each stage is meticulously executed to achieve the desired outcomes.

Agile Data Science:

Adapted from the principles of agile methodologies in software development, agile data science emphasizes iterative and collaborative approaches to project execution. This methodology enables data scientists and business analysts to adapt to changing requirements, incorporate feedback, and deliver incremental value throughout the project lifecycle.

Experimental Design:

Data scientists employ experimental design to formulate and conduct experiments that test hypotheses and uncover causal relationships between variables. This rigorous approach to experimentation is instrumental in validating theories and deriving actionable insights from data.

Tools in Data Science

Programming Languages:

Python and R are widely used programming languages in data science due to their extensive libraries and robust ecosystem of tools and packages. These languages offer a rich set of functionalities for data manipulation, statistical analysis, and machine learning, making them indispensable tools for data scientists.

Data Manipulation:

Tools such as pandas and dplyr are instrumental for data cleaning, transformation, and preprocessing. These libraries provide data scientists with the capability to manipulate and analyze datasets, ensuring that the data is in a suitable format for further analysis and modeling.

Visualization:

Libraries such as matplotlib, seaborn, and ggplot2 offer powerful visualization capabilities, enabling data scientists to create compelling and insightful visual representations of the data. Effective visualization is essential for communicating findings and patterns to stakeholders, facilitating informed decision-making.

Machine Learning Frameworks:

Frameworks such as TensorFlow, PyTorch, and scikit-learn provide data scientists with a suite of tools for building and deploying machine learning models. These frameworks offer a wide array of algorithms and techniques for tasks such as classification, regression, and clustering, empowering data scientists to develop predictive models and algorithms.

Big Data Technologies:

The advent of big data has necessitated the utilization of specialized technologies such as Apache Spark, Hadoop, and Apache Flink. These distributed computing platforms enable data scientists to process and analyze large-scale datasets efficiently, leveraging parallel processing and distributed storage to handle the complexities of big data.

Understanding these fundamentals equips data scientists and business analysts with the knowledge and skills necessary to tackle real-world data challenges effectively. By leveraging the principles, methodologies, and tools of data science, organizations can harness the power of data to drive informed decision-making, gain competitive advantage, and unlock new opportunities for growth and innovation.

In the subsequent chapters of this book, we will delve deeper into the practical applications of data science in the context of business analysis, exploring real-world case studies and best practices for leveraging data science in data analytics, business intelligence, and AI projects. It is within this intersection of data science and business analysis that we find the transformative potential to drive meaningful change and value creation within organizations.

As we embark on this journey into the world of data science for business analysis, we encourage you to embrace the principles and methodologies outlined in this chapter, recognizing the pivotal role that data science plays in shaping the future of data-driven decision-making and strategic business insights.

Data Preprocessing

Data preprocessing is a critical phase in the data science workflow, serving as the foundation for robust and reliable analysis and modeling. In this chapter, we will explore the essential techniques and best practices for cleaning, transforming, and organizing raw data to ensure its suitability for analysis in the context of data analytics, data science, business intelligence, and AI projects.

Importance of Data Preprocessing

Before delving into the specific techniques of data preprocessing, it is essential to understand the significance of this phase in the data science lifecycle. Raw data, often sourced from disparate systems and sources, is seldom in a format that is immediately ready for analysis. Data preprocessing addresses various challenges inherent in raw data, including missing values, inconsistent formats, and disparate scales, ensuring that the data is standardized, consistent, and representative of the underlying phenomena.

Handling Missing Values

Missing values are a common occurrence in real-world datasets, and their presence can significantly impact the validity and reliability of subsequent analyses. Data scientists employ various methods to handle missing values, with two primary approaches being imputation and deletion.

Imputation involves replacing missing values with estimated ones based on statistical measures such as mean, median, or mode. This approach preserves the integrity of the dataset while addressing missing values, albeit with the caveat of potentially introducing bias based on the imputation method chosen.

On the other hand, deletion involves removing instances or features with missing values from the dataset. While this approach ensures the elimination of missing data, it also leads to a reduction in the available data for analysis, potentially impacting the representativeness of the dataset.

Normalization and Scaling

Normalization and scaling techniques are employed to ensure that features within the dataset are comparable and do not unduly influence analyses due to disparate scales or units. Common approaches to normalization include

Min-Max scaling, which rescales features to a specific range, and Z-score normalization, which standardizes features by subtracting the mean and dividing by the standard deviation.

Normalization and scaling are particularly crucial in the context of algorithms sensitive to feature magnitudes, such as distance-based methods or optimization algorithms, where disparate scales can lead to skewed results and biased model performance.

Encoding Categorical Variables

Categorical variables, often denoting qualitative attributes, necessitate encoding into numerical form for compatibility with machine learning algorithms. Common encoding techniques include one-hot encoding and label encoding, each offering distinct advantages based on the nature of the categorical data.

One-hot encoding creates binary columns for each category, allowing for the representation of categorical variables as a series of zeros and ones. This method is particularly useful for nominal categorical variables with no inherent order.

Label encoding, on the other hand, assigns a unique numerical label to each category, thereby transforming categorical variables into ordinal representations. This approach is suitable for ordinal categorical variables where the order of categories holds significance.

Feature Engineering

Feature engineering encompasses the creation of new features or the transformation of existing ones to enhance the performance of machine learning models. This process often involves domain expertise to derive meaningful features that capture underlying patterns and relationships within the data.

Techniques such as polynomial features, interaction terms, and dimensionality reduction through principal component analysis (PCA) are instrumental in enriching the feature space and capturing complex interactions within the data. Feature engineering serves as a creative and iterative process, where the efficacy of engineered features is evaluated through model performance and interpretability.

Data Preprocessing in Practice

The techniques and best practices of data preprocessing outlined in this chapter form the bedrock for effective data analysis, machine learning, and AI model development. As organizations continue to harness the power of data for strategic decision-making and innovation, the role of data preprocessing in ensuring data quality and integrity becomes increasingly paramount.

In the subsequent chapters of this book, we will delve into practical case studies and real-world applications of data preprocessing in the context of data analytics, business intelligence, and AI projects. By understanding and mastering the nuances of data preprocessing, business analysts, data scientists, and professionals across diverse domains can unlock the potential of their data assets, driving actionable insights and transformative outcomes.

As we progress through this exploration of data preprocessing, it is imperative to recognize the indispensable nature of this phase in the data science lifecycle and its pivotal role in enabling organizations to derive value from their data assets. By embracing the principles and best practices of data preprocessing, we pave the way for informed decision-making, predictive modeling, and strategic insights that propel organizations toward sustainable growth and competitive advantage.

Case Study: Data Preprocessing at InfoTech Solutions

Overview

InfoTech Solutions, a hypothetical leading technology firm, embarked on an ambitious project to enhance its data analytics, business intelligence, and AI capabilities. Recognizing the critical importance of data preprocessing in the data science workflow, the company aimed to establish a robust framework for cleaning, transforming, and organizing its vast data repositories. As the Business Analyst (BA) assigned to this project, my role was to oversee the data preprocessing initiative, ensuring the data's suitability for advanced analysis and modeling.

Identifying Stakeholders

- **Data Science Team:** Tasked with the application of machine learning algorithms and predictive modeling.
- **IT Department:** Provided the technical infrastructure and support for data storage, processing, and security.
- **Business Units (BUs):** End-users of the processed data for decision-making, including marketing, sales, and operations departments.
- **Executive Leadership:** Oversaw strategic direction and ensured alignment with organizational objectives.

Tools and Technologies

- **Data Preprocessing and Analysis:** Utilized Python, specifically Pandas and NumPy, for data manipulation, and Scikit-learn for implementing normalization and encoding techniques.
- **Data Visualization:** Tableau for creating intuitive visualizations to identify data inconsistencies and outliers.
- **Cloud Storage:** AWS S3 for secure and scalable data storage solutions.
- **Collaboration and Project Management:** Jira for tracking project tasks and progress.

Implementation Process

Phase 1: Data Collection and Preprocessing

- **Collaboration:** Worked alongside the IT department to aggregate data from various sources, including customer interactions, transaction records, and external databases.
- **Cleaning:** Utilized Python scripts to address missing values through imputation methods, where the mean value substituted missing numeric data, and deletion for instances where data absence was substantial, ensuring minimal bias introduction.

Phase 2: Normalization, Scaling, and Encoding

- **Normalization and Scaling:** Implemented Min-Max scaling for features requiring rescaling to a specific range and Z-score normalization for standardizing features, ensuring comparability across different units and scales.
- **Encoding Categorical Variables:** Applied one-hot encoding for nominal variables and label encoding for ordinal variables to transform qualitative attributes into a machine-readable format.

Phase 3: Feature Engineering

- **Innovation:** Engaged with domain experts within BUs to identify potential new features that could enhance model accuracy.
- **Implementation:** Deployed techniques such as PCA for dimensionality reduction to improve algorithm efficiency and uncover latent patterns in the data.

Outcomes

- **Enhanced Data Quality:** The comprehensive preprocessing approach led to a standardized, consistent dataset ready for advanced analytical processes.
- **Improved Model Performance:** The normalization, scaling, and feature engineering efforts significantly boosted the performance of predictive models, providing more accurate and reliable insights.
- **Streamlined Decision-Making:** Business units benefited from the processed data, utilizing it to drive strategic decisions and achieve operational efficiencies.

Challenges and Solutions

- **Data Quality Assurance:** Continuous monitoring and updating of preprocessing scripts were required to adapt to new data types and sources, ensuring ongoing data integrity.
- **Stakeholder Engagement:** Regular workshops and presentations were conducted to demonstrate the value of preprocessing efforts, fostering a data-driven culture across the organization.

Conclusion

The data preprocessing initiative at InfoTech Solutions exemplifies the transformative impact of systematic data cleaning, normalization, and feature engineering on an organization's analytical capabilities. By establishing a robust framework for preprocessing, InfoTech Solutions unlocked the full potential of its data assets, paving the way for informed strategic decision-making, enhanced predictive modeling, and a competitive advantage in the technology sector. This case study underscores the pivotal role of Business Analysts in guiding data-centric projects, highlighting the essential techniques and best practices for preparing data for the complex world

Exploratory Data Analysis (EDA)

Exploratory Data Analysis (EDA) serves as the foundational stage in understanding the inherent structure and characteristics of the data before embarking on modeling and analysis. This chapter delves into the pivotal role of EDA in unraveling data patterns, relationships, and trends, and elucidates the techniques and methodologies employed in this critical phase of the data analysis process.

Importance of Exploratory Data Analysis (EDA)

EDA represents the essential first step in the data analysis pipeline, enabling practitioners to gain profound insights into the nature of the data and its underlying patterns. By conducting EDA, analysts, data scientists, and business intelligence professionals can comprehend the distribution of variables, identify outliers, discern relationships between features, and detect potential data anomalies that may impact subsequent modeling and analysis. Through

EDA, the stage is set for informed decision-making, hypothesis generation, and the formulation of analytical strategies that are rooted in a comprehensive understanding of the data landscape.

Descriptive Statistics

Descriptive statistics form the bedrock of EDA, providing a succinct summary of the key characteristics and distributions within the data. Common descriptive statistics include measures of central tendency such as the mean, median, and mode, providing insights into the typical or central values of the variables. Additionally, measures of dispersion such as the standard deviation, range, and variance offer a glimpse into the spread or variability of the data points. These statistics enable analysts to grasp the central tendencies, variability, and shape of the data distributions, laying the groundwork for further exploration and analysis.

Data Visualization

Data visualization techniques play a pivotal role in EDA, offering a powerful means to uncover patterns, trends, and relationships within the data. Visual representations such as histograms facilitate the exploration of variable distributions, shedding light on the frequency and spread of values within each variable. Scatter plots, on the other hand, enable the visualization of relationships and correlations between pairs of variables, providing insights into potential associations and trends. Box plots offer a concise portrayal of the distribution and variability of a variable, aiding in the identification of outliers and the comparison of multiple distributions. Through data visualization, complex data structures and interrelationships are distilled into visually interpretable forms, empowering practitioners to discern underlying patterns and anomalies.

Correlation Analysis

Correlation analysis serves as a fundamental technique within EDA, allowing practitioners to unravel the relationships and dependencies between variables. By computing correlation coefficients, such as Pearson's correlation coefficient or Spearman's rank correlation, analysts can quantify the strength and direction of linear associations between pairs of variables. This facilitates the identification of variables that exhibit strong correlations, enabling the prioritization of influential features for subsequent modeling and analysis. Furthermore, correlation analysis unveils potential multicollinearity, guiding the selection of variables for predictive modeling and regression analyses.

Dimensionality Reduction

In the realm of high-dimensional data, dimensionality reduction techniques are instrumental in distilling complex data structures into lower-dimensional representations that preserve the essential patterns and relationships. Principal Component Analysis (PCA) stands as a prominent method for dimensionality reduction, transforming high-dimensional data into a reduced set of orthogonal components that capture the maximum variance within the data. This enables analysts to uncover the intrinsic structure of the data, identify dominant patterns, and visualize the data in a reduced dimensional space. Additionally, t-distributed Stochastic Neighbor Embedding (t-SNE) offers a powerful approach for visualizing high-dimensional data in two or three dimensions, providing intuitive insights into the inherent clusters, similarities, and dissimilarities within the data.

In essence, dimensionality reduction techniques facilitate the compression of data while preserving essential information, thereby enabling practitioners to navigate and comprehend high-dimensional data spaces effectively.

Real-World Applications of EDA

To expound upon the practical significance of EDA, we will delve into real-world applications and case studies that underscore the impact of thorough exploratory data analysis across diverse domains and industries. These case studies will illuminate how EDA has driven actionable insights, informed strategic decision-making, and facilitated the development of robust predictive models in the realms of data analytics, data science, business intelligence, and AI projects.

Case Study: Enhancing Business Insights at Insight360 Inc. Through Exploratory Data Analysis (EDA)

Background

Insight360 Inc., a hypothetical leading data analytics firm, recognized the need to deepen its understanding of vast datasets to improve service offerings and client satisfaction. Embarking on a project to leverage Exploratory Data Analysis (EDA) as a foundational step in their data analysis pipeline, Insight360 aimed to uncover hidden patterns, relationships, and trends within their data, setting the stage for informed decision-making and strategic planning.

Role of the Business Analyst

As the Business Analyst (BA) for this project, I was tasked with orchestrating the EDA initiative, bridging the gap between technical data analysis processes and business objectives. My role involved coordinating with various stakeholders, guiding the EDA process, and ensuring that the insights generated were actionable and aligned with Insight360's strategic goals.

Identification of Stakeholders

- **Data Science Team:** Responsible for conducting EDA, applying statistical models, and generating insights.
- **IT Department:** Provided the necessary infrastructure and data management support.
- **Marketing and Sales Departments:** Beneficiaries of the insights for developing targeted strategies.
- **Executive Leadership:** Relied on the outcomes for strategic decision-making and resource allocation.
- **Clients:** Indirect stakeholders interested in the enhanced analytics service offerings.

Tools and Technologies

- **Data Analysis and Visualization:** Utilized Python with Pandas for data manipulation, Matplotlib, and Seaborn for visualization, providing comprehensive EDA capabilities.
- **Statistical Analysis:** R language, known for its advanced statistical packages, facilitated in-depth descriptive statistics and correlation analysis.
- **Dimensionality Reduction:** Employed scikit-learn for Principal Component Analysis (PCA) and t-SNE to handle high-dimensional datasets effectively.
- **Collaboration Software:** Slack and Asana ensured seamless communication and project management across teams.

Implementation Process

Gather Background Information

In collaboration with the Data Science team, we aggregated internal and client datasets, ensuring they were comprehensive, clean, and organized for analysis. This preparatory work was crucial for a successful EDA process.

Discover Business Objectives

Insight360 aimed to:

- Uncover underlying data patterns to inform product development.
- Identify key customer segments for targeted marketing.
- Enhance predictive modeling for future business trends.

Scope Definition

The EDA project's scope included a thorough investigation of datasets using descriptive statistics, advanced data visualization, correlation analysis, and dimensionality reduction techniques. The project explicitly excluded data modeling and predictive analysis, which were earmarked as subsequent phases post-EDA.

Enterprise Analysis and Requirement Planning

An enterprise analysis revealed the need for a robust, scalable data analytics framework that could handle diverse and large datasets. Requirements were established for data quality, security, and access control, ensuring compliance with data protection regulations.

Investigate the Situation and Identify Improvements

- **Descriptive Statistics:** Provided a foundational understanding of the datasets, highlighting central tendencies, variability, and distribution shapes.
- **Data Visualization:** Utilized histograms, scatter plots, and box plots to visually explore data distributions, relationships, and identify outliers.
- **Correlation Analysis:** Conducted to quantify the strength and direction of relationships between variables, highlighting potential features for further analysis.
- **Dimensionality Reduction:** PCA and t-SNE techniques were applied to complex datasets, revealing intrinsic data structures and simplifying the visualization of high-dimensional data.

Outcomes

- **Enhanced Business Insights:** EDA facilitated a deeper understanding of data characteristics, guiding more informed decision-making and strategic planning.
- **Targeted Marketing Strategies:** Customer segmentation analysis informed the development of personalized marketing campaigns, increasing engagement and ROI.
- **Operational Efficiency:** Inventory and service offerings were optimized based on insights into customer behavior and product performance, significantly improving operational efficiency.

Challenges and Solutions

- **Data Quality Assurance:** Implemented rigorous data preprocessing steps to ensure the high quality and reliability of the datasets analyzed.
- **Stakeholder Engagement:** Regular workshops and presentations were conducted to demonstrate the value of EDA findings, fostering a culture of data-driven decision-making across the organization.

Conclusion

The strategic application of EDA at Insight360 Inc. underscored the critical role of exploratory data analysis in uncovering actionable business insights. By systematically employing descriptive statistics, data visualization, correlation analysis, and dimensionality reduction techniques, the firm was able to navigate complex datasets effectively, laying the groundwork for subsequent modeling and analysis. This case study highlights the indispensable function of the Business Analyst in guiding EDA initiatives, bridging technical processes with strategic business objectives, and ensuring that data analytics efforts translate into tangible business value.

Machine Learning

Fundamentals

Machine learning represents a pivotal area within the realm of data analytics, data science, business intelligence, and AI projects, revolutionizing the landscape of predictive modeling, pattern recognition, and decision-making through the utilization of computational algorithms and statistical techniques. In this chapter, we will delve into the foundational principles and key concepts pertaining to machine learning, elucidating the core components, types, and methodologies that underpin this transformative field.

1. Introduction to Machine Learning

Machine learning, at its essence, entails the development of computational models that can autonomously learn from data, discern patterns, and make predictions or decisions without being explicitly programmed. This paradigm shift from traditional rule-based programming to data-driven learning has engendered a profound transformation in the realms of predictive analysis, classification, clustering, and anomaly detection, empowering organizations to leverage the latent insights within their data for informed decision-making and strategic planning.

2. Types of Machine Learning

a. Supervised Learning

Supervised learning stands as a cornerstone within the domain of machine learning, encompassing the training of models on labeled data to make predictions or decisions. Through the utilization of historical data comprising input features and corresponding output labels, supervised learning algorithms aim to discern the underlying patterns and relationships, enabling the models to generalize and make accurate predictions on new, unseen data. Notable applications of supervised learning include classification tasks, where models categorize input data into predefined classes, and regression tasks, where models predict continuous output values based on input features.

b. Unsupervised Learning

In contrast to supervised learning, unsupervised learning operates on unlabeled data, seeking to unveil hidden patterns, structures, or groupings within the data without explicit guidance. Unsupervised learning algorithms encompass a diverse array of techniques, including clustering, dimensionality reduction, and anomaly detection, enabling practitioners to distill complex data into comprehensible representations and uncover latent insights that may elude human intuition.

c. Semi-Supervised Learning

Semi-supervised learning represents an amalgamation of supervised and unsupervised learning paradigms, where models are trained on a limited amount of labeled data and a vast reservoir of unlabeled data. This hybrid approach leverages the complementary strengths of labeled and unlabeled data, accommodating scenarios where acquiring labeled data may be resource-intensive or impractical. By harnessing the potential within unlabeled data to refine the learned representations and decision boundaries, semi-supervised learning fosters the development of robust models capable of addressing real-world data challenges.

d. Reinforcement Learning

Reinforcement learning embodies a distinctive paradigm within machine learning, where autonomous agents interact with an environment, learn from the consequences of their actions, and adapt their behaviors to maximize cumulative rewards. This dynamic process of trial and error, reinforced by feedback from the environment, underpins the acquisition of optimal decision-making policies in domains such as robotics, game playing, and autonomous systems. By navigating the trade-off between exploration and exploitation, reinforcement learning algorithms engender the development of adaptive, goal-oriented agents capable of navigating complex, uncertain environments.

3. Key Components of Machine Learning

a. Algorithms

At the core of machine learning lie a diverse array of algorithms that encapsulate the computational methodologies for learning patterns, making predictions, and inferring structures from data. From classic algorithms such as linear regression and decision trees to modern techniques including deep learning and ensemble methods, the landscape of machine learning algorithms offers a rich tapestry of tools that cater to diverse data modalities and learning objectives.

b. Model Evaluation

The evaluation of machine learning models stands as a critical facet in assessing their predictive performance, generalization capabilities, and robustness. Through the utilization of metrics such as accuracy, precision, recall, F1-score, and area under the receiver operating characteristic curve (AUC-ROC), practitioners can quantify the efficacy of models in classification tasks, regression tasks, and anomaly detection, thereby guiding the selection of optimal models and tuning of algorithmic parameters.

4. Ethical Considerations in Machine Learning

The pervasive integration of machine learning in diverse domains and industries underscores the imperative of ethical considerations in the development, deployment, and utilization of machine learning models. The potential ramifications of biased data, discriminatory predictions, and unintended consequences necessitate a conscientious approach to algorithmic fairness, transparency, and accountability, ensuring that machine learning systems operate in alignment with ethical principles and societal values.

Predictive Modeling

3.1 Understanding Predictive Modeling

Predictive modeling is a powerful technique that leverages the principles of machine learning to forecast future outcomes based on historical data. It involves the development of statistical models that can make predictions, identify patterns, and discern relationships within the data to facilitate informed decision-making. By synthesizing historical data and discerning underlying patterns, predictive modeling empowers organizations to anticipate future trends, mitigate risks, optimize processes, and capitalize on opportunities, thereby driving strategic insights and competitive advantage.

3.2 Applications of Predictive Modeling

The applications of predictive modeling span a myriad of domains, ranging from finance and marketing to healthcare and manufacturing. In finance, predictive modeling is employed for credit scoring to assess the creditworthiness of borrowers, fraud detection to identify anomalous transactions, and stock price forecasting to make informed investment decisions. In marketing, predictive modeling is utilized for customer segmentation, churn prediction, and personalized recommendation systems, enabling organizations to optimize marketing strategies and enhance customer engagement. In healthcare, predictive modeling supports disease diagnosis, patient prognosis, and healthcare resource allocation, facilitating early intervention and personalized care. Similarly, in manufacturing, predictive modeling is instrumental for predictive maintenance, quality control, and supply chain optimization, fostering operational efficiency and cost reduction.

3.3 Evaluation Metrics for Predictive Modeling

The assessment of predictive model performance is pivotal in gauging the efficacy, generalization capabilities, and robustness of the models. Various evaluation metrics are employed to quantify the predictive accuracy, reliability, and discriminatory power of the models across different domains and tasks.

- Mean Squared Error (MSE): A measure of the average squared difference between the predicted values and the actual values, commonly used in regression tasks to evaluate the predictive accuracy of continuous outcomes.

- R-squared (R^2): A statistical measure that represents the proportion of the variance in the dependent variable that is predictable from the independent variables, offering insights into the goodness of fit of the regression model.

- Area Under the Curve (AUC): A metric utilized in binary classification tasks to assess the discriminatory power of the model, representing the ability to distinguish between positive and negative instances.

- Precision, Recall, and F1-Score: Metrics employed in classification tasks to evaluate the model's performance in identifying true positive, false positive, true negative, and false negative instances, providing insights into the model's precision and recall trade-off.

- Receiver Operating Characteristic (ROC) Curve: A graphical representation of the true positive rate against the false positive rate, offering a visual assessment of the model's discriminatory power across different thresholds.

3.4 Types of Predictive Models

a. Linear Regression

Linear regression represents a fundamental predictive modeling technique for modeling the relationship between a dependent variable and one or more independent variables. It aims to identify the linear relationship between the input features and the continuous outcome variable, enabling the prediction of future values based on historical data patterns.

b. Logistic Regression

Logistic regression is a predictive modeling approach utilized for binary classification tasks, where the model predicts the probability of an event occurring or not occurring. It is widely employed in scenarios such as churn prediction, fraud detection, and risk assessment, where the outcome variable is binary in nature.

c. Decision Trees

Decision trees are tree-like predictive models that recursively partition the data based on the input features, enabling the classification or regression of the data into distinct segments. They are characterized by their interpretability, enabling practitioners to discern the decision-making process and discern the most influential features.

d. Random Forest

Random forest represents an ensemble learning method comprising multiple decision trees, each trained on a subset of the data and features. By aggregating the predictions of individual trees, random forest models enhance predictive accuracy, robustness, and resistance to overfitting, making them well-suited for complex, high-dimensional data.

e. Gradient Boosting Machines (GBM)

Gradient boosting machines entail an iterative ensemble learning approach that sequentially builds a series of weak predictive models, each aimed at minimizing the loss function of the preceding model. By iteratively refining the model predictions based on the residual errors, GBM models excel in capturing complex, non-linear relationships within the data, offering superior predictive performance.

f. Neural Networks

Neural networks, inspired by the structure of the human brain, represent deep learning models capable of learning complex patterns and representations within the data. They are characterized by their hierarchical structure of interconnected nodes, or neurons, and are instrumental in tasks such as image recognition, natural language processing, and time series forecasting.

Case Study: Transformative Analytics at InsightfulData Inc.

Background

InsightfulData Inc., a hypothetical leading data analytics company, embarked on a project to overhaul its predictive modeling capabilities. The initiative aimed to enhance predictive accuracy, streamline operational processes, and deliver tailored solutions to clients across various industries, including finance, healthcare, and e-commerce.

Role of the Business Analyst

As the Business Analyst (BA) on this pivotal project, my role encompassed liaising between the technical team and business stakeholders, defining project scope, and ensuring the analytics solutions developed met our strategic objectives and client needs.

Identification of Stakeholders

- **Executive Team:** Provided strategic oversight and allocated resources for the analytics initiative.
- **Data Science Team:** Comprised of experts in machine learning and data analytics who developed and implemented predictive models.
- **IT Department:** Ensured infrastructure support for high-volume data processing and model deployment.
- **Sales and Marketing Teams:** Utilized analytical insights to refine customer engagement strategies.
- **Clients:** Businesses across sectors relying on our analytics capabilities for data-driven decision-making.

Tools and Technologies

- **Linear and Logistic Regression:** Utilized within Python's SciKit-Learn library, these models provided foundational predictive insights for continuous outcomes and binary classification tasks, respectively.
- **Decision Trees and Random Forest:** Implemented via SciKit-Learn to facilitate both simple and complex classification and regression tasks with enhanced interpretability and accuracy.
- **Gradient Boosting Machines (GBM):** Leveraged through the XGBoost and LightGBM frameworks for superior predictive performance in capturing complex data relationships.
- **Neural Networks:** Deployed using TensorFlow and Keras for deep learning tasks requiring the analysis of unstructured data, such as image and natural language processing.
- **Data Visualization and Reporting:** Tableau and Microsoft Power BI were employed to present model outcomes and insights in an accessible manner to stakeholders.

Implementation Process

a. Project Inception

The initial phase involved gathering requirements from our clients and stakeholders, identifying key predictive tasks that could significantly impact their operations, such as fraud detection, customer churn prediction, and demand forecasting.

b. Model Development and Validation

The Data Science team embarked on developing various predictive models:

- **Linear and Logistic Regression** models were first to be developed, providing baseline performance metrics for tasks like sales forecasting and customer churn prediction.
- **Decision Trees** offered insights into the decision-making process, particularly useful in credit risk assessment.
- **Random Forest** models enhanced accuracy in complex scenarios, such as fraud detection, by aggregating insights from multiple decision trees.
- **Gradient Boosting Machines (GBM)** tackled tasks with intricate data patterns, significantly improving upon baseline models in areas like demand forecasting.
- **Neural Networks** were reserved for high-complexity tasks requiring the analysis of large-scale unstructured data, such as image recognition for security systems and sentiment analysis for market research.

c. Stakeholder Engagement and Feedback

Regular workshops and presentations were organized to demonstrate the models' capabilities, gather feedback, and iteratively refine our solutions to better align with client expectations and market demands.

d. Deployment and Monitoring

Deployed models were integrated into client operations, with continuous monitoring in place to track performance and adapt to changing data landscapes.

Outcomes

- **Enhanced Predictive Accuracy:** The diversified modeling approach led to significant improvements in predictive tasks across client projects.
- **Operational Efficiency:** Streamlined processes and precise forecasting models improved client satisfaction and operational productivity.
- **Strategic Decision-Making:** Clients leveraged our insights to make informed strategic decisions, leading to competitive advantages in their respective markets.

Challenges and Solutions

- **Data Quality and Integration:** Ensuring high-quality, integrated data was paramount. Collaborative efforts with the IT department facilitated the establishment of robust data pipelines and preprocessing mechanisms.
- **Model Interpretability:** To address stakeholder concerns regarding model complexity, particularly with Random Forest and GBM, efforts were made to enhance interpretability through feature importance metrics and visualization techniques.
- **Adapting to Rapid Technological Advances:** The fast-paced evolution of machine learning required ongoing education and training for the Data Science team, ensuring our methodologies remained cutting-edge.

Conclusion

InsightfulData Inc.'s analytics project underscored the transformative potential of applying a comprehensive suite of predictive modeling techniques to business analytics. By strategically leveraging linear regression, logistic regression, decision trees, random forests, GBM, and neural networks, we not only elevated our predictive modeling capabilities but also empowered our clients with deep insights, driving growth and operational excellence. This case study exemplifies the crucial role of Business Analysts in bridging the gap between advanced analytics and practical business applications, highlighting the importance of collaboration, adaptability, and continuous learning in the ever-evolving field of data science.

3.5 Best Practices for Predictive Modeling

a. Data Preprocessing: Prior to building predictive models, it is imperative to preprocess the data by addressing missing values, encoding categorical variables, and standardizing or normalizing the features. This ensures that the data is conducive to model training and enables the models to effectively discern underlying patterns.

b. Feature Selection: The identification of relevant features is pivotal in enhancing the predictive accuracy and interpretability of the models. Through techniques such as feature importance analysis and dimensionality reduction, practitioners can discern the most influential features and refine the model inputs.

c. Model Selection and Evaluation: The selection of appropriate predictive models and the rigorous evaluation of their performance are crucial in identifying the optimal model for the given task. By leveraging cross-validation techniques and robust evaluation metrics, practitioners can ascertain the predictive efficacy and generalization capabilities of the models.

d. Model Interpretability: The interpretability of predictive models is paramount in fostering trust, transparency, and actionable insights. Techniques such as feature importance analysis, partial dependence plots, and model-agnostic interpretability methods enable practitioners to elucidate the decision-making process and discern the model's underlying mechanisms.

Case Study: Enhancing Predictive Analytics at NexusTech Solutions

Overview

NexusTech Solutions, a hypothetical leading technology firm, sought to refine its product recommendation system to improve customer experience and drive sales. Recognizing the potential of advanced predictive modeling, NexusTech embarked on a project to overhaul its analytics capabilities. As a Business Analyst (BA) at NexusTech, I was tasked with managing this project, ensuring that best practices in predictive modeling were adhered to, and aligning the project with strategic business objectives.

Identification of Stakeholders

- **Executive Team:** Provided strategic oversight and allocated resources.
- **Data Science Team:** Led the development and implementation of predictive models.
- **IT Department:** Ensured the technical infrastructure supported data preprocessing and model deployment.
- **Marketing Department:** Utilized insights from the predictive models to tailor customer outreach.
- **Customers:** Benefitted from more personalized product recommendations.

Tools and Technologies

- **Data Preprocessing:** Python libraries such as Pandas for data manipulation and SciKit-Learn for encoding and normalization.
- **Feature Selection:** Tools like XGBoost for feature importance analysis and PCA (Principal Component Analysis) for dimensionality reduction.
- **Model Development and Evaluation:** TensorFlow and SciKit-Learn for building and evaluating a variety of machine learning models.
- **Model Interpretability:** SHAP (SHapley Additive exPlanations) and LIME (Local Interpretable Model-agnostic Explanations) for explaining model predictions.
- **Collaboration and Project Management:** JIRA for project tracking and Slack for team communication.

Implementation Process

Data Preprocessing

The project commenced with a comprehensive data preprocessing phase. Collaborating with the IT department, we ensured all customer interaction and transaction data was collected and cleaned. This stage involved filling missing values, encoding categorical variables, and standardizing features to prepare the dataset for effective model training.

Feature Selection

Working alongside the Data Science team, we employed feature importance analysis using XGBoost and conducted dimensionality reduction with PCA. This process helped identify the most relevant features for predicting customer product preferences, streamlining the inputs for model training.

Model Selection and Evaluation

We explored several predictive models, including decision trees, ensemble methods, and neural networks, to identify the best fit for NexusTech's recommendation system. Utilizing cross-validation and robust evaluation metrics like AUC-ROC and F1 scores, the team rigorously assessed each model's performance and generalization capabilities.

Model Interpretability

Understanding the importance of model transparency, we applied SHAP and LIME techniques to elucidate how the models made predictions. This not only fostered trust among stakeholders but also provided actionable insights for the Marketing Department to refine customer outreach strategies.

Outcomes

- **Enhanced Customer Experience:** The revamped recommendation system offered more accurate and personalized product suggestions, significantly improving customer satisfaction.
- **Increased Sales:** By effectively predicting customer preferences, NexusTech saw a marked increase in sales and customer retention rates.
- **Operational Efficiency:** The streamlined feature set and optimized models enhanced the efficiency of NexusTech's analytics operations.

Challenges and Solutions

- **Data Privacy and Security:** Ensured all data handling processes complied with GDPR and other relevant regulations, maintaining customer trust.
- **Stakeholder Alignment:** Regularly engaged with stakeholders through workshops and presentations to demonstrate the value and functionality of the predictive models, ensuring their support and buy-in.

Conclusion

NexusTech Solutions' journey in enhancing its predictive analytics capabilities exemplifies the strategic application of best practices in predictive modeling. By meticulously preprocessing data, selecting relevant features, evaluating and interpreting models, we not only achieved but exceeded our project objectives. This case study underscores the pivotal role of the Business Analyst in navigating the complexities of predictive modeling projects, bridging the gap between technical execution and strategic business goals, and ultimately driving significant improvements in customer experience and business performance.

3.6 Ethical Considerations in Predictive Modeling

The integration of predictive modeling in diverse domains necessitates a conscientious approach to ethical considerations, transparency, and accountability. The potential ramifications of biased predictions, discriminatory outcomes, and unintended consequences underscore the imperative of ethical safeguards to ensure the responsible development, deployment, and utilization of predictive models. By addressing issues of algorithmic fairness, interpretability, and privacy preservation, practitioners can foster the ethical and equitable application of predictive modeling, aligning with societal values and ethical principles.

Data Analytics Essentials

Introduction to Data Analytics Techniques

Introduction to Data Analytics Techniques

In the rapidly evolving landscape of data analytics, the role of a Business Analyst (BA) is crucial in harnessing the power of data to drive insightful decision-making and strategic planning. This chapter aims to provide BAs with a comprehensive understanding of their responsibilities and the foundational techniques used in data analytics, including descriptive and diagnostic analytics. By delving into these techniques, BAs can gain a deeper appreciation for the significance of data-driven insights in the context of their projects, whether they pertain to Data Science, Business Intelligence, or AI initiatives.

The Importance of Data Analytics for Business Analysts

As a BA, it is imperative to recognize the pivotal role that data analytics plays in shaping business strategies and informing operational decisions. The ability to interpret and derive meaningful insights from data is a skill set that is increasingly in demand, particularly in the realm of business analysis. Data analytics empowers BAs to uncover patterns, trends, and anomalies within the data, thereby enabling them to provide valuable recommendations and support evidence-based decision-making processes.

Foundational Techniques in Data Analytics

Descriptive Analytics:

Descriptive analytics serves as the cornerstone of data analysis, offering a retrospective view of historical data to unveil patterns, trends, and anomalies. By summarizing and visualizing past data, BAs can glean valuable insights into the performance of a business, identify emerging trends, and recognize potential areas for improvement. For instance, consider a scenario where a retail company employs descriptive analytics to analyze sales data over the past year. By leveraging this technique, the company can identify seasonal sales patterns, pinpoint popular products, and ascertain the impact of marketing campaigns on consumer behavior.

Diagnostic Analytics:

Building upon the foundation of descriptive analytics, diagnostic analytics delves deeper into the underlying causes and reasons behind observed trends or anomalies within the data. This technique seeks to unearth the 'why' behind the 'what,' thereby empowering BAs to unravel the root causes of specific business outcomes. For example, a BA working in the healthcare sector may utilize diagnostic analytics to investigate the factors contributing to patient readmission rates. By scrutinizing the data, the BA can uncover correlations between readmissions and various clinical indicators, leading to actionable insights for improving patient care and reducing readmission rates.

Examples and Case Studies:

To illustrate the practical application of descriptive and diagnostic analytics, consider the following case studies:

Case Study 1: Revolutionizing Retail Analytics at GlobalFusion Inc.

Background

GlobalFusion Inc., a hypothetical multinational retail giant, was grappling with uneven sales performance and inventory inefficiencies across its worldwide stores. An initial review indicated discrepancies in customer behavior and product preferences across regions, necessitating a comprehensive analytical approach to unearth actionable insights.

Role of the Business Analyst

As the lead Business Analyst (BA) on this project, my responsibility was to coordinate the efforts between different stakeholders, oversee the data analytics process, and ensure the derived insights effectively informed strategic decisions.

Identification of Stakeholders

- **Corporate Executive Team:** Set the strategic direction and provided the necessary resources.
- **Regional Store Managers:** Offered insights into local market dynamics and implemented region-specific strategies.
- **Marketing Departments:** Utilized analytics to craft personalized marketing and product offerings.
- **Supply Chain Partners:** Adjusted logistical operations based on inventory management improvements.
- **Customers:** The ultimate beneficiaries of optimized product offerings and enhanced shopping experiences.

Tools and Technologies

- **Data Analytics Platform:** Utilized Microsoft Power BI for its comprehensive data integration, reporting, and analytics capabilities.
- **Data Preprocessing Tools:** Employed Python, with libraries like Pandas and NumPy, for cleaning and preparing the dataset for analysis.
- **Collaboration Software:** Microsoft Teams facilitated communication across departments and geographic locations.

Implementation Process

Gather Background Information

In collaboration with data scientists, we aggregated transactional data, customer feedback, and regional sales reports to form a unified dataset for analysis.

Discover Business Objectives

The primary aims were to amplify sales in lagging regions, heighten customer satisfaction through tailored marketing, and refine inventory management for operational efficiency.

Evaluate Options

After considering various analytics solutions, the decision was to enhance our existing Power BI setup with advanced data modeling and machine learning capabilities for deeper consumer insights.

Scope Definition

The project scope encompassed analyzing customer transaction patterns, applying descriptive and diagnostic analytics, and rolling out targeted marketing and inventory strategies based on analytical findings.

Enterprise Analysis and Requirement Planning

Analyzed the retail ecosystem to identify the need for an agile, scalable analytics solution that could rapidly adapt to market trends and customer behavior changes.

Investigate the Situation and Identify Improvements

Descriptive analytics exposed regional variances in product popularity, while diagnostic analytics traced sales performance to factors like economic conditions, seasonal trends, and marketing effectiveness.

Evaluate Improvements and Solutions

Implemented bespoke inventory management tactics and localized marketing campaigns, markedly improving sales metrics and customer engagement in targeted regions.

Outcomes

- **Enhanced Sales Performance:** Tailored strategies led to a significant uptick in sales, particularly in previously underperforming markets.
- **Improved Customer Satisfaction:** Data-driven product offerings and marketing strategies heightened customer engagement and loyalty.
- **Optimized Inventory Management:** Advanced analytics facilitated more accurate stock levels, reducing overheads and bolstering supply chain operations.

Challenges and Solutions

- **Data Quality Assurance:** Established rigorous data cleansing and normalization protocols to ensure high data integrity.
- **Stakeholder Alignment:** Conducted regular briefings and workshops to align stakeholder expectations and foster a data-driven culture across the organization.

Conclusion

Through strategic application of descriptive and diagnostic analytics, GlobalFusion Inc. transformed its retail operations, achieving its objectives of boosting sales, enhancing customer satisfaction, and streamlining inventory management. This case study underscores the critical role of a Business Analyst in navigating complex analytics projects, showcasing the power of data visualization and pattern recognition in driving actionable business insights.

Case Study 2: Advancing Healthcare Analytics at MedCare Health

Background

MedCare Health, a hypothetical leading healthcare provider, faced critical challenges in addressing disparities and optimizing service delivery across its network. Preliminary analysis of patient demographic data and healthcare utilization patterns revealed significant variations in access to and outcomes of healthcare services among different patient cohorts and regions.

Role of the Business Analyst

As the Business Analyst (BA) for this initiative, my primary responsibility was to facilitate the integration of advanced analytics into MedCare Health's operations. This involved coordinating with stakeholders, overseeing the analytics process, and ensuring that insights derived were actionable and aligned with MedCare Health's objectives.

Identification of Stakeholders

- **Healthcare Providers:** Doctors and nurses who required insights to improve patient care.
- **Patients:** The direct beneficiaries of improved healthcare outcomes.
- **Insurance Companies:** Interested in data-driven models to adjust policies and coverage.
- **Government Health Agencies:** Focused on public health outcomes and healthcare equity.
- **Community Organizations:** Advocated for patient groups, particularly in underserved regions.

Tools and Technologies

- **Advanced Analytics Platform:** SAS for healthcare analytics, known for its robust data manipulation and advanced statistical capabilities.
- **Machine Learning Frameworks:** TensorFlow, for developing predictive models based on patient data.
- **Data Visualization Tools:** Tableau, for creating interactive dashboards that present analytics outcomes in an understandable format.
- **Secure Data Storage:** HIPAA-compliant cloud storage solutions for patient data confidentiality and integrity.

Implementation Process

Gather Background Information

Collaborated with IT and clinical data teams to compile comprehensive datasets, including patient demographics, treatment records, and outcome metrics, ensuring compliance with data protection regulations.

Discover Business Objectives

MedCare Health aimed to:

- Enhance the quality of patient care and outcomes.
- Address healthcare disparities affecting treatment effectiveness.
- Allocate healthcare resources more efficiently across its network.

Evaluate Options

After reviewing several analytics and machine learning solutions, the team decided to utilize a combination of SAS for data analysis and TensorFlow for developing predictive models tailored to healthcare applications.

Scope Definition

Defined the project's scope to include the analysis of healthcare utilization and patient outcomes, leveraging both descriptive and diagnostic analytics to inform the development of targeted healthcare programs.

Enterprise Analysis and Requirement Planning

Conducted an enterprise analysis to identify the requirement for a comprehensive analytics framework that could integrate diverse data sources and support real-time predictive modeling.

Investigate the Situation and Identify Improvements

Using descriptive analytics, we identified patterns of healthcare service distribution and areas of under-service. Diagnostic analytics then helped to pinpoint factors contributing to disparities, such as gaps in service availability and variances in patient healthcare-seeking behavior.

Evaluate Improvements and Solutions

Implemented targeted healthcare intervention strategies, including personalized care programs and adjustments in resource allocation to underserved areas, leading to improved healthcare outcomes and reduced treatment disparities.

Outcomes

- **Enhanced Patient Care:** The analytics-driven approach led to significant improvements in treatment outcomes and patient satisfaction.
- **Reduced Healthcare Disparities:** Targeted interventions addressed gaps in care, ensuring equitable access to healthcare services across patient groups.
- **Optimized Resource Allocation:** Data insights allowed for more efficient distribution of healthcare resources, maximizing the impact of MedCare Health's services.

Challenges and Solutions

- **Data Privacy and Security:** Adopted stringent data protection measures and conducted regular audits to safeguard patient information.
- **Continuous Model Refinement:** Established protocols for the ongoing evaluation and adjustment of predictive models to reflect emerging healthcare trends and patient needs.

Conclusion

The integration of healthcare analytics at MedCare Health exemplifies the transformative power of data in improving healthcare delivery and outcomes. By adopting a structured analytical approach, MedCare Health addressed critical challenges, enhancing service delivery and patient care across its network. This case study highlights the pivotal role of Business Analysts in steering healthcare analytics projects, underscoring the importance of leveraging data to drive informed decisions and strategic healthcare initiatives

Data Visualization and Pattern Recognition

Data Visualization and Storytelling

In today's fast-paced business environment, where data analytics, data science, business intelligence, and AI projects play a pivotal role in driving organizational success, the importance of data visualization cannot be overstated. Data visualization serves as a powerful tool for conveying insights and recommendations to stakeholders, enabling effective decision-making and facilitating clear communication across all levels of an organization. In this chapter, we will delve into the critical role of data visualization in data-driven projects and its impact on the work of business analysts.

Data visualization refers to the graphical representation of data and information. It involves using visual elements such as charts, graphs, and dashboards to present complex data in a clear and understandable format. The visual representation of data allows stakeholders to quickly grasp key trends, patterns, and relationships within the data, making it an indispensable tool for business analysts involved in data analytics, data science, business intelligence, and AI projects.

One of the primary benefits of data visualization is its ability to distill large and complex datasets into meaningful and actionable insights. Through the use of visual representations, business analysts can effectively communicate the findings of their analysis to stakeholders, providing them with a clear and intuitive understanding of the underlying data. This, in turn, empowers stakeholders to make informed decisions based on the insights derived from the data visualization, ultimately driving business performance and strategic direction.

In data-driven projects, business analysts often find themselves at the forefront of translating raw data into valuable insights for decision-makers. This is where data visualization plays a crucial role. By presenting data in a visually compelling manner, business analysts can effectively convey the significance of their findings and recommendations to stakeholders who may not have the technical expertise to interpret raw data. This ability to bridge the gap between complex data and non-technical stakeholders is essential in ensuring that data-driven insights are effectively utilized to drive business outcomes.

Furthermore, data visualization enhances the storytelling aspect of data analysis. By crafting compelling narratives through visual representations of data, business analysts can create a compelling and engaging narrative that resonates with stakeholders. This approach not only facilitates a deeper understanding of the data but also fosters a sense of connection and engagement among stakeholders, thereby increasing buy-in and support for data-driven initiatives.

The Role of Business Analysts in Data Visualization:

Business Analysts (BAs) play a critical role in leveraging data visualization techniques to communicate insights and drive informed decision-making within their organizations. By transforming raw data into visually compelling representations, BAs enable stakeholders to grasp complex information more readily and derive actionable intelligence from the data. Through the strategic use of charts, graphs, and dashboards, BAs facilitate the dissemination of key business metrics and performance indicators, empowering stakeholders to make data-driven decisions.

Types of Data Visualization Techniques:

1. Charts and Graphs:

- Bar charts, line graphs, scatter plots, and pie charts are commonly used to represent numerical data and relationships between variables. These visualizations allow BAs to showcase trends, comparisons, and distributions in the data, aiding in the identification of patterns and anomalies.

2. Dashboards:

- Dashboards provide a comprehensive overview of key performance indicators (KPIs) and metrics, consolidating diverse data sources into a unified display. BAs utilize dashboards to present real-time insights, monitor business operations, and track progress towards organizational goals.

3. Geographic Mapping:

- Geographic maps visualize spatial data, enabling BAs to identify regional trends, target specific markets, and analyze the geographical distribution of customers or resources. This visualization technique is particularly valuable for businesses with diverse geographical footprints.

4. Infographics:

- Infographics combine visual elements, such as icons and illustrations, with data to convey complex information in a visually engaging manner. BAs leverage infographics to simplify intricate concepts and make data more accessible to non-technical audiences.

Tools for Data Visualization

In the previous section, we discussed the critical role of data visualization in data-driven projects and its impact on the work of business analysts. Now, we will delve into the specific tools commonly used for data visualization, providing a comprehensive overview of their features and applications. As business analysts seek to harness the power of visual storytelling in their data-driven projects, understanding the capabilities of these tools is essential for creating compelling visual narratives that empower stakeholders to make informed decisions and drive business outcomes.

1. Power BI

Power BI is a powerful business analytics tool developed by Microsoft. It enables users to visualize and share insights from their data, providing interactive dashboards and reports. One of the key strengths of Power BI is its seamless integration with a wide range of data sources, making it a versatile tool for business analysts working with diverse datasets. With its intuitive interface and robust visualization capabilities, Power BI empowers business analysts to create rich, interactive visualizations that convey complex data in a clear and compelling manner. Additionally, Power BI offers advanced features such as natural language queries, AI-powered insights, and real-time data visualization, making it a valuable asset for data-driven projects across various industries.

2. Tableau

Tableau is a leading data visualization tool that excels in helping users gain insights into their data. Its drag-and-drop interface allows for the creation of interactive dashboards and visualizations without the need for extensive coding or technical expertise. Tableau's ability to handle large datasets and its wide array of visualization options make it a popular choice among business analysts. Furthermore, Tableau's seamless integration with numerous data sources and its robust sharing and collaboration features enable business analysts to create impactful visual narratives and effectively communicate data-driven insights to stakeholders. With its emphasis on user-friendly design and powerful analytics capabilities, Tableau is a valuable tool for business analysts seeking to elevate their data visualization efforts.

3. D3.js

D3.js, short for Data-Driven Documents, is a JavaScript library that enables the creation of dynamic, interactive data visualizations in web browsers. While D3.js requires a deeper understanding of programming and web technologies, it offers unparalleled flexibility and customization options for creating bespoke visualizations. Business analysts with a technical background can leverage D3.js to craft highly tailored visual representations of their data, incorporating interactive elements and animation for engaging storytelling. D3.js is particularly well-suited for projects that demand unique and innovative visualizations, allowing business analysts to push the boundaries of data storytelling and create immersive experiences for stakeholders.

4. Python Libraries: Matplotlib, Seaborn, and Plotly

In addition to standalone data visualization tools, business analysts can harness the power of Python libraries such as Matplotlib, Seaborn, and Plotly to create compelling visualizations within the Python ecosystem. Matplotlib is a versatile library for creating static, interactive, and animated visualizations, providing a wide range of plot types and customization options. Seaborn, built on top of Matplotlib, offers a high-level interface for creating aesthetically pleasing statistical graphics. Its focus on concise and informative visualizations makes it a valuable asset for business analysts conducting exploratory data analysis and communicating insights. Plotly, on the other hand, specializes in interactive visualizations and dashboards, enabling business analysts to create dynamic and responsive visual narratives for their data-driven projects. The integration of these Python libraries with data analysis and machine learning workflows further enhances the capabilities of business analysts in leveraging data visualization for impactful storytelling and decision-making.

5. QlikView and Qlik Sense

QlikView and Qlik Sense are powerful data visualization and business intelligence platforms known for their associative data model, which allows users to explore and understand the relationships within their data. These platforms enable business analysts to create interactive and dynamic visualizations that uncover hidden insights and facilitate data discovery. With features such as in-memory data processing, self-service analytics, and collaborative storytelling, QlikView and Qlik Sense empower business analysts to create data-driven narratives that drive meaningful conversations and actions within their organizations. The ability to seamlessly integrate with various data sources and provide real-time data visualizations makes QlikView and Qlik Sense valuable assets for business analysts seeking to harness the full potential of their data for driving business impact.

6. Google Data Studio

Google Data Studio is a free and intuitive data visualization tool that allows business analysts to create dynamic and interactive reports and dashboards. With its seamless integration with Google's suite of data sources, including Google Analytics, Google Ads, and BigQuery, Google Data Studio provides a user-friendly platform for visualizing and sharing insights from diverse datasets. Business analysts can leverage Google Data Studio to create compelling visual narratives, collaborate with stakeholders, and drive data-driven decision-making within their organizations. The platform's customizable and shareable reports enable business analysts to deliver impactful insights that resonate with stakeholders and drive organizational transformation.

7. R Shiny

R Shiny is a web application framework for creating interactive data visualizations and dashboards using the R programming language. Business analysts with expertise in R can utilize Shiny to develop customized and interactive visualizations that facilitate data exploration and storytelling. With its ability to seamlessly integrate R's statistical and data analysis capabilities with interactive web applications, R Shiny empowers business analysts to create engaging and responsive visual narratives that enable stakeholders to interact with and derive insights from the data. The flexibility and extensibility of R Shiny make it a valuable tool for business analysts looking to elevate their data visualization efforts and deliver impactful data-driven stories.

Techniques for Compelling Data Visualizations

The ability to create compelling and informative data visualizations is a critical skill for business analysts working on data-driven projects. In this chapter, we will delve into techniques for creating engaging and informative data visualizations, including best practices for design, storytelling, and incorporating data narratives. By mastering these techniques, business analysts can effectively communicate insights and drive meaningful actions within their organizations.

1. Understanding the Audience

Before embarking on the creation of data visualizations, it is essential for business analysts to understand their audience. Different stakeholders may have varying levels of familiarity with the data and its context, as well as differing priorities and decision-making needs. By understanding the audience's knowledge level and information needs, business analysts can tailor their visualizations to effectively convey the most relevant insights and drive impactful actions.

2. Storytelling Through Visuals

Effective data visualizations go beyond presenting numbers and statistics; they tell a story that engages and informs the audience. Business analysts should approach data visualization as a form of visual storytelling, using the narrative structure to guide the audience through the data and its implications. By incorporating elements of storytelling, such as setting the context, introducing conflict or challenges, and providing resolution or actionable insights, business analysts can create visual narratives that resonate with stakeholders and drive meaningful decision-making.

3. Data Narratives and Annotations

Incorporating data narratives and annotations within visualizations can provide additional context and guidance to the audience. Business analysts can use annotations to highlight key insights, trends, or anomalies within the data, guiding the audience's attention to the most critical aspects of the visualization. Additionally, integrating data narratives – concise explanations or interpretations of the data – can help stakeholders understand the significance of the insights presented and make informed decisions based on the visualized information.

4. Design Principles for Effective Visualizations

The design of data visualizations plays a crucial role in their effectiveness. Business analysts should adhere to design principles that promote clarity, simplicity, and visual appeal. This includes considerations such as choosing appropriate chart types for the data, using color effectively to convey information and highlight key points, and ensuring the overall layout and composition of the visualization is intuitive and easy to comprehend. By applying sound design principles, business analysts can create visualizations that are both aesthetically pleasing and informative.

5. Interactive and Dynamic Elements

Interactive and dynamic elements can enhance the engagement and impact of data visualizations. Business analysts can leverage the capabilities of visualization tools such as Power BI, Tableau, and D3.js to create interactive dashboards, allowing stakeholders to explore the data, drill down into specific details, and gain deeper insights. By incorporating interactive elements, business analysts can empower stakeholders to interact with the data, fostering a deeper understanding and facilitating informed decision-making.

6. Visual Hierarchy and Emphasis

Visual hierarchy is a fundamental principle in designing effective data visualizations. Business analysts should carefully consider the visual hierarchy within their visualizations, using techniques such as varying the size, color, and positioning of elements to guide the audience's attention and emphasize key insights. By establishing a clear visual hierarchy, business analysts can ensure that stakeholders focus on the most critical aspects of the data and derive meaningful insights from the visualized information.

7. Iterative Design and Feedback

Creating compelling data visualizations often requires an iterative design process. Business analysts should be open to refining and improving their visualizations based on feedback from stakeholders. By seeking input from the audience and incorporating their perspectives, business analysts can ensure that the visualizations effectively address the audience's information needs and drive meaningful actions. Iterative design and feedback loops are essential for refining visual narratives and maximizing their impact.

In conclusion, mastering the techniques for creating compelling data visualizations is a key aspect of the business analyst's toolkit. By understanding the audience, embracing storytelling, incorporating data narratives and annotations, adhering to design principles, leveraging interactive elements, establishing visual hierarchy, and embracing iterative design, business analysts can create visual narratives that effectively communicate insights and drive impactful actions within their organizations. Effective data visualizations empower stakeholders to make informed decisions and drive business outcomes through the power of visual storytelling.

Pattern Recognition

Pattern recognition involves identifying regularities or patterns within data. It's crucial in data analytics for uncovering meaningful insights and predicting future trends. Machine learning algorithms often utilize pattern recognition techniques to classify data or make predictions based on observed patterns.

The Role of Business Analysts in Pattern Recognition:

BAs collaborate with data scientists and machine learning experts to apply pattern recognition techniques in identifying trends, anomalies, and predictive patterns within the data. By understanding the business context and the specific objectives of pattern recognition, BAs contribute to the formulation of relevant hypotheses and the selection of appropriate algorithms for pattern identification and prediction.

Types of Pattern Recognition Techniques:

1. Supervised Learning:

- In supervised learning, BAs work with data scientists to train machine learning models using labeled data, enabling the models to recognize patterns and make predictions based on known outcomes. This technique is valuable in scenarios where historical data can be used to predict future trends or behaviors.

2. Unsupervised Learning:

- Unsupervised learning techniques, such as clustering and association analysis, allow BAs and data scientists to identify hidden patterns and groupings within the data without predefined labels. These techniques can reveal unexpected insights and relationships, guiding decision-making processes.

3. Time-series Analysis:

- Time-series analysis involves identifying patterns and trends in sequential data, such as stock prices, sensor readings, or seasonal sales data. BAs collaborate with data experts to apply statistical methods and machine learning algorithms to extract meaningful patterns from time-varying data.

Best Practices in Pattern Recognition:

To effectively harness pattern recognition techniques, BAs should adhere to best practices that optimize the accuracy and relevance of pattern identification and prediction:

- Collaborate with Data Experts:

- Partner with data scientists, machine learning engineers, and statisticians to leverage their expertise in selecting and applying appropriate pattern recognition algorithms.

- Validate Patterns and Predictions:

- Validate identified patterns and predictive models using rigorous testing and validation techniques to ensure their reliability and generalizability.

- Incorporate Business Context:

- Integrate business domain knowledge and contextual insights into the pattern recognition process, aligning the identified patterns with the strategic objectives and operational needs of the organization.

- Continuously Refine Models:

- Iteratively refine pattern recognition models based on feedback, new data, and evolving business requirements to ensure their ongoing relevance and accuracy.

Examples of Data Visualization and Pattern Recognition in Business Analytics:

To illustrate the practical application of data visualization and pattern recognition in business analytics, consider the following examples:

Case Study: Leveraging Data Visualization to Enhance Business Decisions at Apex Solutions

Overview

Apex Solutions, a hypothetical multinational corporation with a diverse product portfolio, faced challenges in synthesizing vast amounts of sales data to inform decision-making processes. Recognizing the potential of data visualization in simplifying complex datasets, the company embarked on a project to implement a comprehensive sales performance dashboard. This case study explores the practical application of data visualization in business analytics, focusing on the development and impact of the sales performance dashboard.

Role of the Business Analyst

As the Business Analyst (BA) for Apex Solutions, I was tasked with bridging the gap between the sales team's informational needs and the technical capabilities offered by modern data visualization tools. My responsibilities included defining the project scope, selecting the appropriate data visualization tool, overseeing the dashboard's development, and ensuring its alignment with business objectives.

Identification of Stakeholders

- **Sales Team:** Primary users of the dashboard, requiring access to real-time sales data to drive strategic sales initiatives.
- **Marketing Department:** Interested in correlating marketing efforts with sales outcomes to gauge campaign effectiveness.
- **Executive Leadership:** Sought a high-level overview of sales performance to guide corporate strategy.
- **IT Department:** Provided technical support in integrating the dashboard with existing data systems and ensuring data security.

Tools and Technologies Selected

After evaluating several data visualization platforms, Tableau was chosen for its robust data integration capabilities, interactive visualization features, and user-friendly interface. Tableau's ability to connect directly to Apex Solution's sales databases and provide real-time analytics made it an ideal choice for this project.

Implementation Process

Defining Dashboard Requirements

Working collaboratively with the sales and marketing teams, I gathered requirements for the dashboard, including key performance indicators (KPIs), desired visualizations, and access levels for various user groups.

Dashboard Development

Leveraging Tableau, I developed a comprehensive sales performance dashboard that provided:

- **Interactive Charts and Graphs:** Representing sales data across different product categories, geographic regions, and time frames.
- **Trend Identification Features:** Allowing users to spot sales trends and patterns easily.
- **Marketing Campaign Analysis:** Enabling the marketing team to correlate sales data with specific marketing activities.

Training and Deployment

I organized training sessions for the sales team and other stakeholders to ensure they were proficient in using the dashboard. Following successful training, the dashboard was deployed across the organization.

Outcomes

- **Enhanced Decision-Making:** The sales performance dashboard empowered the sales team to make data-driven decisions, optimizing sales strategies and improving overall performance.
- **Increased Marketing ROI:** Marketing campaigns were refined based on insights gained from the

dashboard, leading to increased return on investment.
- **Strategic Business Insights:** Executive leadership gained a clear understanding of sales dynamics, informing strategic planning and resource allocation.

Challenges and Solutions

- **Data Integration:** Initially, integrating real-time data from various sources into Tableau was challenging. This was addressed by working closely with the IT department to streamline data pipelines.
- **User Adoption:** Encouraging widespread adoption of the dashboard required demonstrating its value through case studies and success stories, highlighting how it could simplify complex data analysis and enhance decision-making.

Conclusion

The implementation of a sales performance dashboard at Apex Solutions exemplifies the transformative power of data visualization in business analytics. By converting complex sales data into accessible and actionable insights, the dashboard has become an invaluable tool for the sales team, marketing department, and executive leadership. This case study underscores the critical role of the Business Analyst in facilitating data-driven decision-making processes, showcasing the practical application of data visualization in achieving business objectives.

Case Study: Leveraging Data Visualization to Transform Business Analytics at Horizon Enterprises

Overview

Horizon Enterprises, a hypothetical mid-sized consumer goods company, recognized the potential of data to drive strategic decisions but faced challenges in interpreting complex datasets and translating them into actionable insights. The company embarked on an initiative to harness the power of data visualization in its business analytics, aiming to enhance decision-making processes across various departments.

Project Genesis

As the Business Analyst spearheading this initiative, I identified the need for a more intuitive approach to data analysis that could democratize data access and understanding across Horizon Enterprises. The goal was to move beyond traditional spreadsheets and reports, making data more accessible and actionable for decision-makers at all levels.

Stakeholder Identification

- **Executive Team:** Provided strategic direction and funding.
- **Sales and Marketing Teams:** Primary users of the sales performance dashboards.
- **IT Department:** Ensured technical feasibility and data security.
- **Data Science Team:** Assisted in data preparation and establishing metrics.
- **External Design Consultants:** Offered expertise in UI/UX design for dashboard development.

Practical Application of Data Visualization

Example : Sales Performance Dashboard

The first major deliverable of the project was the development of a comprehensive Sales Performance Dashboard. This tool was designed to offer an at-a-glance view of sales metrics across different dimensions, including product categories, geographic regions, and time frames.

Implementation Steps

1. **Data Aggregation:** Collaborated with the IT and Data Science teams to aggregate sales data from various sources, ensuring accuracy and completeness.
2. **Dashboard Design:** Worked with external design consultants to create a user-friendly interface that presented data through interactive charts and graphs.
3. **Metric Definition:** Defined key performance indicators (KPIs) with the sales and marketing teams to ensure the dashboard focused on the most impactful data.
4. **Tool Selection:** Chose Tableau as the BI tool for its robust data visualization capabilities and interactive features.
5. **Training and Rollout:** Conducted workshops for the sales and marketing teams, highlighting how to interpret the dashboard and make data-driven decisions.

Outcomes

- **Trend Identification:** The dashboard enabled the sales team to quickly identify sales trends, adjusting strategies to capitalize on opportunities or address downturns.
- **Marketing Impact Assessment:** By overlaying marketing campaign data with sales performance, the marketing team could directly measure campaign effectiveness.
- **Informed Decision-Making:** The visual representation of data facilitated evidence-based decisions, leading to optimized sales strategies and improved performance.

Additional Applications

Building on the success of the Sales Performance Dashboard, Horizon Enterprises expanded its data visualization initiatives to include:

- **Inventory Optimization Dashboards:** Enabled the supply chain team to maintain optimal stock levels by visualizing inventory turnover rates and identifying potential shortages or overstocks.
- **Customer Satisfaction Insights:** Utilized customer survey data to visualize satisfaction trends, helping the customer service team improve engagement and resolve issues proactively.

Challenges Overcome

- **Data Silos:** Initially, disparate data sources posed integration challenges. A unified data warehouse solution was implemented to centralize data.
- **User Adoption:** Some stakeholders were hesitant to rely on the new tool. Ongoing training and demonstration of quick wins helped in gaining buy-in.

Conclusion

The initiative to integrate data visualization into business analytics at Horizon Enterprises marked a significant turning point in how the company leveraged data for strategic decision-making. By making complex datasets understandable and actionable, data visualization empowered teams across the organization to uncover insights, identify trends, and make informed decisions that drove business success. As a Business Analyst, guiding this transformation not only highlighted the value of visual data in analytics but also underscored the importance of collaboration, continuous learning, and user-centric design in driving organizational change.

Case Study: Enhancing Customer Engagement at Optima Retail Group Through Data Visualization and Pattern Recognition

Overview

Optima Retail Group, a hypothetical multinational retail corporation, recognized the need to refine its marketing strategies to better meet the diverse needs of its customer base. By leveraging data visualization and pattern recognition for customer segmentation analysis, Optima aimed to categorize its customers into distinct groups, facilitating more personalized marketing efforts. As a Business Analyst (BA) at Optima, I spearheaded this initiative, guiding the process from data collection to the implementation of targeted strategies.

Identifying Stakeholders

- Marketing Department: Key beneficiaries of the customer segmentation, requiring detailed insights to tailor marketing campaigns.
- Data Science Team: Tasked with applying unsupervised learning techniques for customer segmentation.
- IT Department: Provided the necessary technical support and data infrastructure.
- Customer Service Team: Utilized segmentation insights to enhance customer interactions and service offerings.
- Executive Leadership: Overseen the strategic direction and approved resource allocation for the initiative.

Tools and Technologies

- Data Preprocessing and Analysis: Python, specifically libraries like Pandas for data manipulation and SciKit-Learn for implementing unsupervised learning algorithms such as k-means clustering.
- Data Visualization: Tableau for creating interactive charts and visualizations that clearly depict customer segments and their characteristics.
- Data Storage: AWS cloud services for secure and scalable data storage solutions.
- Collaboration and Project Management: Trello for project tracking and Microsoft Teams for stakeholder communication.

Implementation Process

Step 1: Data Collection and Preprocessing

Collaborated with the IT and Data Science teams to aggregate customer data from various sources, including transaction records, customer feedback, and online behavior metrics. We focused on cleaning the data, handling missing values, normalizing numerical data, and encoding categorical variables, ensuring it was primed for analysis.

Step 2: Application of Unsupervised Learning Techniques

Working closely with the Data Science team, we applied k-means clustering to the preprocessed dataset. The algorithm parsed through the data, unveiling natural groupings based on purchasing behavior, demographic attributes, and other relevant characteristics without predefined labels.

Step 3: Data Visualization

Utilizing Tableau, I developed a series of visualizations, including scatter plots and heat maps, to represent the identified customer segments. These visual tools enabled us to present the segmentation results in an easily digestible format, facilitating pattern recognition among different customer groups.

Step 4: Insight Generation and Strategy Development

The insights derived from the segmentation analysis informed the Marketing Department's development of targeted campaigns. For instance, we identified a "Loyal Luxury" segment, characterized by high spending and frequent purchases, and tailored premium service offerings to this group.

Step 5: Implementation and Monitoring

After launching the targeted marketing campaigns, we closely monitored their performance using KPIs such as customer retention rates and segment-specific average order values. This monitoring allowed us to assess the effectiveness of our segmentation strategy and make necessary adjustments.

Benefits:

- Enhanced personalization in marketing strategies led to improved customer engagement and satisfaction.
- Increased efficiency in resource allocation for marketing efforts, focusing on the most profitable customer segments.

Challenges:

- Ensuring the ongoing accuracy and quality of customer data required continuous efforts in data management and cleansing.
- The dynamic nature of customer behavior necessitated regular updates to the segmentation model to reflect changing patterns and preferences.

Conclusion

The customer segmentation project at Optima Retail Group illustrates the powerful synergy between data visualization, pattern recognition, and business analytics. By transforming complex datasets into actionable insights, we enabled Optima to engage its customers more effectively, driving satisfaction and loyalty. This case study underscores the importance of a structured analytical approach, stakeholder collaboration, and the judicious use of technology in harnessing data's full potential to achieve business objectives.

Statistical Analysis in Data Analytics

Statistical analysis plays a pivotal role in the realm of data analytics, providing the means to extract meaningful insights, identify trends, and make informed decisions based on empirical evidence. In this session, we will delve into the multifaceted landscape of statistical analysis, exploring its fundamental principles, diverse applications, and its indispensable role in driving business analytics, data science, business intelligence, and AI projects.

Understanding Statistical Analysis:

At its core, statistical analysis encompasses the application of statistical methods to analyze and interpret data, unraveling the underlying patterns, relationships, and distributions within datasets. The fundamental objective of statistical analysis is to derive actionable intelligence from data, enabling organizations to make strategic decisions, mitigate risks, and capitalize on opportunities.

Statistical Methods and Techniques:

Statistical analysis encompasses a broad spectrum of methods and techniques, each tailored to address specific analytical objectives and data characteristics. Some of the key statistical methods integral to data analytics include:

1. Descriptive Statistics:

- Descriptive statistics provide a comprehensive summary of the key features of a dataset, offering insights into central tendencies, variability, and distributions of the data. Measures such as mean, median, mode, variance, and standard deviation are employed to characterize and contextualize the data.

2. Inferential Statistics:

- Inferential statistics facilitates the generalization of insights derived from a sample to the broader population, enabling analysts to draw conclusions, make predictions, and test hypotheses. Techniques like hypothesis testing, confidence intervals, and regression analysis are instrumental in inferential statistics.

3. Regression Analysis:

- Regression analysis elucidates the relationships between variables within the data, enabling analysts to model and predict outcomes based on the interplay of independent and dependent variables. Linear regression, logistic regression, and polynomial regression are prominent techniques within this domain.

4. Hypothesis Testing:

- Hypothesis testing enables analysts to make inferences about the characteristics of a population based on sample data, allowing for the validation or rejection of hypotheses. It serves as a critical tool in substantiating the significance of observations and drawing informed conclusions.

5. Clustering and Classification:

- Clustering techniques, such as K-means clustering and hierarchical clustering, categorize data points into distinct clusters based on similarity measures. Classification methods, including decision trees and support vector machines, assign categorical labels to data instances based on their attributes.

Role of Statistical Analysis

Statistical analysis serves as the bedrock of data analytics, underpinning the process of data exploration, pattern recognition, and predictive modeling. Its contributions to the field of business analytics, data science, business intelligence, and AI projects are manifold:

1. Uncovering Patterns and Trends:

- Statistical analysis enables analysts to discern hidden patterns, trends, and anomalies within the data, revealing actionable insights that drive strategic decision-making and business optimization.

2. Predictive Modeling and Forecasting:

- Through the application of statistical models and techniques, analysts can develop predictive models that forecast future trends, behaviors, and outcomes, providing organizations with the foresight to anticipate market dynamics and consumer preferences.

3. Risk Mitigation and Decision Support:

- Statistical analysis empowers organizations to assess risks, validate assumptions, and make evidence-based decisions, fostering a data-driven culture that prioritizes empirical evidence over conjecture.

4. Performance Evaluation and Optimization:

- Statistical analysis facilitates the evaluation of business performance, enabling organizations to measure the efficacy of strategies, identify areas for improvement, and optimize operational processes.

Statistical Analysis in Business Analysis:

In the context of business analysis, statistical analysis is instrumental in elucidating the quantitative dimensions of business operations, market dynamics, and consumer behavior. Business analysts leverage statistical methods to derive actionable insights and shape strategic initiatives:

1. Market Research and Segmentation:

- By employing statistical analysis, business analysts can segment markets, gauge consumer preferences, and discern market trends, facilitating targeted marketing strategies and product positioning.

2. Performance Metrics and KPIs:

- Statistical analysis aids business analysts in establishing key performance indicators (KPIs), benchmarking performance metrics, and evaluating the impact of business initiatives within their organizations.

3. Decision Support Systems:

- Business analysts harness statistical analysis to develop decision support systems that facilitate informed decision-making, scenario analysis, and risk assessment, empowering stakeholders to make strategic choices grounded in empirical evidence.

Real-world Applications of Statistical Analysis:

The impact of statistical analysis reverberates across diverse industries and domains, manifesting in an array of real-world applications that underscore its pervasive influence:

1. Financial Forecasting and Risk Management:

- In the realm of finance, statistical analysis is instrumental in forecasting stock prices, assessing investment risks, and modeling financial derivatives, enabling organizations to navigate the complexities of financial markets with precision.

2. Healthcare Analytics and Epidemiology:

- Statistical analysis underpins healthcare analytics, facilitating the identification of disease patterns, the evaluation of treatment efficacy, and the modeling of epidemiological trends, thereby advancing public health initiatives and clinical decision-making.

3. Customer Relationship Management and Predictive Analytics:

- In the domain of customer relationship management, statistical analysis fuels predictive analytics, enabling organizations to anticipate customer churn, forecast purchasing behavior, and personalize customer experiences based on data-driven insights.

4. Operations Research and Process Optimization:

- Statistical analysis empowers organizations to optimize operational processes, streamline supply chain management, and enhance resource allocation through the application of quantitative modeling and statistical optimization techniques.

Tools and Techniques for Analytics

In the ever-evolving landscape of data analytics, the array of tools and techniques at our disposal is as diverse as it is essential. From data wrangling and manipulation to advanced visualization and machine learning, the tools and techniques available to data analysts, data scientists, business intelligence professionals, and AI practitioners are instrumental in unraveling the complexities of data and transforming it into actionable insights. This chapter delves deep into the multifaceted toolkit that empowers professionals to navigate the intricacies of data analytics, data science, business intelligence, and AI projects.

Fundamental Tools for Data Analysis:

1. Microsoft Excel:

Microsoft Excel stands as a stalwart in the arsenal of data analysts, offering a versatile platform for data cleaning, manipulation, analysis, and visualization through its familiar interface of spreadsheets. Its functionalities extend from basic data formatting and filtering to advanced statistical analysis and visualization, making it an indispensable tool in the realm of data analytics.

2. Python:

Python has emerged as a powerhouse in the domain of data analysis and manipulation, owing to its rich ecosystem of libraries such as Pandas and NumPy for data processing and manipulation, and Matplotlib for advanced data visualization. Its intuitive syntax and extensive community support have positioned Python as a favored language for data analytics and have fueled its widespread adoption across diverse industries.

3. R:

Designed specifically for statistical computing and graphics, R has garnered substantial traction in both academia and industry due to its robust statistical libraries and visualization capabilities. Its prowess in statistical analysis, coupled with its extensibility through the development of custom packages, renders R an indispensable tool for data analysts and statisticians alike.

4. Jupyter Notebook:

Jupyter Notebook presents a paradigm shift in the realm of data analytics by providing an open-source web application that enables the creation and sharing of documents containing live code, visualizations, and narrative text. Its interactive nature fosters a collaborative and reproducible environment for data analysis, making it an invaluable tool for documenting and sharing analytical workflows.

Cloud-Based Tools for Data Analytics:

1. Microsoft Power BI:

Microsoft Power BI serves as a transformative tool that converges disparate data sources into coherent and visually immersive insights. Its capabilities span from intuitive dashboard creation to advanced data modeling and are instrumental in empowering organizations to extract meaningful insights from their data.

2. Google Cloud AutoML:

Google Cloud AutoML has democratized machine learning by providing developers with limited expertise in the field with the means to develop and deploy machine learning models tailored to their specific use cases. Its user-friendly interface and automated model training capabilities have streamlined the process of machine learning model development, making it accessible to a broader audience.

3. Google Data Studio:

Google Data Studio has redefined the landscape of data visualization and reporting by enabling users to seamlessly transform data into customizable reports and dashboards. Its intuitive drag-and-drop interface, coupled with its integration with a myriad of data sources, has empowered organizations to demonstrate data-driven insights in a visually compelling manner.

4. Tableau Online:

Tableau Online has emerged as a pivotal platform for organizations to share and collaborate on data visualizations and insights. Its interactive dashboards and advanced analytics capabilities have facilitated the dissemination of data-driven insights within organizations and have fostered a culture of data-driven decision-making.

Advanced Data Analysis and Machine Learning Tools:

1. TensorFlow:

TensorFlow, an open-source machine learning framework developed by Google, has gained widespread adoption in the domain of deep learning and neural network modeling. Its flexible architecture and extensive library of pre-built models have positioned it as a cornerstone in the development of advanced machine learning applications, spanning from image recognition to natural language processing.

2. Apache Spark:

Apache Spark has revolutionized the realm of big data analytics by offering a unified analytics engine for large-scale data processing. Its distributed computing capabilities, coupled with its support for advanced analytics and machine learning, have rendered it instrumental in the realm of big data analytics and real-time data processing.

3. Scikit-learn:

Scikit-learn, a versatile machine learning library for Python, has emerged as a go-to tool for data scientists due to its comprehensive suite of algorithms and utilities for machine learning tasks. Its user-friendly interface and extensive documentation have democratized machine learning by making complex algorithms accessible to a broader audience of data analysts and scientists.

4. Amazon SageMaker:

Amazon SageMaker has streamlined the process of building, training, and deploying machine learning models on the cloud. Its integrated development environment and automated model tuning capabilities have accelerated the adoption of machine learning within organizations, making it a pivotal tool for implementing machine learning solutions at scale.

Emerging Trends and Future Directions:

As the field of data analytics continues to evolve, several emerging trends and future directions are poised to shape the landscape of tools and techniques:

1. Automated Machine Learning (AutoML):

The emergence of AutoML platforms, such as Google Cloud AutoML and Amazon SageMaker, signals a paradigm shift in democratizing machine learning by automating the model development process and making it accessible to a broader audience of developers and analysts.

2. Augmented Analytics:

Augmented analytics, powered by advancements in artificial intelligence and natural language processing, is poised to revolutionize the realm of data analytics by offering automated insights, natural language querying, and automated data preparation, thereby empowering a broader spectrum of users to derive insights from data.

3. Extended Reality (XR) Data Visualization:

The integration of extended reality technologies, including virtual reality and augmented reality, into data visualization and analytics is set to redefine the landscape of data exploration and storytelling by offering immersive and interactive data experiences that transcend traditional two-dimensional visualizations.

4. Quantum Computing for Advanced Analytics:

The advent of quantum computing is poised to revolutionize the realm of advanced analytics by offering unprecedented computational capabilities for solving complex optimization, simulation, and machine learning problems, thereby unlocking new frontiers in data analytics and predictive modeling.

Business Intelligence in Modern Business Analysis

The Essence of Business Intelligence

In today's fast-paced and data-driven business landscape, the need for efficient and strategic decision-making has never been more critical. As organizations strive to gain a competitive edge, they increasingly rely on Business Intelligence (BI) to turn raw data into actionable insights. This session seeks to define BI and explore its significance in contemporary business environments. It will also delve into the key components of BI, including data warehousing, data mining, and BI reporting tools.

Defining Business Intelligence

Business Intelligence, often abbreviated as BI, refers to the technologies, applications, and practices used to collect, integrate, analyze, and present business information. It encompasses a wide range of tools and methodologies designed to support better business decision-making. At its core, BI empowers organizations to transform raw data into meaningful and useful information for strategic planning, operational improvements, and competitive advantage.

The Significance of Business Intelligence in Contemporary Business Environments

In today's hyperconnected and data-rich world, the significance of Business Intelligence cannot be overstated. BI enables organizations to gain a comprehensive understanding of their operations, customers, and market trends. By leveraging BI tools and techniques, companies can uncover hidden patterns, identify emerging opportunities, and mitigate potential risks. Moreover, BI empowers decision-makers to make informed choices based on data-driven insights rather than intuition or guesswork.

The Key Components of Business Intelligence

1. Data Warehousing

A fundamental component of Business Intelligence, data warehousing involves the process of collecting and storing large volumes of structured and unstructured data from various sources. Data warehouses serve as centralized repositories, consolidating data from disparate systems and enabling efficient data analysis. By organizing data in a structured manner, organizations can easily access and analyze information to derive actionable insights.

2. Data Mining

Data mining is the process of discovering patterns, correlations, and anomalies within large datasets to extract valuable information. Leveraging statistical and machine learning algorithms, data mining techniques enable organizations to uncover hidden trends, customer preferences, and market dynamics. This allows businesses to make strategic decisions based on predictive analytics and data-driven forecasts.

3. BI Reporting Tools

BI reporting tools form the interface through which users interact with BI systems to access and visualize data. These tools facilitate the creation of customized reports, dashboards, and data visualizations, enabling stakeholders to gain a comprehensive view of the organization's performance and key metrics. By presenting data in a user-friendly and intuitive manner, BI reporting tools empower decision-makers to derive insights and drive strategic initiatives.

BI Tools and Technologies

In the ever-evolving landscape of Business Intelligence (BI), the selection and utilization of the right tools and technologies are critical to the success of data analytics, data science, business intelligence, and AI projects. This chapter aims to provide a comprehensive overview of popular BI tools and technologies, their features, strengths, and application areas. Furthermore, it will offer guidelines for selecting the most suitable BI tool based on organizational needs.

Introduction to BI Tools and Technologies

BI tools and technologies encompass a diverse array of software applications and platforms designed to facilitate the collection, integration, analysis, and visualization of business data. These tools play a pivotal role in enabling organizations to transform raw data into actionable insights, thereby empowering informed decision-making and strategic planning. From traditional reporting and analytics solutions to cutting-edge cloud-based platforms, the BI ecosystem offers a wide spectrum of options tailored to meet the diverse needs of modern enterprises.

Popular BI Tools: Tableau, Power BI, and QlikView

Tableau:

Tableau stands as one of the leading players in the realm of data visualization and analytics. Its intuitive interface and robust features make it a preferred choice for organizations seeking to derive actionable insights from their data. Tableau offers seamless connectivity to a wide range of data sources, enabling users to create interactive dashboards, visualizations, and reports with unparalleled ease. The platform's drag-and-drop functionality and robust data exploration capabilities empower users to uncover hidden patterns and trends, making it an invaluable tool for data discovery and exploratory analysis.

Power BI:

Developed by Microsoft, Power BI has emerged as a flagship BI tool, offering a comprehensive suite of features for data preparation, data discovery, and interactive dashboards. With its seamless integration with Microsoft's ecosystem, including Azure services and Excel, Power BI provides a unified platform for data analysis and visualization. The tool's intuitive interface and powerful data modeling capabilities enable users to create compelling visualizations and share insights across the organization. Moreover, Power BI's support for natural language queries and AI-powered analytics further enhances its appeal as a versatile BI solution.

QlikView:

QlikView stands out for its associative data model, which enables users to explore data relationships and associations dynamically. This unique approach to data analysis allows for unparalleled flexibility and agility in uncovering insights and making data-driven decisions. QlikView's in-memory processing engine facilitates rapid data access and analysis, empowering users to gain real-time insights into their business operations. Additionally, the platform's robust security features and scalability make it a suitable choice for organizations seeking a comprehensive BI solution.

Microsoft SQL Server BI Stack

In addition to Power BI, Microsoft offers a comprehensive suite of BI tools and technologies within its SQL Server ecosystem, catering to diverse data analytics and reporting requirements.

SQL Server Reporting Services (SSRS):

SSRS remains a stalwart in the realm of enterprise reporting, providing a robust platform for creating, publishing, and managing reports. Integrated with Power BI, SSRS offers a comprehensive reporting solution, enabling organizations to deliver pixel-perfect reports and interactive visualizations to stakeholders. With its support for a wide range of data sources and flexible report delivery options, SSRS continues to be a preferred choice for organizations with sophisticated reporting needs.

SQL Server Analysis Services (SSAS):

SSAS empowers organizations with advanced data analytics capabilities, allowing the creation of multidimensional and tabular models for in-depth data analysis. By leveraging SSAS, organizations can build analytical models that enable complex calculations, predictive analytics, and data mining. This enables business users and data analysts to gain insights into historical performance, forecast trends, and make informed decisions based on comprehensive data analysis.

Azure Analysis Services:

As organizations increasingly embrace cloud-based solutions, Azure Analysis Services provides a scalable and enterprise-grade platform for data modeling and analytics in the cloud. By leveraging Azure Analysis Services, organizations can benefit from the flexibility and agility of cloud computing while harnessing the power of advanced data modeling and analytics capabilities. This enables businesses to perform large-scale data analysis and gain insights from diverse data sources, driving strategic decision-making and operational efficiency.

Excel Integration:

Power BI's seamless integration with Excel offers a compelling advantage for users familiar with Excel's interface and data modeling capabilities. By enabling the import of data models and reports from Excel into Power BI, organizations can leverage existing Excel-based analyses and seamlessly transition to a more robust and interactive BI platform. This integration facilitates a smooth transition for users, empowering them to explore data, create visualizations, and share insights within the Power BI environment.

Selecting the Right BI Tool Based on Organizational Needs

The selection of the most suitable BI tool is contingent upon the specific needs and objectives of an organization. When embarking on the evaluation and selection process, several key considerations come into play:

1. Data Sources and Integration:

Organizations must assess the compatibility of BI tools with their existing data sources and the ease of integrating diverse data sets. The ability to seamlessly connect to on-premises and cloud-based data sources, as well as third-party applications, is crucial for ensuring comprehensive data analysis and visualization.

2. Scalability and Performance:

Scalability and performance considerations are paramount, particularly for organizations dealing with large volumes of data and complex analytical requirements. The BI tool's capacity to handle growing data volumes, concurrent user access, and complex queries is pivotal in meeting the evolving needs of the organization.

3. User Interface and Accessibility:

The user interface and accessibility of the BI tool play a critical role in user adoption and engagement. Intuitive and user-friendly interfaces, coupled with support for mobile and web-based access, contribute to a seamless user experience and enhanced collaboration across the organization.

4. Advanced Analytics and AI Capabilities:

Organizations seeking to leverage advanced analytics, machine learning, and AI-powered insights must evaluate the BI tool's capabilities in these domains. The integration of predictive analytics, natural language processing, and automated insights generation can provide a competitive edge in driving data-driven decision-making.

5. Total Cost of Ownership:

An in-depth analysis of the total cost of ownership, encompassing licensing fees, implementation costs, maintenance, and training expenses, is essential for making informed investment decisions. Organizations must weigh the upfront costs against the long-term value and return on investment offered by the BI tool.

6. Security and Compliance:

The BI tool's security features, data governance capabilities, and adherence to regulatory compliance standards are paramount, particularly for organizations handling sensitive and confidential data. Robust security measures and compliance frameworks are imperative for safeguarding data integrity and ensuring regulatory adherence.

The BI Process: From Data to Insights

Data Warehousing in Business Intelligence

In the realm of Business Intelligence (BI), the process of transforming raw data into actionable insights relies heavily on the effective aggregation and management of data. This is where the role of data warehousing becomes pivotal. Data warehousing refers to the process of collecting, storing, and organizing data from various sources into a central repository, enabling organizations to perform complex analytics and generate meaningful business intelligence. This session will delve into the significance of data warehousing in BI, explore its components, and elucidate best practices for designing and implementing robust data warehousing solutions.

Understanding Data Warehousing

At its core, a data warehouse serves as a centralized repository that consolidates data from disparate sources within an organization, including transactional systems, relational databases, and external data feeds. This unified view of data allows businesses to analyze historical trends, track performance metrics, and derive insights that facilitate informed decision-making. Data warehousing also supports the integration of structured and unstructured data, enabling organizations to leverage a wide spectrum of data types for comprehensive analytics.

Components of Data Warehousing

A well-architected data warehouse comprises several key components that collectively contribute to its functionality and effectiveness in delivering business insights:

1. Extract, Transform, Load (ETL) Processes: ETL processes are responsible for extracting data from source systems, transforming it into a consistent format, and loading it into the data warehouse. This stage involves data cleansing, normalization, and enrichment to ensure the quality and integrity of the data being ingested.

2. Data Storage: The data warehouse utilizes a structured storage model optimized for query performance and analytical processing. This often involves the use of dimensional modeling techniques, such as star and snowflake schemas, to organize data into easily accessible and analyzable structures.

3. Metadata Management: Metadata, or data about the data, plays a crucial role in data warehousing, providing context and lineage for the stored information. Effective metadata management facilitates data governance, lineage tracking, and query optimization within the data warehouse environment.

4. Business Intelligence Tools Integration: Data warehousing integrates seamlessly with BI tools, enabling users to access, analyze, and visualize data stored in the warehouse through intuitive dashboards, reports, and ad-hoc querying interfaces.

Significance of Data Warehousing in BI

The role of data warehousing in BI extends beyond mere data storage; it serves as the foundation for generating actionable insights and facilitating informed decision-making. By consolidating data from disparate sources into a unified repository, data warehousing enables organizations to perform advanced analytics, including trend analysis, predictive modeling, and performance monitoring. Furthermore, data warehousing supports the integration of historical and real-time data, providing a comprehensive view of organizational operations and market dynamics.

Best Practices for Designing Data Warehousing Solutions

Designing and implementing an effective data warehousing solution requires adherence to best practices that ensure optimal performance, scalability, and data governance. The following best practices are instrumental in developing robust data warehousing solutions for BI projects:

1. Requirements Analysis: Conduct a thorough analysis of business requirements, data sources, and analytical use cases to define the scope and objectives of the data warehouse. This analysis serves as the foundation for designing a data model that aligns with the organization's BI needs.

2. Data Modeling: Employ dimensional modeling techniques to design a schema that optimizes query performance and facilitates analytical querying. Dimensional modeling enables efficient navigation of data for reporting and analysis, supporting the creation of intuitive and insightful visualizations.

3. Data Quality Management: Implement robust data quality processes to ensure the accuracy, consistency, and completeness of data stored in the warehouse. Data cleansing, deduplication, and validation mechanisms are essential for maintaining high-quality data for analytics and reporting.

4. Performance Optimization: Optimize the data warehouse for query performance by employing indexing, partitioning, and materialized views to accelerate data retrieval and analysis. Performance tuning is crucial for delivering responsive and efficient BI capabilities to users.

5. Scalability and Elasticity: Design the data warehouse with scalability in mind, allowing for the accommodation of growing data volumes and evolving analytical requirements. Cloud-based data warehousing solutions offer elasticity and on-demand scalability, providing flexibility in resource allocation based on changing workloads.

6. Data Security and Governance: Implement robust data security measures and governance policies to protect sensitive information and ensure compliance with regulatory requirements. Data access controls, encryption, and auditing mechanisms are essential components of a secure data warehousing environment.

7. Integration with BI Tools: Ensure seamless integration between the data warehouse and BI tools, enabling users to access and analyze data effectively through intuitive and user-friendly interfaces. This integration enhances the usability and adoption of BI capabilities within the organization.

Implementing BI in Business Analysis

Business Intelligence (BI) has become an indispensable tool for extracting actionable insights from data, facilitating informed decision-making, and fostering a data-driven culture within organizations. In this session, we will delve into the strategic role of BI in business analysis, explore the core components of a BI system, and provide a step-by-step approach for implementing BI solutions within the framework of business analysis practices. Additionally, we will examine the integration of BI with business analysis workflows, address challenges in BI implementation, and explore future directions and emerging trends in the BI landscape.

The Strategic Role of BI in Business Analysis

BI for Enhanced Decision-Making

One of the primary objectives of BI is to empower organizations with the ability to make data-driven decisions. By providing timely, accurate, and actionable insights, BI supports decision-makers at all levels of the organization in evaluating performance, identifying opportunities, and mitigating risks. Through intuitive visualizations and interactive dashboards, BI facilitates the interpretation of complex data, enabling stakeholders to gain valuable insights and drive strategic initiatives.

Core Components of a BI System

Data Warehousing

Data warehousing plays a critical role in the BI landscape by providing a centralized repository for storing and organizing data from various sources. It enables organizations to consolidate disparate data sets, including structured and unstructured data, into a unified platform, facilitating comprehensive analytics and reporting. The architecture of a data warehouse is designed to optimize query performance and support analytical processing, allowing users to extract meaningful insights from vast volumes of data.

Analytics and Reporting

Analytics methodologies and reporting techniques form the backbone of BI systems, enabling organizations to derive actionable insights from data. Advanced analytical tools facilitate the exploration of historical trends, predictive modeling, and performance monitoring, empowering decision-makers to anticipate market dynamics and strategic opportunities. Reporting capabilities within BI systems provide stakeholders with intuitive and customizable visualizations, empowering them to interpret data and make informed decisions.

Dashboards and Visualization

Dashboards and data visualization tools are instrumental in communicating complex data insights effectively. By presenting data in a visually compelling and interactive manner, organizations can facilitate the rapid comprehension of key performance indicators, trends, and outliers. Effective visualization enhances the accessibility and interpretability of data, enabling stakeholders to derive actionable insights and drive strategic initiatives based on compelling evidence.

Implementing BI Solutions: A Step-by-Step Approach

Assessment and Planning

The successful implementation of a BI solution begins with a comprehensive needs assessment to identify business requirements and objectives. By engaging stakeholders across various functional areas, organizations can gain a holistic understanding of the analytical needs and challenges they face. This assessment forms the basis for defining the scope, architecture, and key performance indicators (KPIs) for the BI system, aligning it with the strategic goals of the organization.

Tool Selection

Selecting the right BI tools and technologies is crucial for aligning the BI system with organizational needs and infrastructure. Organizations must evaluate the scalability, compatibility, and ease of integration of BI tools to ensure that they meet current and future analytical requirements. Additionally, considerations such as user interface intuitiveness, support for ad-hoc querying, and mobile accessibility play a pivotal role in selecting BI tools that resonate with the user community and foster adoption.

Development and Deployment

The development and deployment phase of a BI project encompasses the design, implementation, testing, and rollout of the BI solution. Best practices for developing a robust BI system include iterative prototyping, user feedback incorporation, and performance tuning. User training and support are critical components of the deployment phase, ensuring that stakeholders are equipped with the knowledge and skills necessary to leverage the BI system effectively.

Integrating BI with Business Analysis Practices

Bridging Data Analysis and Business Strategy

The integration of BI insights into business analysis workflows is essential for informing strategic planning and operational improvements. By aligning data-driven insights with business objectives, organizations can optimize resource allocation, identify growth opportunities, and mitigate risks. Business analysts play a pivotal role in translating data insights into actionable strategies, leveraging BI to foster a culture of continuous improvement and innovation.

Case Study: Implementing Business Intelligence (BI) in Retail Operations

Overview

A prominent retail chain embarked on a transformative journey to incorporate Business Intelligence (BI) within its operations. The initiative aimed to refine operational efficiency, elevate customer satisfaction, and bolster decision-making processes. As the Business Analyst spearheading this BI project, my role was to navigate the project from conceptualization through to execution, ensuring alignment with business goals and stakeholder expectations.

Identification of Stakeholders

- **Internal Stakeholders:**
  - **Executive Team:** Provided strategic direction and approvals.
  - **IT Department:** Oversaw the technical implementation, including integration and data management.
  - **Marketing Division:** Utilized BI insights for campaign strategies and customer engagement.
  - **Sales Managers and Store Managers:** Benefited directly from real-time data for inventory and sales management.
- **External Stakeholders:**
  - **Suppliers:** Influenced by inventory management improvements.
  - **Customers:** Impacted by enhanced personalization and service quality.
  - **Technology Partners:** Provided BI tools and ongoing support.

Discovery of Business Objectives

The BI initiative focused on key objectives:

- Streamlining inventory management for increased efficiency.
- Enhancing customer personalization and engagement strategies.
- Empowering data-driven decisions for sales optimization and product placement.

Evaluation of Options

A comprehensive evaluation of BI tools considered scalability, ease of integration, user experience, and cost-effectiveness. The selection ranged from industry-leading BI software like Tableau for dashboard creation and Microsoft Power BI for analytics, to custom solutions developed in-house for specialized needs.

Scope Definition

The project's scope was meticulously defined to include:

- Seamless integration of BI tools with existing Point of Sale (POS) systems and inventory software.
- Development of intuitive dashboards for real-time insights into sales and inventory.
- Leveraging customer data analytics for targeted marketing campaigns, excluding unnecessary hardware overhauls.

Enterprise Analysis and Requirement Planning

A deep dive into the organizational context underscored the necessity for a BI solution adept at managing vast transactional datasets. A detailed plan covered training needs, data governance frameworks, and mechanisms for continuous system support.

Investigation and Improvement Identification

Initial assessments exposed:

- Inventory management inefficiencies causing stock discrepancies.
- A gap in leveraging real-time data for agile decision-making in pricing and promotions.
- Suboptimal utilization of customer data in crafting marketing strategies.

Evaluation of Improvements and Solutions

The BI solution implementation facilitated:

- Dashboards for immediate visibility into sales trends and inventory levels, optimizing stock management.
- Advanced customer segmentation analytics, enabling precise marketing initiatives.
- Strategic insights guiding store layout, product positioning, and promotional activities.

Outcomes and Impact

The BI project significantly transformed the retailer's operations, delivering:

- Enhanced inventory turnover through dynamic management.
- Increased sales from personalized marketing efforts.
- Informed strategic decisions leading to optimized operational practices.

Challenges and Considerations

Adopting BI was not without its hurdles. Key challenges such as maintaining high data quality standards and facilitating employee adoption were tackled through exhaustive training programs and robust support mechanisms.

Conclusion

This case study highlights the pivotal role of BI in modernizing retail operations. The strategic integration of BI technologies, underpinned by a structured project management approach, has set a benchmark for operational excellence, customer centricity, and strategic agility in the retail sector. As a Business Analyst, guiding this BI project to fruition not only underscored the value of aligning technology with business goals but also reinforced the importance of stakeholder engagement and adaptive solutioning in navigating the complexities of digital transformation in retail.

Overcoming Challenges in BI Implementation

Data Quality and Governance

Common challenges related to data quality, consistency, and governance can significantly impact the success of BI projects. Organizations must implement robust data quality processes, data cleansing mechanisms, and governance frameworks to ensure the accuracy and integrity of the data being analyzed. By establishing data quality standards and governance policies, organizations can instill confidence in the reliability and relevance of BI insights, fostering trust and adoption across the organization.

Stakeholder Engagement

Securing stakeholder buy-in and fostering a culture that values data-driven insights are critical success factors for BI initiatives. Organizations must invest in change management strategies, communication plans, and user engagement activities to drive awareness, acceptance, and adoption of the BI system. By involving stakeholders in the design and implementation process, organizations can address user needs and expectations, ensuring that the BI system resonates with the user community and delivers tangible value.

Scalability and Flexibility

As organizations evolve, so do their analytical requirements. Ensuring that the BI system is scalable and adaptable to meet evolving business needs is essential for its long-term relevance and sustainability. Cloud-based BI solutions offer scalability and flexibility, enabling organizations to accommodate growing data volumes, changing user demands, and dynamic market conditions. By embracing agile methodologies and continuous improvement practices, organizations can evolve their BI capabilities in tandem with their business growth and transformation.

Case Study: Transforming Data into Insights at Zenith Retailers

Background

Zenith Retailers, a hypothetical mid-sized company in the competitive retail sector, faced significant challenges in harnessing the full potential of their data to drive decision-making and improve operational efficiencies. Recognizing the need for a comprehensive Business Intelligence (BI) solution, Zenith embarked on a BI project aimed at enhancing data quality and governance, engaging stakeholders effectively, and ensuring system scalability and flexibility.

Challenge Overview

Zenith Retailers struggled with:

- **Data Quality and Governance:** Disparate data sources led to inconsistencies, inaccuracies, and a lack of trust in the data.
- **Stakeholder Engagement:** Resistance from various departments fearing the change would disrupt their current processes.
- **Scalability and Flexibility:** The existing system couldn't adapt to the rapidly changing business environment and increasing data volumes.

Project Initiation

As the Business Analyst leading this initiative, my first task was to outline a structured approach for the BI implementation, focusing on addressing the core challenges head-on.

Identifying Stakeholders

- **Executive Team:** Their strategic vision was crucial for aligning the BI project with business goals.
- **IT Department:** Managed the technical aspects of the BI solution, ensuring proper integration and data security.
- **Sales and Marketing Divisions:** Primary users of the BI system, requiring real-time insights into customer behavior and market trends.
- **Data Governance Team:** Tasked with establishing data quality standards and governance policies.

- **External Technology Partners:** Provided the BI tools and platforms, and assisted with implementation and support.

Tools and Technologies Selected

- **BI Platform:** Tableau for its user-friendly dashboards and powerful analytics capabilities.
- **Data Management:** Talend for data integration and quality management.
- **Cloud Infrastructure:** AWS for scalable storage and computing resources.
- **Collaboration Platform:** Microsoft Teams for facilitating communication and collaboration among project team members and stakeholders.

Implementation Process

Data Quality and Governance

- **Process Establishment:** Developed a comprehensive data governance framework defining data ownership, quality standards, and cleansing procedures.
- **Tool Implementation:** Leveraged Talend for data integration and cleansing, ensuring high data quality and consistency across sources.

Stakeholder Engagement

- **Change Management:** Initiated a series of workshops and training sessions to familiarize users with the BI tools and the value of data-driven insights.
- **Feedback Loops:** Established regular feedback sessions to address user concerns and adapt the BI solution to better meet departmental needs.

Scalability and Flexibility

- **Cloud Adoption:** Transitioned to AWS cloud infrastructure to ensure the BI system's scalability and flexibility.
- **Agile Methodology:** Adopted agile practices for continuous improvement of the BI system based on evolving business requirements and user feedback.

Outcomes

- **Enhanced Data Integrity:** Through robust data quality processes and governance, Zenith Retailers achieved high data accuracy, fostering trust in BI insights.
- **Improved Stakeholder Buy-In:** Comprehensive engagement strategies led to widespread adoption of the BI system, with departments actively leveraging data for decision-making.
- **Adaptable BI System:** The cloud-based, agile BI solution scaled with the business, accommodating new data sources and analytical needs as Zenith Retailers grew.

Challenges and Solutions

- **Data Resistance:** Initial resistance was overcome through targeted change management efforts,

highlighting the BI system's benefits through success stories and quick wins.
- **Technical Hurdles:** Encountered and resolved through close collaboration with IT and external technology partners, ensuring seamless integration and system performance.

Conclusion

The BI project at Zenith Retailers exemplifies how addressing key challenges in data quality, stakeholder engagement, and system scalability can transform a retail company's operations. By focusing on these areas, Zenith Retailers not only overcame initial hurdles but also laid a foundation for continuous growth and innovation. As the Business Analyst at the helm, steering the project through its complexities to a successful outcome underscored the value of a structured, stakeholder-focused approach in unlocking the true potential of BI in the retail industry.

Future Directions in BI

Emerging Trends in BI

The future of BI is characterized by emerging trends that leverage advanced technologies such as Artificial Intelligence (AI) and machine learning to enhance analytical capabilities. The integration of AI and machine learning in BI systems enables predictive and prescriptive analytics, empowering organizations to anticipate trends, forecast outcomes, and automate decision-making processes. Additionally, advancements in natural language processing and augmented analytics are poised to revolutionize the accessibility and usability of BI for a broader user community.

Preparing for an Evolving BI Landscape

Staying current with BI technologies and practices is essential for organizations to maintain a competitive advantage in an evolving landscape. Continuous learning, skills development, and knowledge sharing initiatives are instrumental in equipping business analysts with the expertise needed to harness the full potential of BI. Additionally, organizations must cultivate a culture of innovation and experimentation, fostering a mindset that embraces change and adapts to emerging trends in BI. By investing in ongoing education and exploration of new BI capabilities, organizations can position themselves as leaders in leveraging data for strategic advantage.

Advancing With BI: Predictive and Prescriptive Analytics

Advancing BI with Predictive and Prescriptive Analytics

As the landscape of business intelligence (BI) continues to evolve, the integration of predictive and prescriptive analytics has emerged as a transformative force, empowering organizations to harness the full potential of their data. In this session, we will explore the advancements in BI towards predictive and prescriptive analytics, discuss their applications in solving complex business problems, and provide real-world examples of how these advanced analytics techniques inform strategic decisions, drive operational efficiencies, and unlock new opportunities for growth and innovation.

Evolution of BI towards Predictive and Prescriptive Analytics

The evolution of BI from descriptive and diagnostic analytics to predictive and prescriptive analytics represents a paradigm shift in the way organizations leverage data to drive strategic decision-making. While descriptive and diagnostic analytics focus on understanding historical data and identifying the root causes of past events, predictive and prescriptive analytics enable organizations to anticipate future outcomes and recommend actionable strategies to optimize performance and mitigate risks proactively.

Applications in Solving Complex Business Problems

Predictive Analytics: Anticipating Future Trends

Predictive analytics leverages statistical algorithms, machine learning models, and data mining techniques to forecast future trends, behaviors, and outcomes based on historical data patterns. Organizations can apply predictive analytics to a wide range of business challenges, including demand forecasting, customer churn prediction, risk assessment, and fraud detection, enabling them to make proactive decisions that drive operational efficiencies, optimize resource allocation, and capitalize on emerging opportunities.

Prescriptive Analytics: Recommending Actionable Strategies

Prescriptive analytics takes predictive insights a step further by recommending actionable strategies to achieve desired outcomes and mitigate risks. By simulating multiple decision scenarios and evaluating their potential impact, prescriptive analytics enables organizations to optimize resource allocation, improve operational processes, and drive strategic initiatives with confidence. Real-time prescriptive analytics empowers decision-makers to make informed choices that align with organizational goals, maximize performance, and adapt to dynamic market conditions.

Applications of Advanced Analytics in BI

Operational Optimization

Organizations can leverage predictive and prescriptive analytics within the BI framework to optimize operational processes, improve resource allocation, and enhance productivity. By analyzing historical data patterns and simulating potential outcomes, predictive and prescriptive analytics enable organizations to identify operational bottlenecks, anticipate supply chain disruptions, and optimize production schedules, driving operational efficiencies and cost savings.

Strategic Decision-Making

Predictive and prescriptive analytics play a pivotal role in informing strategic decisions by providing decision-makers with actionable insights that anticipate market trends, customer preferences, and competitive dynamics. Organizations can leverage predictive analytics to forecast demand patterns, identify emerging market opportunities, and optimize pricing strategies, while prescriptive analytics empowers decision-makers to evaluate multiple decision scenarios and recommend strategies that align with organizational objectives and market dynamics.

Risk Mitigation

By applying advanced analytics techniques, organizations can proactively identify and mitigate risks across various domains, including financial risk, operational risk, and compliance risk. Predictive analytics enables organizations to forecast potential risks and their impact, while prescriptive analytics recommends risk mitigation strategies that align with regulatory requirements and organizational objectives. By integrating advanced analytics into the BI framework, organizations can strengthen their risk management practices and safeguard against potential threats.

Examples of Predictive Analytics Informing Strategic Decisions

Demand Forecasting in Retail

A leading retail chain leverages predictive analytics to forecast demand patterns for its products, enabling it to optimize inventory levels, streamline supply chain operations, and capitalize on emerging market trends. By analyzing historical sales data, customer demographics, and market dynamics, the organization anticipates demand fluctuations and tailors its inventory management strategies to meet customer needs while minimizing excess inventory costs.

Customer Churn Prediction in Telecommunications

A telecommunications provider applies predictive analytics to anticipate customer churn by analyzing customer usage patterns, service interactions, and demographic factors. By identifying customers at risk of churn, the organization can proactively engage them with targeted retention offers, personalized service enhancements, and proactive customer support, driving customer loyalty and reducing churn rates.

Credit Risk Assessment in Financial Services

A financial institution utilizes predictive analytics to assess credit risk by analyzing customer credit profiles, transaction history, and market indicators. By forecasting potential credit defaults and assessing the associated risks, the organization can make informed lending decisions, optimize credit portfolio management, and mitigate potential financial losses, ensuring sound risk management practices and regulatory compliance.

Real-World Applications of Prescriptive Analytics

Supply Chain Optimization in Manufacturing

A manufacturing company employs prescriptive analytics to optimize its supply chain operations by evaluating multiple production scenarios, demand forecasts, and resource constraints. By simulating production schedules, inventory levels, and distribution strategies, the organization identifies cost-effective supply chain configurations, minimizes inventory holding costs, and enhances production agility, driving operational efficiencies and customer satisfaction.

Dynamic Pricing Strategies in E-Commerce

An e-commerce platform utilizes prescriptive analytics to recommend dynamic pricing strategies that align with market demand, competitive dynamics, and customer preferences. By simulating pricing scenarios, demand elasticity, and competitor pricing strategies, the organization can optimize its pricing models, maximize revenue generation, and adapt to dynamic market conditions, driving profitability and market competitiveness.

Operational Process Optimization in Healthcare

A healthcare facility integrates prescriptive analytics into its operational processes to optimize resource allocation, patient flow, and staffing schedules. By simulating patient arrival patterns, treatment workflows, and resource utilization, the organization identifies optimal operational configurations, minimizes patient wait times, and maximizes resource utilization, enhancing patient care and operational efficiency.

Challenges and Best Practices

Addressing Data Quality Challenges in Business Intelligence Systems

As organizations increasingly rely on Business Intelligence (BI) systems to drive strategic decision-making and operational efficiency, the importance of high-quality, reliable data cannot be overstated. In this session, we will address the critical challenges related to data quality in BI systems, explore best practices for ensuring data governance, and discuss strategies for fostering a data-driven culture that values and prioritizes data quality.

The Significance of Data Quality in BI Systems

Data quality is the foundation of effective BI systems, as the insights and decisions derived from these systems are only as reliable as the underlying data. High-quality data is accurate, consistent, timely, complete, and relevant, enabling organizations to make informed decisions and gain a competitive advantage. However, maintaining data quality poses significant challenges, ranging from data silos and inconsistencies to data entry errors and lack of data governance.

Addressing Data Quality Challenges

Data Silos and Inconsistencies

One of the primary challenges in BI systems is the existence of data silos, where data is fragmented and isolated across different departments or systems within an organization. This fragmentation leads to inconsistencies in data definitions, duplicate records, and conflicting information, undermining the reliability of BI insights. Organizations must address data silos by implementing data integration and standardization strategies, ensuring that data is harmonized and accessible across the enterprise.

Data Entry Errors and Inaccuracies

Data entry errors, such as typos, missing values, and incorrect formats, can significantly compromise the accuracy of BI insights. These errors often stem from manual data entry processes or inadequate data validation checks. To mitigate data entry errors, organizations should invest in automated data capture technologies, implement data quality validation rules, and establish data stewardship programs to ensure that data is cleansed and validated at the point of entry.

Timeliness and Completeness

Timely and complete data is essential for BI systems to provide actionable insights. Delays in data availability or missing data can hinder decision-making and lead to suboptimal outcomes. Organizations must establish data governance policies that define data capture processes, data validation timelines, and data completeness standards to ensure that BI systems are fueled with up-to-date and comprehensive data.

Best Practices for Data Governance

Implementing effective data governance policies is paramount to ensuring data quality in BI systems. Data governance encompasses the processes, policies, and standards for managing and safeguarding organizational data assets. Key best practices for data governance in BI systems include:

Clear Data Ownership and Accountability: Assigning clear ownership and accountability for data assets ensures that individuals or teams are responsible for maintaining data quality and consistency.

Data Quality Standards and Metrics: Establishing data quality standards and defining metrics for data accuracy, completeness, timeliness, and consistency enables organizations to monitor and measure data quality against predefined benchmarks.

Data Stewardship and Data Quality Management: Designating data stewards who are responsible for overseeing data quality management activities, such as data profiling, cleansing, and enrichment, fosters a culture of data stewardship and accountability.

Data Integration and Master Data Management: Implementing data integration solutions and master data management practices ensures that data is unified, standardized, and consistent across the organization, reducing the impact of data silos and inconsistencies.

Cultivating a Data-Driven Culture

Fostering a data-driven culture is essential for instilling a mindset that values and prioritizes data quality in BI systems. Organizations can cultivate a data-driven culture by:

Promoting Data Literacy: Providing training and resources to enhance data literacy among employees enables individuals to understand the importance of data quality and empowers them to contribute to data governance efforts.

Recognizing and Rewarding Data Quality Contributions: Acknowledging and incentivizing individuals or teams that actively contribute to data quality improvements fosters a culture of accountability and continuous improvement.

Embedding Data Quality in Decision-Making Processes: Integrating data quality checks and validation steps into decision-making processes ensures that data quality is a fundamental consideration in strategic initiatives and operational workflows.

Artificial Intelligence Basics

As the field of data analytics, data science, business intelligence, and AI continues to evolve, machine learning (ML) remains at the forefront, driving innovation and transformation across various industries. In this session, we will delve into an in-depth exploration of machine learning, including its algorithms, the types of learning paradigms such as supervised, unsupervised, and reinforcement learning, and the fundamental role it plays in the broader landscape of artificial intelligence.

Artificial Intelligence Basics: Fundamentals and Machine Learning

Artificial Intelligence (AI)

Artificial Intelligence (AI) is a multidisciplinary field that encompasses the development of intelligent systems capable of performing tasks that typically require human intelligence. These tasks include problem-solving, understanding natural language, recognizing patterns, and learning from experience. The ultimate goal of AI is to create systems that can mimic cognitive functions such as learning, reasoning, and problem-solving.

Fundamentals of AI

To gain a comprehensive understanding of AI, it is essential to grasp its core concepts, which include machine learning, natural language processing, computer vision, robotics, and expert systems. These components collectively contribute to the development of AI systems that are capable of emulating human-like cognitive abilities. Machine learning, in particular, is a subset of AI that focuses on enabling machines to learn from data without being explicitly programmed.

Machine Learning (ML)

Machine learning is a subset of AI that empowers systems to learn from data, identify patterns, and make decisions or predictions iteratively. It eliminates the need for explicit programming by utilizing algorithms to learn from the data provided. The process of machine learning involves training models on large datasets and enabling them to make data-driven decisions, thus enhancing their predictive capabilities.

Supervised Learning

Supervised learning is a prominent technique within machine learning where models are trained on labeled data, meaning that the input-output pairs are provided. The objective of supervised learning is for the algorithm to learn to map input to output accurately by minimizing the error between predicted and actual outputs. This approach is widely used in tasks such as classification and regression, where the model learns to make predictions based on labeled training data.

Unsupervised Learning

In contrast to supervised learning, unsupervised learning involves training models on unlabeled data to uncover inherent patterns and structures within the data. This type of learning is particularly useful for tasks such as clustering, where the goal is to group similar data points together, and dimensionality reduction, which aims to reduce the complexity of the data while retaining its essential characteristics. Unsupervised learning techniques are instrumental in uncovering hidden insights within large and unstructured datasets.

Reinforcement Learning

Reinforcement learning represents a paradigm within machine learning where an agent learns to make sequential decisions by interacting with an environment. The agent receives feedback in the form of rewards or penalties based on its actions, guiding its learning process. This form of learning is prevalent in scenarios such as game playing, robotics, and autonomous systems, where the agent continually refines its decision-making abilities based on the feedback it receives from the environment.

Understanding the Fundamentals

Understanding the fundamentals of machine learning is paramount for individuals venturing into the realm of artificial intelligence, particularly in its application to diverse domains such as data analytics, data science, business intelligence, and AI projects. It is imperative to comprehend the nuances of supervised, unsupervised, and reinforcement learning, as well as the underlying algorithms that drive these learning paradigms. Mastery of these concepts equips professionals with the knowledge and skills required to harness the power of machine learning in solving complex problems and driving innovation in today's data-driven world.

In the following sections, we will delve deeper into the individual components of machine learning, exploring the intricacies of various algorithms, their applications, and the evolving landscape of AI-driven technologies. By gaining a comprehensive understanding of machine learning, readers will be equipped with the foundational knowledge to navigate the complexities of modern data analytics, data science, business intelligence, and AI projects.

Natural Language Processing (NLP)

In the realm of data analytics, data science, business intelligence, and AI, Natural Language Processing (NLP) stands as a fundamental pillar, enabling the extraction of valuable insights from unstructured text data. This session will delve into an in-depth exploration of NLP techniques, their applications in text analysis, sentiment analysis, language translation, and speech recognition, supported by real-world examples and case studies that showcase the transformative potential of NLP across diverse industries.

Introduction

Natural Language Processing (NLP) is a branch of artificial intelligence that focuses on enabling machines to understand, interpret, and generate human language in a manner that is both meaningful and contextually relevant. NLP encompasses a broad spectrum of applications, ranging from language understanding and generation to speech recognition and language translation, all aimed at facilitating seamless interactions between humans and machines.

Text Analysis

Text analysis, a core application of NLP, entails the extraction of meaningful insights from unstructured text data, such as articles, social media posts, customer reviews, and more. NLP techniques empower organizations to process and analyze vast volumes of textual information, uncovering valuable patterns, sentiments, and trends that drive informed decision-making and strategic business initiatives.

Sentiment Analysis

Sentiment analysis, also known as opinion mining, leverages NLP to discern and quantify the sentiment expressed within textual content. By analyzing the emotional tone and polarity of textual data, organizations can gauge public opinion, customer satisfaction, and market trends, enabling them to adapt their strategies, products, and services in response to the sentiments expressed by their target audience.

Language Translation

Language translation represents another pivotal application of NLP, facilitating the seamless conversion of text from one language to another. NLP-driven translation systems have undergone significant advancements, harnessing deep learning and neural network models to achieve human-level accuracy and fluency in language translation, thereby breaking down language barriers and fostering global collaboration and communication.

Speech Recognition

NLP plays a critical role in speech recognition, enabling machines to comprehend and transcribe spoken language into text. This capability underpins the development of virtual assistants, interactive voice response systems, and voice-operated devices, revolutionizing the way humans interact with technology and unlocking new avenues for hands-free communication and task automation.

Real-World Applications and Case Studies

To illustrate the practical impact of NLP across diverse industries, let us delve into real-world examples and case studies that exemplify the transformative potential of NLP in driving innovation, enhancing user experiences, and unlocking new opportunities for businesses.

Case Study: Revolutionizing Healthcare Through NLP Data Mining and Analysis

Background

In the era of digital healthcare, the ability to efficiently process and analyze the vast amounts of unstructured data generated daily is paramount. This case study delves into a transformative project at a leading healthcare institution aimed at leveraging Natural Language Processing (NLP) to mine and analyze unstructured healthcare data. As a Business Analyst, I was tasked with orchestrating this ambitious project, from its inception through to its implementation, working closely with various stakeholders to ensure its success.

Project Initiation

Objective: The primary goal was to harness NLP technologies to extract meaningful information from unstructured data sources such as Electronic Health Records (EHRs), clinical notes, and medical research papers. This initiative aimed to enhance patient care, accelerate disease detection, and drive medical research innovations.

Stakeholders Identified:

- **Healthcare Professionals:** Doctors, nurses, and clinical staff who require access to patient information and research data.
- **Data Science Team:** Specialists in NLP and data analysis tasked with developing the algorithms and models.
- **IT Department:** Responsible for integrating the NLP solutions into existing healthcare systems.
- **Patients:** The ultimate beneficiaries of improved diagnosis and treatment plans.
- **Research Community:** Researchers looking for new insights in medical literature.

Planning Phase

Needs Assessment: Conducted interviews and surveys with healthcare professionals to identify key challenges and opportunities in data utilization. Reviewed existing data management systems for integration capabilities.

Technology Selection: Evaluated various NLP tools and platforms, considering factors such as accuracy, scalability, compatibility, and cost. Tools like TensorFlow for machine learning, NLTK for language processing, and Apache Spark for big data processing were shortlisted.

Project Plan Development: Outlined the project timeline, milestones, resource allocation, and risk management strategies. Adopted an agile project management approach to allow for flexibility and continuous improvement.

Execution Phase

Data Collection and Preprocessing: Worked with the IT department to aggregate data from EHRs, clinical notes, and research papers. Employed data preprocessing techniques to clean and normalize the data, making it suitable for NLP analysis.

Development of NLP Models: Collaborated with the data science team to develop and train NLP models for named entity recognition, sentiment analysis, and topic modeling. Ensured models were trained on diverse datasets to improve accuracy and reduce bias.

Integration with Healthcare Systems: Partnered with software developers and the IT department to integrate the NLP solutions into the healthcare institution's systems, enabling seamless access to structured insights for healthcare professionals.

Testing and Validation: Conducted comprehensive testing phases, including unit testing, system integration testing, and user acceptance testing, with continuous feedback loops from end-users to refine the solutions.

Monitoring and Control

Performance Metrics: Established key performance indicators (KPIs) such as improvement in diagnosis accuracy, reduction in data processing time, and user satisfaction levels to monitor the project's impact.

Stakeholder Updates: Regularly communicated progress, challenges, and adjustments to stakeholders through meetings, reports, and dashboards, ensuring transparency and stakeholder engagement.

Outcomes and Benefits

- **Improved Patient Care:** Enabled healthcare professionals to access accurate and comprehensive patient data swiftly, leading to better-informed diagnosis and personalized treatment plans.
- **Accelerated Disease Detection:** Facilitated early detection of diseases through the analysis of clinical notes and EHRs, significantly improving patient outcomes.
- **Enhanced Research Capabilities:** Unlocked new insights from medical research papers, advancing the field of medical research.

Lessons Learned

- The importance of cross-functional collaboration cannot be overstated. Engaging stakeholders at every

project stage ensured alignment and maximized project outcomes.
- Data quality is paramount. Investing time in data preprocessing significantly improved the accuracy of NLP models.
- Flexibility is key. Adopting an agile approach allowed the team to adapt to unforeseen challenges and refine the project scope as needed.

Conclusion

This project underscored the transformative potential of NLP in healthcare, from enhancing patient care to propelling medical research forward. As a Business Analyst, navigating the complexities of this project was a challenging yet rewarding experience that highlighted the importance of strategic planning, stakeholder engagement, and agile project management in achieving digital transformation in healthcare

Case Study: Implementing NLP for Enhanced Customer Experience in Retail

Situation

A leading retail conglomerate sought to elevate its understanding of customer sentiments to refine its service and product offerings. Traditional feedback mechanisms were slow and failed to capture the nuanced perspectives of a varied customer base.

Objective

The primary objective was to deploy an NLP-powered sentiment analysis system to automate the analysis of customer feedback across diverse channels, including social media, customer surveys, and online product reviews. This initiative aimed to extract and categorize sentiments to inform business strategies effectively.

Stakeholders

- **Retail Management Team:** Oversight of project implementation and results integration into business strategies.
- **IT and Data Science Teams:** Development and maintenance of the NLP system.
- **Marketing Department:** Utilization of insights for campaign strategy.
- **Product Development Teams:** Integration of customer feedback into product innovation.
- **Customers:** Indirect participants providing the data through feedback.

Tools and Technologies

- **NLP Frameworks:** Utilization of TensorFlow for model training and NLTK for natural language processing tasks.
- **Data Analytics Platforms:** Integration with platforms like Tableau for visualizing sentiment trends and feedback patterns.
- **Customer Relationship Management (CRM) System:** To aggregate and manage customer feedback data.

Implementation Steps

1. **Data Aggregation:** Coordinated with the IT department to integrate data streams from various feedback

channels into a central repository.
2. **Preprocessing and Analysis:** The Data Science team undertook the cleaning and normalization of text data to prepare for NLP analysis. Utilized NLP techniques to detect, extract, and classify sentiment from textual feedback.
3. **Integration with Business Processes:** Worked with the Marketing and Product Development teams to ensure insights from the sentiment analysis were actionable and accessible.
4. **Continuous Learning:** Established mechanisms for the NLP system to learn from new data continuously, enhancing its accuracy and relevance.

Impact

- **Deep Insights:** Achieved a comprehensive understanding of customer sentiments, preferences, and dissatisfaction points.
- **Tailored Marketing Strategies:** Enabled the development of marketing campaigns that resonated with specific customer segments.
- **Refined Product Offerings:** Product adjustments and innovations were informed by direct customer feedback and sentiment trends.
- **Enhanced Customer Satisfaction:** Directly addressed customer concerns, leading to improved loyalty and brand perception.

Challenges

- **Data Quality and Volume:** Managing vast amounts of unstructured data required sophisticated preprocessing techniques to ensure data quality.
- **Cultural and Linguistic Variations:** Ensuring the NLP system accurately understood sentiments across different languages and cultural contexts posed a significant challenge.
- **Integration with Existing Systems:** Seamlessly integrating the NLP system with existing CRM and data analytics platforms required close coordination across teams.

Lessons Learned

- **Cross-functional Collaboration is Key:** Effective communication and collaboration between business analysts, data scientists, and departmental teams were crucial for the project's success.
- **The Value of Real-Time Insights:** The ability to analyze and act on customer sentiments in real-time significantly impacted business decisions and strategies.
- **Flexibility and Scalability:** Building a system that could adapt to evolving customer feedback trends and scale as the business grows was essential for long-term success.

Conclusion

By leveraging NLP for sentiment analysis, the retail conglomerate transformed its approach to understanding customer feedback, enabling data-driven decisions that significantly enhanced customer satisfaction and informed business strategies. This case study underscores the power of NLP to transform unstructured data into actionable business insights, marking a milestone in the retail sector's journey towards innovation and customer-centricity.

Computer Vision

Computer vision, a foundational field within the realm of data analytics, data science, business intelligence, and AI, encompasses the study and application of techniques that enable machines to interpret and understand visual information, such as images and videos. By leveraging the principles of computer vision, organizations can unlock a myriad of capabilities, including image recognition, object detection, video analysis, and more, laying the groundwork for transformative innovations across diverse industries.

Principles of Computer Vision

At the core of computer vision lie fundamental principles that facilitate the extraction of valuable insights from visual data. Image processing, pattern recognition, machine learning, and deep learning form the bedrock of computer vision, empowering machines to perceive, analyze, and derive meaningful interpretations from visual content.

Image Recognition

Image recognition, a pivotal application of computer vision, entails the automatic identification and categorization of objects, scenes, and patterns within images. By harnessing advanced algorithms and deep learning models, machines can discern and classify visual content, enabling a spectrum of applications, ranging from facial recognition and biometric authentication to content-based image retrieval and visual search engines.

Object Detection

Object detection, a cornerstone of computer vision, revolves around the identification and localization of specific objects within images or videos. Through the utilization of sophisticated techniques such as convolutional neural networks (CNNs) and region-based algorithms, machines can not only recognize objects but also delineate their precise spatial coordinates, underpinning applications in autonomous vehicles, surveillance systems, and industrial automation.

Video Analysis

Video analysis, an extension of computer vision, encompasses the extraction of insights and patterns from video data, enabling machines to comprehend motion, track objects, and discern temporal relationships within visual sequences. From action recognition and behavior analysis to video summarization and surveillance, the application of computer vision in video analysis transcends traditional boundaries, fostering a new era of intelligent video processing and understanding.

Deep Learning in Computer Vision

The advent of deep learning has revolutionized the landscape of computer vision, endowing machines with unprecedented capabilities to learn and extract intricate features from visual data. Convolutional neural networks (CNNs), recurrent neural networks (RNNs), and generative adversarial networks (GANs) represent just a few of the powerful deep learning architectures that have propelled the field of computer vision to new heights, enabling breakthroughs in image generation, style transfer, and image captioning.

Real-World Applications and Case Studies

To exemplify the practical impact of computer vision across diverse industries, let us delve into real-world examples and case studies that showcase the transformative potential of computer vision in driving innovation, enhancing user experiences, and unlocking new opportunities for businesses.

Case Study: Implementing Computer Vision in Autonomous Vehicle Development

Background

The evolution of autonomous vehicles marks a significant innovation within the automotive industry, poised to transform transportation through enhanced safety, efficiency, and convenience. Central to this advancement is computer vision technology, which equips vehicles with human-like perception abilities to navigate complex environments.

The Challenge

The primary challenge in the autonomous vehicle sector is ensuring these vehicles can navigate safely and efficiently in varied and unpredictable road conditions. This includes the accurate real-time detection and interpretation of objects, road signs, pedestrians, and other vehicles, under different weather and lighting conditions.

Objective

As a Business Analyst at a leading automotive company, my objective was to oversee the integration of advanced computer vision algorithms into our autonomous vehicle prototypes to address these navigation challenges.

Stakeholders

- **R&D Team:** Engineers and computer vision specialists developing the algorithms.
- **Test Drivers and Safety Analysts:** Personnel involved in real-world testing and safety validation.
- **Legal and Compliance Team:** Ensuring the project adheres to regulatory standards.
- **Marketing and Consumer Insights Team:** Analyzing market trends and consumer readiness.
- **Investors and Board Members:** Providing oversight and funding for the project.

Solution Overview

The solution involved deploying a combination of computer vision techniques, including:

- **Semantic Segmentation:** To understand road layouts, differentiate objects, and identify drivable surfaces.
- **Object Detection:** To recognize and locate objects within the vehicle's vicinity using CNNs and deep learning.
- **Real-Time Decision Making:** To process visual data for immediate navigational decisions, enhancing safety and efficiency.

Tools and Technologies

- **Hardware:** High-resolution cameras and LiDAR sensors for data capture.
- **Software:** TensorFlow and PyTorch for developing and training deep learning models.
- **Data Processing:** Onboard computing systems capable of executing complex algorithms in real-time.

Implementation Steps

1. **Data Collection:** Equipped vehicles with sensors and cameras to gather environmental visual data.
2. **Algorithm Development:** R&D team developed and fine-tuned computer vision algorithms for semantic segmentation and object detection.
3. **Prototype Testing:** Initial tests in controlled environments, followed by extensive real-world road tests under various conditions to validate performance.
4. **Stakeholder Engagement:** Regular updates and demonstrations to stakeholders to ensure alignment and address concerns.
5. **Compliance and Safety Protocols:** Worked with legal and safety analysts to ensure the technology meets all regulatory requirements and safety standards.

Impact

- **Enhanced Safety:** The technology significantly reduces accident risks associated with human error.
- **Improved Traffic Flow:** Optimizes driving patterns, contributing to reduced congestion.
- **Increased Accessibility:** Offers mobility solutions for those unable to drive.
- **Environmental Advantages:** Promotes reduced emissions through efficient navigation and supports the integration of electric vehicles.

Challenges

- **System Reliability:** Ensuring consistent performance under extreme conditions remains a hurdle.
- **Ethical and Legal Issues:** Navigating the moral implications and legal framework surrounding autonomous vehicles.
- **Public Acceptance:** Building trust in autonomous vehicle safety and reliability is crucial for widespread adoption.

Conclusion

The application of computer vision in autonomous vehicles represents a leap forward in making transportation safer, more efficient, and accessible. Through careful planning, development, and testing, this project highlights the potential of computer vision to revolutionize the automotive industry, setting a path toward a future where autonomous vehicles become a common aspect of everyday mobility. Continuous advancements in technology, along with a focus on safety and regulatory compliance, are key to overcoming remaining challenges and fully unlocking the transformative power of autonomous driving.

Case Study: Enhancing Retail Operations and Customer Experience with Computer Vision

Overview

In an era where the retail industry faces intense competition, a leading global retailer embarked on a transformative journey by integrating computer vision technology into its operations. This initiative aimed to revolutionize the shopping experience by monitoring foot traffic, analyzing customer behavior, and optimizing store layouts. As a Business Analyst, I played a pivotal role in steering this digital transformation, ensuring the successful implementation of computer vision technologies to improve operational efficiency and personalize customer interactions.

Challenge

The retailer confronted several obstacles that hindered its competitiveness and customer satisfaction, including inefficient queue management, a lack of detailed insights into customer interactions with products, and suboptimal store layouts.

Solution Development

The retailer adopted a computer vision system across its network of stores, comprising the following strategic components:

1. **Foot Traffic Monitoring:** Installation of cameras at key points to track customer movements, aiding in the analysis of peak hours and staffing optimization.
2. **Customer Behavior Analysis:** Deployment of algorithms to interpret how customers engage with products, identifying high-demand items and store hotspots.
3. **Queue Management:** Real-time assessment of checkout lines to dynamically open additional registers, enhancing customer satisfaction by reducing wait times.
4. **Store Layout Optimization:** Utilization of heatmaps from traffic and interaction data to inform strategic changes in store design, aiming to maximize engagement and sales.
5. **Personalized Experiences:** Leveraging loyalty program data to deliver customized marketing messages and promotions to customers based on their in-store behavior.

Implementation Process

As a Business Analyst, my role encompassed several key activities:

- **Stakeholder Engagement:** Collaborated with IT, operations, marketing, and external technology partners to align on project goals and milestones.
- **Technology Selection:** Evaluated and selected computer vision and analytics tools, emphasizing scalability, accuracy, and integration capabilities.
- **Pilot Testing:** Oversaw the pilot implementation in select stores to refine the technology setup and gather preliminary insights.
- **Data Privacy Compliance:** Worked closely with legal teams to ensure all data collection and analysis adhered to privacy laws and regulations.
- **Training and Change Management:** Facilitated training sessions for store staff and management on the new system and processes.

Results

The introduction of computer vision technology led to remarkable outcomes:

- **Operational Efficiency:** Streamlined operations and queue management contributed to a 30% decrease in checkout wait times.
- **Enhanced Customer Insights:** The detailed analysis offered actionable insights for inventory, marketing,

and product placement strategies.
- **Sales Growth:** Targeted improvements in store layout and marketing initiatives drove a 20% sales increase in key categories.
- **Personalization:** The integration of in-store behavior with loyalty programs significantly elevated the customer experience.

Challenges and Considerations

The project faced hurdles, including addressing privacy concerns and ensuring the secure handling of customer data. It was crucial to anonymize and protect data to maintain customer trust. Additionally, the computer vision algorithms required ongoing adjustments to keep pace with evolving customer behaviors and store configurations.

Conclusion

This case study demonstrates the power of computer vision to transform the retail sector. By harnessing this technology, the retailer not only optimized its operations but also crafted more personalized and engaging shopping experiences. Balancing innovation with privacy concerns and continuously adapting to retail dynamics were essential for achieving sustainable growth and customer satisfaction.

Case Study: Revolutionizing Medical Diagnostics with Computer Vision

Overview

In the rapidly evolving healthcare landscape, the integration of computer vision into medical imaging and diagnostic support systems represents a significant leap forward. This case study delves into the journey of a leading healthcare institution as it embraces computer vision technologies to enhance diagnostic accuracy and improve patient care outcomes.

Role of the Business Analyst

As a Business Analyst, my responsibility was to bridge the gap between medical professionals' diagnostic needs and the technical capabilities offered by computer vision technology. This involved understanding the clinical requirements, identifying suitable technological solutions, and overseeing the project's implementation process.

Implementation Process

Identifying Stakeholders

- **Medical Professionals:** Their insights were crucial in understanding the diagnostic challenges and integrating computer vision solutions into clinical workflows.
- **Patients:** The primary beneficiaries of improved diagnostic accuracy and efficiency.
- **IT and Data Science Teams:** Tasked with the technical development, implementation, and maintenance of the computer vision systems.
- **Regulatory Bodies:** Ensured that the solution complied with healthcare regulations and patient data protection laws.

Discovering Business Objectives

The project aimed to:

- Significantly enhance diagnostic accuracy through advanced image analysis.
- Enable early disease detection, particularly for conditions like cancer, by pinpointing anomalies with greater precision.
- Streamline the diagnostic process, making it more time and resource-efficient.

Evaluating Options

After reviewing various computer vision platforms, we prioritized those offering high accuracy, seamless integration with existing medical imaging tools, scalability, and regulatory compliance.

Scope Definition

The project scope was meticulously outlined to include:

- The development and integration of deep learning models capable of analyzing various medical imaging data, including X-rays and MRI scans.
- Model training on a comprehensive dataset of medical images to ensure accuracy in anomaly detection.
- Creation of an intuitive interface for medical professionals.
- Upholding data security and patient privacy standards.

Enterprise Analysis and Requirements Planning

A detailed analysis highlighted the need for robust computational infrastructure and established criteria for data privacy, model accuracy, and system interoperability.

Investigating the Situation

An initial investigation into existing diagnostic processes pinpointed limitations in early disease detection and a concerning rate of diagnostic errors, presenting computer vision as a viable solution.

Evaluating Improvements

The computer vision system brought about considerable improvements in diagnostic accuracy and efficiency, particularly in early detection efforts, thereby enhancing patient care.

Outcome and Impact

The implementation of computer vision technologies yielded:

- An increase in disease detection accuracy and early intervention capabilities.
- More efficient diagnostic processes, significantly reducing patient wait times.
- Notably improved patient outcomes through timely and accurate diagnoses.

Challenges and Considerations

The project encountered hurdles, including acquiring sufficient training data for the models and addressing the interpretability of the models' decisions. Continuous model training and updates were essential to keep pace with evolving diagnostic needs.

Conclusion

This case study underscores the profound impact of integrating computer vision in medical imaging and diagnostic support, highlighting a milestone in the use of technology to advance healthcare. Through careful planning, stakeholder engagement, and continuous improvement, we have significantly enhanced diagnostic accuracy, streamlined processes, and, most importantly, improved patient outcomes, setting a new standard in medical diagnostics.

Computer vision stands at the forefront of technological innovation, reshaping the landscape of data analytics, data science, business intelligence, and AI with its ability to interpret and derive insights from visual information.

Other AI Applications

Examining real-world applications of AI in recommendation systems, chatbots, autonomous vehicles, and more.

AI Applications

Artificial Intelligence (AI) has emerged as a transformative force, revolutionizing businesses and industries by enabling machines to perform cognitive functions typically associated with human intelligence. From recommendation systems and chatbots to autonomous vehicles and healthcare diagnostics, the applications of AI have permeated diverse domains, driving innovation, enhancing user experiences, and unlocking new opportunities for businesses. In this chapter, we will delve into real-world examples and case studies that showcase the practical impact of AI across various industries, shedding light on the transformative potential of AI in driving innovation and shaping the future of business analytics and AI-driven technologies.

Recommendation Systems

Recommendation systems, a cornerstone of AI applications, have redefined the landscape of e-commerce, entertainment, and content consumption by providing personalized recommendations to users. Leveraging advanced machine learning algorithms and collaborative filtering techniques, recommendation systems analyze user behavior, preferences, and historical data to deliver tailored suggestions, thereby enhancing user engagement, driving sales, and fostering customer loyalty. Companies such as Amazon, Netflix, and Spotify have successfully harnessed the power of recommendation systems to curate personalized product recommendations, movie selections, and music playlists, thereby enriching user experiences and optimizing content delivery.

Chatbots and Virtual Assistants

Chatbots and virtual assistants represent another compelling application of AI, revolutionizing customer service, support, and interaction across diverse industries. By integrating natural language processing (NLP) and machine learning algorithms, chatbots can engage in intelligent conversations, understand user queries, and provide relevant information and assistance, thereby streamlining customer interactions and augmenting operational efficiency. From automated customer support and virtual concierge services to voice-activated assistants and personalized recommendations, chatbots have empowered businesses to deliver seamless, personalized experiences while optimizing resource utilization and enhancing customer satisfaction.

Healthcare Diagnostics and Disease Prediction

AI has emerged as a transformative force in healthcare, empowering medical professionals with advanced diagnostic tools, predictive analytics, and personalized treatment recommendations. By leveraging machine learning models and deep learning algorithms, AI can analyze medical images, genomic data, and patient records to detect anomalies, predict disease progression, and optimize treatment plans, ultimately improving patient outcomes and healthcare delivery. From early detection of diseases and precision medicine to drug discovery and clinical decision support, AI-driven healthcare applications hold the potential to revolutionize medical diagnostics, treatment, and patient care, fostering a new era of personalized and data-driven healthcare solutions.

Financial Fraud Detection and Risk Management

In the financial sector, AI applications have played a critical role in detecting fraudulent activities, mitigating risks, and enhancing security measures. By leveraging machine learning algorithms and anomaly detection techniques, AI systems can analyze vast volumes of financial transactions, identify suspicious patterns, and flag potential fraudulent activities in real time, thereby safeguarding financial institutions and their customers from fraudulent behavior and cyber threats. Furthermore, AI-driven risk management solutions can assess credit risks, optimize investment portfolios, and enhance regulatory compliance, enabling financial institutions to make data-driven decisions and mitigate financial risks effectively.

Business Analysis Basis-Requirements Elicitation and Analysis

Techniques for Gathering Business Requirements

As a business analyst, the process of gathering business requirements is a fundamental step in the successful execution of data-driven projects. The ability to collect detailed and accurate business requirements is crucial in ensuring that the end product meets the needs and expectations of stakeholders. In this session, we will explore various techniques such as interviews, surveys, observations, and brainstorming sessions that are essential for translating business strategy into powerful data Solutions.

1. Interviews

One of the most effective techniques for gathering business requirements is conducting interviews with stakeholders and subject matter experts. During these interviews, the business analyst engages in in-depth conversations to elicit information about the project scope, objectives, constraints, and desired outcomes. By asking targeted questions and actively listening to the responses, the business analyst can capture valuable insights that inform the development of comprehensive business requirements.

Interviews provide an opportunity to delve into the specific needs of individual stakeholders, allowing the business analyst to gain a nuanced understanding of their perspectives and priorities. Additionally, conducting interviews fosters open communication and collaboration, establishing a foundation of trust and rapport that is essential for successful requirement gathering.

2. Surveys

In situations where engaging with a large number of stakeholders is necessary, surveys are a valuable tool for gathering business requirements. Surveys allow the business analyst to reach a broader audience and collect quantitative and qualitative data on the needs and preferences of stakeholders. By designing targeted survey questions and distributing them through appropriate channels, the business analyst can gather diverse perspectives and identify common themes and patterns across the stakeholder group.

When analyzing survey responses, the business analyst can identify trends and prioritize requirements based on the collective input of the stakeholders. Surveys provide a systematic approach to gathering business requirements and can complement other techniques by providing a comprehensive view of stakeholder perspectives.

3. Observations

In certain scenarios, observing the current business processes and workflows can provide invaluable insights into the underlying requirements for a data-driven project. By immersing themselves in the operational environment, business analysts can identify pain points, inefficiencies, and opportunities for improvement. Observations enable the business analyst to gain a firsthand understanding of how the business operates and identify areas where data analytics, data science, business intelligence, or AI solutions can drive meaningful impact.

Furthermore, observations can uncover implicit requirements that stakeholders may not explicitly articulate during interviews or surveys. By observing interactions, workflows, and decision-making processes, the business analyst can uncover hidden requirements that are essential for developing a comprehensive understanding of the business context.

4. Brainstorming Sessions

Collaborative brainstorming sessions offer a platform for stakeholders to collectively generate and refine business requirements in a structured and creative manner. By bringing together diverse perspectives and expertise, brainstorming sessions foster ideation and innovation, leading to the discovery of novel requirements and potential solutions. Business analysts facilitate these sessions by guiding the discussion, capturing ideas, and synthesizing them into actionable requirements.

Brainstorming sessions encourage active participation and engagement from stakeholders, empowering them to contribute to the development of business requirements. Additionally, the iterative nature of brainstorming allows for the exploration of alternative approaches and the refinement of requirements through collaborative feedback and discussion.

In conclusion, mastering the techniques for gathering business requirements is essential for driving the success of data analytics, data science, business intelligence, and AI projects. By leveraging interviews, surveys, observations, and brainstorming sessions, business analysts can capture the diverse and nuanced needs of stakeholders, leading to the development of comprehensive and accurate business requirements. These techniques empower business analysts to navigate the complexities of requirement gathering and pave the way for the successful execution of data-driven projects.

Practical Implementation of Digital Transformation in Retail Banking: A Comprehensive Case Study

Background

In the dynamic landscape of retail banking, a prominent bank initiated a digital transformation project with the aspiration to redefine customer experience, elevate operational efficiency, and harness the power of data analytics for delivering personalized banking services. The cornerstone of this project's success was the meticulous gathering and analysis of business requirements, a task that necessitated a synergistic collaboration among business analysts, stakeholders, and subject matter experts.

Techniques for Gathering Business Requirements

To ensure a robust foundation for the digital transformation, a multifaceted approach was adopted to gather business requirements:

1. Interviews

Business analysts conducted exhaustive interviews with a wide array of internal stakeholders, including bank executives, branch managers, IT staff, and customer service representatives. These interactions provided valuable insights into the existing operational challenges, expectations from the digital overhaul, and specific functionalities desired in the new banking platform. This method proved instrumental in grasping the intricate requirements from various organizational perspectives.

Practical Implementation:

- **Scheduled Sessions:** Interviews were meticulously planned to cover all relevant departments within the bank.
- **Structured Questionnaires:** Tailored questionnaires were developed to ensure comprehensive coverage of

all pertinent areas.
- **Documentation:** All insights and requirements gathered were documented in a centralized repository for subsequent analysis and reference.

2. Surveys

To capture the voices of a broader audience, including customers and frontline employees, targeted surveys were deployed. These surveys were designed to extract feedback on current service satisfaction levels, digital features of interest, and areas yearning for improvement. The analysis of survey responses illuminated significant trends and customer preferences, which played a pivotal role in prioritizing the project's requirements.

Practical Implementation:

- **Digital Platforms:** Utilized online survey tools for widespread distribution and ease of analysis.
- **Segmented Surveys:** Surveys were tailored to specific customer segments to capture nuanced feedback.
- **Feedback Loop:** Results were shared with relevant teams to inform decision-making and strategy development.

3. Observations

Business analysts undertook field observations across several bank branches and existing digital platforms. These firsthand insights into the day-to-day operations unveiled inefficiencies in customer service and gaps in the digital service offerings. Observing the customer journey in action was key to pinpointing crucial enhancements needed in the digital platform to streamline operations and enrich customer interactions.

Practical Implementation:

- **Observation Schedule:** Planned visits during peak and off-peak hours to observe a range of interactions.
- **Technology Use:** Leveraged video and audio recording tools (with consent) for accurate documentation.
- **Immediate Feedback:** Provided real-time suggestions for quick wins in customer service improvement.

4. Brainstorming Sessions

Diverse stakeholder groups were convened in brainstorming sessions to foster innovative ideas for the digital platform and to deliberate potential challenges and solutions. This inclusive approach ensured that the project encapsulated a broad spectrum of requirements and inventive solutions to address them.

Practical Implementation:

- **Facilitated Workshops:** Employed professional facilitators to guide discussions and ensure productive outcomes.
- **Idea Management Software:** Used digital tools to capture and categorize ideas for easy retrieval and assessment.
- **Cross-functional Teams:** Encouraged participation from across departments to ensure a holistic view of the project.

Outcome

The amalgamation of interviews, surveys, observations, and brainstorming sessions culminated in a nuanced understanding of organizational and customer needs. This led to the creation of a digital banking platform characterized by:

- Personalized banking experiences, powered by advanced data analytics.
- Streamlined internal processes for enhanced operational efficiency.
- An integrated omnichannel experience, enabling customers to fluidly transition between physical branches and digital services.

Impact

The bank's digital transformation project markedly improved customer satisfaction, catalyzing increased retention and the acquisition of new customers. Furthermore, the bank observed a reduction in operational costs due to the optimization of processes and an uptick in revenue from newly introduced digital services.

Conclusion

This case study underscores the paramount importance of comprehensive business requirements gathering in the fruition of successful digital transformation projects. By leveraging a blend of interviews, surveys, observations, and brainstorming sessions, the retail bank ensured the alignment of its digital transformation initiative with both its internal objectives and customer expectations, thereby achieving significant business benefits and superior customer experiences.

Documenting Business Requirements

As a business analyst, the ability to effectively document business requirements is paramount to the success of data analytics, data science, business intelligence, and AI projects. Documentation serves as the bridge between the insights gathered from stakeholders and the tangible solutions that will be developed to address their needs. In this session, we will explore the importance of documenting business requirements, the key elements of effective documentation, and best practices for ensuring clarity, traceability, and alignment with project objectives.

Importance of Documenting Business Requirements

Documenting business requirements is essential for several reasons. Firstly, it provides a clear and structured representation of the needs, expectations, and constraints identified during the requirements gathering phase. This documentation serves as a reference point for all project stakeholders, ensuring that everyone is aligned on the scope and objectives of the project. Additionally, it facilitates communication and collaboration among cross-functional teams, enabling a shared understanding of the business context and requirements.

Furthermore, well-documented business requirements serve as a basis for making informed decisions throughout the project lifecycle. They provide a foundation for prioritizing features, defining acceptance criteria, and validating the success of the solution against the originally identified needs. Moreover, documentation supports the traceability of requirements, enabling stakeholders to understand the rationale behind specific design and development decisions, and to track changes and their impacts over time.

Key Elements of Effective Documentation

Effective documentation of business requirements encompasses several key elements that contribute to its clarity, completeness, and usability. These elements include:

1. Business Needs and Objectives: The documentation should clearly articulate the business needs, goals, and objectives that the solution aims to address. This provides the context for understanding the significance and impact of the requirements.

2. Stakeholder Requirements: It is crucial to capture the specific needs and expectations of each stakeholder group. This includes functional, non-functional, and technical requirements, as well as any constraints or dependencies that may influence the solution design.

3. Use Cases and User Stories: Use cases and user stories provide a narrative description of how the solution will be used and the value it will deliver to end users. They serve as concrete examples that illustrate the functionality and behavior of the proposed solution.

4. Acceptance Criteria: Clearly defined acceptance criteria outline the conditions that must be met for a requirement to be considered successfully implemented. This ensures that the solution aligns with the intended outcomes and meets the expectations of stakeholders.

5. Assumptions and Constraints: Documenting assumptions and constraints helps to delineate the boundaries within which the solution must operate. This provides transparency regarding any limitations or dependencies that may impact the implementation and performance of the solution.

Best Practices for Documentation

To ensure that business requirements are documented effectively, it is important to adhere to best practices that promote clarity, consistency, and accessibility. Some best practices include:

1. Standardized Templates: Using standardized templates for documenting business requirements ensures a consistent format and structure across all project documentation. This facilitates readability and comprehension for all stakeholders.

2. Version Control: Implementing version control mechanisms for the documentation helps to track changes, revisions, and updates over time. This ensures that stakeholders are working with the most current and accurate information.

3. Collaboration and Review: Encouraging collaboration and seeking input from relevant stakeholders during the documentation process fosters a sense of ownership and ensures that all perspectives are considered. Additionally, conducting regular reviews of the documentation helps to validate its accuracy and completeness.

4. Clear and Concise Language: Using clear and concise language in the documentation helps to eliminate ambiguity and misinterpretation. Avoiding technical jargon and acronyms that may not be universally understood ensures that the documentation is accessible to all stakeholders.

5. Traceability and Cross-Referencing: Establishing traceability links and cross-references within the documentation enables stakeholders to navigate between related requirements and understand their interdependencies. This promotes a holistic view of the solution and its constituent parts.

By adhering to these best practices, business analysts can ensure that the documentation of business requirements is comprehensive, unambiguous, and aligned with the needs and expectations of stakeholders.

Implementing a CRM System at XYZ Corporation: A Strategic Initiative to Enhance Customer Engagement and Drive Growth

Background

In the fast-paced retail industry, maintaining robust customer relationships and streamlining sales operations are pivotal for sustaining growth. XYZ Corporation, a front-runner in the retail sector, acknowledged the imperative need to enhance its customer engagement and sales methodologies. The corporation embarked on an initiative to implement a Customer Relationship Management (CRM) system, aimed at augmenting customer satisfaction, optimizing sales processes, and catalyzing revenue growth. A Business Analyst (BA) was commissioned to spearhead this venture by documenting the comprehensive business requirements.

The Importance of Documenting Business Requirements

For XYZ Corporation, the meticulous documentation of business requirements was not merely a procedural step but a cornerstone for the project's success. It ensured a shared understanding of the project's aims and scope among all stakeholders, streamlined communication across diverse teams, and provided a solid foundation for decision-making and solution validation. Furthermore, it facilitated the traceability of requirements throughout the project's lifecycle, ensuring steadfast alignment with the corporation's strategic objectives.

Process of Documenting Business Requirements

Identifying Stakeholders

The spectrum of stakeholders encompassed the sales team, customer service representatives, the marketing department, the IT team, and, crucially, the customers themselves. Early engagement with these groups was essential to glean their needs and expectations from the CRM system.

Discovering Business Objectives

The CRM implementation was driven by four primary business objectives:

1. Elevating customer engagement and satisfaction.
2. Streamlining the sales process to enhance efficiency.
3. Gleaning actionable insights into customer behaviors.
4. Bolstering sales and fostering revenue growth.

Through SWOT analysis and focus group discussions, these objectives were refined to ensure alignment with the company's overarching strategic ambitions.

Evaluating Options

The BA undertook a comprehensive evaluation of various CRM solutions, considering critical factors such as customization capabilities, integration potential with existing systems, user-friendliness, and cost-effectiveness. The evaluation spanned cloud-based solutions to on-premise installations, aiming to identify the most fitting solution for XYZ Corporation.

Defining the Scope

The defined project scope included critical elements such as:

- Seamless integration of the CRM system with existing ERP and e-commerce platforms.
- Customizations tailored to the specific needs of the sales and marketing departments.
- Efficient data migration from legacy systems to the new CRM framework.
- Comprehensive training programs for staff to ensure adept usage of the new system.

Non-essentials, like the complete overhaul of the existing e-commerce platform or integration with untested third-party tools, were deliberately excluded from the scope.

Enterprise Analysis and Requirements Planning & Management

An exhaustive enterprise analysis underscored the necessity for a scalable CRM solution, capable of accommodating a burgeoning customer base and evolving business exigencies. The analysis delineated requirements pertaining to data security, system reliability, and adherence to regulatory mandates.

Investigating the Situation and Identifying Improvements

A thorough review of the extant sales processes and customer interaction mechanisms unearthed inefficiencies and improvement avenues. The CRM system was pinpointed as a pivotal solution for automating routine tasks, providing in-depth customer insights, and enabling personalized marketing strategies.

Evaluating Improvements and Solutions

The chosen CRM solution promised a plethora of benefits, including:

- Automated sales workflows to minimize manual data entry and mitigate errors.
- Advanced customer segmentation for bespoke marketing campaigns.
- Access to real-time sales and customer analytics for informed decision-making.
- Enhanced customer service capabilities, significantly boosting customer satisfaction levels.

Key Elements of Effective Documentation

The BA incorporated several key elements into the business requirements documentation to ensure clarity and comprehensiveness:

1. **Business Needs and Objectives:** Articulated the strategic goals aimed to be achieved with the CRM system.
2. **Stakeholder Requirements:** Detailed the specific needs of each stakeholder group, encompassing both functional and technical requirements.
3. **Use Cases and User Stories:** Showcased scenarios illustrating the CRM's application and its advantages to users.
4. **Acceptance Criteria:** Established specific conditions that each requirement must meet to be deemed

fulfilled.
5. **Assumptions and Constraints:** Highlighted planning assumptions and any project constraints.

Best Practices for Documentation

To optimize the effectiveness of the documentation process, the BA adhered to several best practices:

1. **Standardized Templates:** Ensured consistency across all documentation.
2. **Version Control:** Managed revisions meticulously to keep stakeholders informed with the most up-to-date documents.
3. **Collaboration and Review:** Fostered stakeholder engagement in the documentation process and conducted regular reviews to guarantee accuracy.
4. **Clear and Concise Language:** Made the documentation accessible and comprehensible to all stakeholders.
5. **Traceability and Cross-Referencing:** Facilitated easy navigation among related documents and requirements.

Conclusion

By rigorously documenting the business requirements and adhering to best documentation practices, the BA played a pivotal role in ensuring that the CRM system implementation at XYZ Corporation was meticulously aligned with the company's

Conducting Stakeholder Interviews

Stakeholder interviews are a fundamental aspect of the business analysis process. They provide a platform for business analysts to engage with stakeholders, understand their perspectives, and extract valuable insights that will inform the project's direction and requirements. In this chapter, we will explore the intricacies of conducting stakeholder interviews, including the preparation, execution, and follow-up phases. By mastering the art of interviewing stakeholders, business analysts can uncover critical information that will drive the success of data analytics, data science, business intelligence, and AI projects.

Preparation for Stakeholder Interviews

Effective preparation is the cornerstone of successful stakeholder interviews. Prior to conducting interviews, business analysts should undertake the following preparatory steps:

1. Stakeholder Identification: Identify the key stakeholders who possess relevant insights, perspectives, and decision-making authority. This may include business leaders, subject matter experts, end users, and other individuals with a vested interest in the project's outcomes.

2. Objectives Clarification: Clearly define the objectives of the interviews, outlining the specific information and perspectives that need to be elicited from stakeholders. This could include understanding their pain points, expectations, preferences, and constraints.

3. Interview Plan Development: Develop a structured interview plan that outlines the key topics, questions, and probes that will be used to guide the conversation with stakeholders. This plan should ensure that all relevant areas are covered and that the interview remains focused and productive.

4. Logistics Arrangements: Coordinate the logistics of the interviews, including scheduling, location, and any necessary materials or technology required for the interviews. Ensuring that stakeholders are comfortable and well-prepared for the interviews is essential for obtaining valuable insights.

Execution of Stakeholder Interviews

The execution phase of stakeholder interviews requires business analysts to employ active listening, effective communication, and adaptability to the dynamics of the conversation. During this phase, analysts should focus on the following considerations:

1. Establishing Rapport: Begin the interview by establishing a rapport with the stakeholders, creating an environment of trust and openness that encourages them to share their perspectives and insights candidly.

2. Open-Ended Questions: Use open-ended questions to elicit detailed and nuanced responses from stakeholders, allowing them to express their thoughts and experiences in their own words. This approach fosters a deeper understanding of their perspectives and needs.

3. Probing for Clarity: Employ probing techniques to delve deeper into specific topics or responses, seeking clarity and additional context to fully comprehend the nuances of stakeholders' viewpoints.

4. Active Listening: Actively listen to stakeholders' responses, demonstrating genuine interest and attention to their perspectives. This not only validates their contributions but also enables the identification of underlying motivations and concerns.

5. Adaptability: Remain adaptable and responsive to the flow of the conversation, allowing for unexpected insights or deviations from the interview plan that may lead to valuable discoveries.

Follow-up and Analysis of Stakeholder Interviews

After the interviews, the follow-up and analysis phase is crucial for synthesizing the gathered insights and translating them into actionable requirements. This phase involves the following steps:

1. Documentation of Insights: Thoroughly document the insights, perspectives, and findings from the stakeholder interviews, capturing the nuances and key takeaways that will inform the project's requirements and direction.

2. Validation and Alignment: Validate the insights obtained from stakeholder interviews against existing knowledge and project objectives, ensuring that they align with the overarching goals and constraints of the project.

3. Requirement Formulation: Translate the extracted insights into clear and concise requirement statements, use cases, and user stories that reflect the needs, expectations, and preferences of stakeholders.

4. Collaboration with Stakeholders: Engage stakeholders in the review and validation of the formulated requirements, seeking their input and feedback to ensure that the documented requirements accurately represent their perspectives.

5. Iterative Refinement: Iterate on the documented requirements based on stakeholder feedback, refining and enhancing them to reflect a comprehensive and accurate representation of the stakeholders' needs and expectations.

Conducting stakeholder interviews is a pivotal component of the business analyst's toolkit, essential for gathering the diverse perspectives, insights, and expectations of stakeholders in data-driven projects. By mastering the process of preparation, execution, and follow-up, business analysts can extract valuable information that will drive the identification of key project requirements, ensuring that the resulting solutions effectively address the needs and preferences of stakeholders.

Facilitating Workshops

In the realm of business analysis for data analytics, data science, business intelligence, and AI projects, engaging in workshops with stakeholders is a powerful mechanism for fostering collaboration, creativity, and consensus in defining and prioritizing business requirements. This session will provide an in-depth exploration of how business analysts can effectively plan and facilitate workshops to elicit valuable insights, align stakeholder perspectives, and drive the strategic direction of projects. By mastering the art of workshop facilitation, business analysts can leverage the collective expertise and creativity of stakeholders to inform and shape the project's requirements, ultimately contributing to the successful delivery of data-driven solutions.

Planning for Workshops

Effective planning is essential for the success of workshops, ensuring that the objectives are clearly defined, the participants are engaged, and the outcomes align with the project's strategic goals. The following preparatory steps are crucial for planning workshops:

1. Objective Definition: Clearly define the objectives of the workshop, outlining the specific outcomes, decisions, or discussions that need to be achieved. These objectives should be aligned with the project's scope, and they may include the identification of business requirements, prioritization of features, or ideation of solution concepts.

2. Participant Selection: Identify and invite the appropriate stakeholders to participate in the workshop, ensuring representation from diverse perspectives, expertise, and decision-making authority. This may include business leaders, subject matter experts, end users, and other individuals who can contribute valuable insights.

3. Agenda Development: Develop a structured agenda for the workshop, outlining the topics, activities, and time allocations that will guide the flow of the session. The agenda should balance information dissemination, interactive discussions, and collaborative exercises to achieve the desired outcomes.

4. Material Preparation: Prepare any necessary materials, tools, or visual aids that will support the workshop activities, such as whiteboards, flip charts, sticky notes, and facilitation guides. Ensuring that the workshop environment is conducive to creativity and collaboration is essential for achieving meaningful outcomes.

Facilitation of Workshops

The role of the business analyst as a workshop facilitator is to guide the participants through a structured process that encourages active participation, idea generation, and consensus building. During the facilitation phase, business analysts should focus on the following key considerations:

1. Setting the Context: Begin the workshop by setting the context for the discussions, providing a clear overview of the objectives, agenda, and expected outcomes. This sets the stage for productive and focused engagement from the participants.

2. Engaging Activities: Introduce engaging activities and exercises that prompt stakeholders to share their perspectives, generate ideas, and collaborate on defining or prioritizing business requirements. This may include brainstorming sessions, group discussions, affinity mapping, or prioritization exercises.

3. Encouraging Participation: Create an inclusive and supportive environment that encourages all participants to contribute their insights, experiences, and ideas. Facilitate active participation by asking open-ended questions, seeking diverse viewpoints, and valuing the contributions of all stakeholders.

4. Conflict Resolution: Effectively manage any conflicts or divergent opinions that may arise during the workshop, guiding the participants toward constructive discussions and consensus-building. This may involve mediating discussions, clarifying misunderstandings, and ensuring that all perspectives are heard and considered.

5. Decision Making: Guide the participants through decision-making processes to align on key priorities, requirements, or design choices. This may involve voting exercises, consensus-seeking discussions, or structured decision-making frameworks to reach collective agreements.

Capture and Analysis of Workshop Outputs

After the workshop sessions, the capture and analysis of the generated outputs are critical for synthesizing the collective insights, identifying patterns, and translating them into actionable requirements. This phase involves the following steps:

1. Documentation of Outputs: Thoroughly document the outputs, ideas, decisions, and prioritizations that emerged from the workshop sessions, capturing the nuances and rationale behind the identified requirements or strategic directions.

2. Validation and Alignment: Validate the outputs against the project objectives, existing knowledge, and stakeholder expectations, ensuring that they align with the overarching goals and constraints of the project. This may involve cross-referencing the workshop outputs with previous insights gathered from stakeholder interviews or other requirements elicitation activities.

3. Requirement Prioritization: Translate the workshop outputs into clear and prioritized business requirements, features, or solution concepts that reflect the consensus and collective decisions of the participants. This prioritization enables the focus on high-impact deliverables that align with the strategic objectives of the project.

4. Collaboration with Stakeholders: Engage the workshop participants in the review and validation of the captured outputs, seeking their input and feedback to ensure that the documented requirements accurately represent their collective perspectives. This collaborative validation fosters stakeholder buy-in and ownership of the identified priorities.

5. Iterative Refinement: Iterate on the documented outputs based on stakeholder feedback, refining and enhancing them to reflect a comprehensive and accurate representation of the collective insights and decisions generated during the workshops.

Conclusion

Facilitating workshops is a pivotal aspect of the business analyst's toolkit for driving collaboration, creativity, and consensus among stakeholders in data-driven projects. By effectively planning and guiding workshop sessions, business analysts can harness the collective expertise and creativity of stakeholders to define, prioritize, and align on critical business requirements, ultimately shaping the strategic direction of data analytics, data science, business intelligence, and AI projects.

Leveraging Surveys for Requirement Elicitation

Introduction to Surveys

Surveys are a valuable tool for gathering feedback, preferences, and requirements from a wide range of stakeholders, ensuring comprehensive input for the success of data analytics, data science, business intelligence, and AI projects. In this chapter, we will explore the strategic use of surveys in uncovering and prioritizing business requirements, understanding stakeholder perspectives, and validating insights to inform the strategic direction of projects.

The Role of Surveys in Requirement Elicitation

Surveys offer a structured and scalable approach to gather input from diverse stakeholders, including business leaders, subject matter experts, end users, and other individuals who can provide valuable insights. By leveraging surveys, business analysts can elicit a broad range of perspectives, preferences, and requirements, ensuring that the project's deliverables align with the evolving needs of the organization and its stakeholders.

Designing Effective Surveys

The effectiveness of surveys in eliciting valuable requirements hinges on their design and execution. Business analysts should consider the following key aspects when designing surveys for requirement elicitation:

1. Clear Objectives: Define the specific objectives of the survey, outlining the insights, preferences, or decisions that need to be captured. These objectives should be aligned with the project's scope and strategic goals, guiding the design of survey questions and response options.

2. Target Audience: Identify the target audience for the survey, ensuring representation from diverse perspectives, roles, and expertise. Tailoring the survey to the specific characteristics and needs of the audience enhances the relevance and quality of the elicited requirements.

3. Question Structure: Craft clear and concise survey questions that align with the defined objectives, avoiding ambiguity and leading language. The question structure should facilitate meaningful responses and enable the capture of nuanced requirements and preferences.

4. Response Options: Provide well-structured response options that allow participants to express a range of perspectives, priorities, and preferences. Utilizing a mix of closed-ended and open-ended response formats can capture both quantitative data and qualitative insights.

5. Survey Flow: Design the survey flow to guide participants through a logical and coherent sequence of questions, ensuring that the survey is intuitive and engaging. Consider the use of skip logic and branching to tailor the survey experience to individual participant profiles.

Distributing and Collecting Survey Responses

Once the survey is designed, the distribution and collection of responses play a crucial role in maximizing participation and capturing diverse insights. Business analysts should consider the following strategies for effectively distributing and collecting survey responses:

1. Communication Plan: Develop a communication plan to promote the survey, clearly articulating its purpose, the expected time commitment, and the value of the participant's input. Engaging stakeholders through targeted messaging enhances survey participation and response quality.

2. Multi-Channel Distribution: Utilize multiple channels for survey distribution, including email, collaboration platforms, and enterprise communication tools. Leveraging diverse channels increases the reach of the survey and accommodates diverse communication preferences.

3. Incentives and Reminders: Consider implementing incentives for survey participation, such as prize draws or recognition, to motivate stakeholders to provide thoughtful responses. Additionally, sending timely reminders can prompt participation and ensure a high response rate.

4. Data Security and Privacy: Communicate the measures taken to ensure the security and privacy of survey responses, fostering trust and confidence among participants. Clearly outline data protection protocols and use secure survey platforms to safeguard participant information.

Analyzing and Synthesizing Survey Data

The analysis and synthesis of survey data are critical steps in deriving actionable insights and requirements from the collected responses. Business analysts should employ the following techniques to effectively analyze and synthesize survey data:

1. Quantitative Analysis: Utilize statistical methods to analyze quantitative survey responses, identifying trends, patterns, and correlations within the data. This analysis provides quantitative validation of preferences and priorities, informing the prioritization of requirements.

2. Qualitative Coding: Apply qualitative coding techniques to categorize and analyze open-ended survey responses, identifying recurring themes, sentiments, and nuanced requirements. This qualitative analysis enriches the understanding of stakeholder perspectives and uncovers nuanced insights.

3. Cross-Referencing with Stakeholder Profiles: Cross-reference survey data with stakeholder profiles and characteristics to understand how preferences and requirements vary across different roles and perspectives. This segmentation enables targeted insights and requirement prioritization based on stakeholder groups.

4. Synthesizing Insights: Synthesize the analyzed survey data into a coherent and comprehensive representation of stakeholder preferences, priorities, and requirements. This synthesis forms the basis for informed decision-making and the validation of strategic project directions.

Incorporating Survey Insights into Requirements

The insights gleaned from surveys should be incorporated into the broader context of requirement elicitation, aligning with other sources of stakeholder input and project objectives. Business analysts should consider the following strategies for effectively incorporating survey insights into the definition and prioritization of requirements:

1. Requirement Validation: Validate the survey insights against existing knowledge, stakeholder interviews, and other requirement elicitation activities to ensure alignment with the project's strategic goals and constraints. This validation enhances the reliability and relevance of the survey-derived requirements.

2. Collaborative Review: Engage stakeholders in the review and validation of survey-derived requirements, seeking their input and feedback to ensure that the captured insights accurately represent their preferences and priorities. This collaborative review fosters stakeholder buy-in and ownership of the identified requirements.

3. Prioritization Alignment: Align the survey-derived requirements with the prioritization framework established through workshops, interviews, or other requirement elicitation methods. This alignment ensures that the survey insights inform the prioritization of high-impact deliverables aligned with the project's strategic objectives.

4. Iterative Refinement: Iterate on the incorporated survey insights based on stakeholder feedback, refining and enhancing them to reflect a comprehensive and accurate representation of stakeholder preferences and requirements. This iterative refinement ensures that the survey insights evolve in response to stakeholder input and validation.

Digital Transformation of Global Supply Chain Operations: A Case Study on GlobalTech Inc.

Introduction

In an era where operational efficiency and agility are paramount, GlobalTech Inc., a renowned multinational manufacturing entity, confronted pressing challenges stemming from archaic systems and methodologies within its supply chain operations. The imperative to overhaul these outdated mechanisms propelled the organization towards embarking on a journey of digital transformation. The initiative aimed at not only enhancing operational efficiency but also at augmenting real-time visibility into the supply chain and empowering decision-making through digitalization. A cadre of skilled Business Analysts (BAs) was assembled to spearhead this transformative venture, tasked with the critical roles of eliciting, analyzing, and documenting business requirements, and steering the implementation of a comprehensive digital solution.

Requirements Elicitation and Analysis

Techniques for Gathering Business Requirements

The BAs deployed a multifaceted approach to ascertain a comprehensive understanding of the business necessities:

- **Conducting Stakeholder Interviews:** Key stakeholders, including supply chain managers, IT personnel, logistics coordinators, and executives, were interviewed individually. These interactions furnished profound insights into the specific challenges faced and the expectations from the digital overhaul.
- **Facilitating Workshops:** Cross-functional teams were brought together in collaborative workshops to deliberate on existing processes, identify pain points, and conceptualize future state processes. Brainstorming and process mapping techniques were pivotal in these sessions, facilitating a wide-ranging perspective on the requirements.
- **Leveraging Surveys for Requirement Elicitation:** Surveys were disseminated across the organization, reaching frontline employees to collate quantitative data on system usage, performance bottlenecks, and areas ripe for improvement.

Documenting Business Requirements

A comprehensive Business Requirements Document (BRD) was meticulously compiled by the BAs, utilizing standardized templates to ensure uniformity and clarity across the documentation, which included:

- **Business Needs and Objectives:** The strategic objectives of the digital transformation were delineated, emphasizing on reducing lead times, minimizing stockouts, and fostering supplier collaboration.
- **Functional Requirements:** The document elaborated on the functionalities required, such as real-time inventory tracking, automated procurement processes, and advanced analytics for demand forecasting.
- **Non-functional Requirements:** It specified the system performance, security, usability, and integration capabilities with existing ERP systems.
- **Stakeholder Roles and Responsibilities:** The document delineated the involvement and responsibilities of each stakeholder group within the project.
- **Acceptance Criteria:** It outlined the criteria for each requirement that must be fulfilled for the solution to be deemed acceptable.

Tools and Templates

- **Requirement Gathering Tools:** Tools like Jira and Confluence were employed for organizing, tracking, and sharing requirements.
- **Process Mapping Software:** Visio and Lucidchart were utilized for visualizing current and future state processes.
- **Survey Platforms:** SurveyMonkey was leveraged to design and distribute surveys, gathering broad organizational input.
- **Documentation Templates:** Standardized templates for the BRD were adopted to ensure a uniform structure that facilitates comprehension and review.

Stakeholders

- **Internal Stakeholders:** Included supply chain managers, IT staff, logistics coordinators, executives, and frontline employees.
- **External Stakeholders:** Encompassed suppliers, logistics partners, and technology vendors involved in the supply chain operations.

Implementation and Challenges

The implementation phase was characterized by the selection of a cloud-based supply chain management solution that aligned with the documented requirements. The selection was guided by detailed evaluation criteria from the BRD, focusing on integration capabilities with GlobalTech Inc.'s existing ERP system, scalability, and vendor support.

Key Challenges

- **Managing Change Resistance:** Employees accustomed to legacy systems exhibited resistance to change, a hurdle that was addressed through extensive training programs and stakeholder engagement activities.
- **Ensuring Data Accuracy:** The accuracy of data during the migration to the new digital platform was pivotal, tackled through phased migration strategies and parallel run periods to guarantee system reliability.

Outcome

The fruition of GlobalTech Inc.'s digital transformation journey was marked by notable achievements, including a 30% reduction in lead times, a 25% decrease in inventory costs, and a significant improvement in supplier collaboration, culminating in superior product quality and reliability. The project laid a robust foundation for continuous improvement and innovation in supply chain management practices.

Conclusion

This case study underscores the indispensable role of business analysis in catalyzing successful digital transformations. Through meticulous requirements elicitation, analysis, and documentation, the BAs at GlobalTech Inc. were instrumental in bridging the chasm between stakeholder needs and the technological solution. The result was not just a leap towards operational excellence in the supply chain domain but also a benchmark setting a new paradigm for future transformations.

Communication and Stakeholder Management

Effective Communication Strategies

In the realm of data analytics, data science, business intelligence, and AI projects, effective communication is the cornerstone of success. The ability to bridge the gap between business stakeholders and technical teams is paramount in ensuring alignment and clarity in data-driven initiatives. This chapter delves into communication strategies that facilitate understanding, foster collaboration, and ultimately drive the success of projects in the data realm.

Active Listening:

The art of active listening forms the bedrock of effective communication. Engaging in active listening requires giving undivided attention to the speaker, asking clarifying questions, and reflecting back messages for confirmation. This process not only demonstrates respect for the speaker but also ensures accurate understanding, thereby fostering trust and respect among team members. By actively listening, technical teams can gain a deeper understanding of the business requirements and expectations, while business stakeholders feel heard and valued. This creates a collaborative environment that sets the stage for successful project outcomes.

Storytelling:

The power of storytelling lies in its ability to make complex data insights understandable and memorable for business stakeholders. By weaving data into narratives, technical teams can illuminate trends and patterns in a way that resonates with stakeholders, making the abstract tangible. Storytelling not only simplifies complex data but also creates an emotional connection, driving home the significance of the insights and fostering a shared understanding among team members.

Visual Communication Tools:

In the age of data, visual communication tools play a pivotal role in transcending language and educational barriers. Dashboards, infographics, and data visualizations provide a clear understanding of complex information, enabling stakeholders to grasp insights at a glance. These visual tools not only aid in the comprehension of data but also enhance persuasion power, making a compelling case for the insights derived from the data. By leveraging visual communication tools, technical teams can effectively convey complex information to business stakeholders, ensuring alignment and clarity in project objectives.

Clarity in Language:

The use of simple, straightforward language is essential when communicating technical concepts to ensure that all team members are on the same page. Avoiding technical jargon that may be unfamiliar to non-technical stakeholders is crucial in fostering understanding and alignment. Clear and concise language not only facilitates effective communication but also minimizes the risk of misinterpretation, thereby promoting a shared understanding of project goals and requirements.

Feedback Loops:

Establishing regular check-ins where team members can voice concerns, ask questions, and provide updates is instrumental in keeping everyone aligned and engaged. These informal sessions create an open and inclusive atmosphere where every voice is heard, fostering a culture of transparency and collaboration. By incorporating feedback loops into the communication process, technical teams can address concerns and adapt to changing requirements, ensuring that the project remains on track and aligned with business objectives.

Empathy:

Understanding the perspectives, challenges, and motivations of others is essential in transforming interactions and building deeper connections among team members. Empathy plays a pivotal role in bridging the gap between business stakeholders and technical teams, fostering an environment of understanding and cooperation. By considering the business implications of technical work and vice versa, team members can align their efforts towards a common goal, driving the success of data-driven projects.

Leveraging Technology:

In an increasingly digital world, the effective use of collaboration tools, video conferencing software, and project management platforms is critical in enhancing communication, especially in remote work scenarios. Technology not only facilitates seamless interaction but also helps maintain the human connection vital to successful teamwork. By leveraging technology, teams can overcome geographical barriers and ensure that communication remains efficient and effective, regardless of physical distance.

Effective communication, encompassing these strategies, is critical for the success of data-driven projects. It ensures that every team member is engaged, understood, and aligned towards a common goal, ultimately driving the achievement of project objectives and delivering value to the business. By fostering a collaborative environment built on active listening, storytelling, visual communication tools, clarity in language, feedback loops, empathy, and the effective use of technology, organizations can propel their data initiatives towards success.

Stakeholder Expectation Management

What the BA Should Know and Do

As a business analyst, it is imperative to understand the significance of managing stakeholders' expectations in data analytics, data science, business intelligence, and AI projects. The effective management of stakeholder expectations contributes to successful project outcomes by creating a collaborative environment built on transparency, realistic goal setting, regular communication, stakeholder engagement, effective conflict resolution, data-driven decision-making, feedback incorporation, and personalized approaches.

Transparency

Transparency is a foundational element of stakeholder expectation management. By being transparent about project timelines, challenges, and potential risks, the business analyst builds trust and cooperation among all project stakeholders. It is essential to openly address what can realistically be achieved and discuss potential obstacles. Transparency fosters an environment of honesty and openness, setting the stage for successful collaboration and project outcomes.

Realistic Goal Setting

Setting realistic goals is a critical aspect of stakeholder expectation management. While it is important to set goals that stretch the team, they must also remain achievable considering the project scope, resources, and potential obstacles. Crafting goals that motivate without overwhelming the team is akin to navigating through foggy seas with an awareness of capabilities and challenges ahead. Realistic goal setting encourages the team to strive for excellence while ensuring that expectations align with the project's capabilities and constraints.

Regular Updates

Providing regular updates to stakeholders is vital in managing their expectations. Celebrating milestones, addressing concerns, and recalibrating expectations as the project progresses are essential components of effective stakeholder communication. Updates serve as vital touchpoints, keeping all parties in sync and ensuring that everyone is aware of the project's progress. Regular communication fosters a sense of collaboration and transparency, leading to better stakeholder engagement and understanding.

Stakeholder Engagement

Engaging stakeholders in the decision-making process is key to fostering a sense of ownership and commitment. Encouraging open discussions where every voice is valued allows stakeholders to shape the project's direction. By involving stakeholders in decision-making, the business analyst ensures that their perspectives and requirements are considered, leading to a more inclusive and collaborative project environment.

Conflict Resolution

Implementing a robust conflict resolution strategy is essential in managing stakeholders' expectations. Active listening, acknowledgment of differing viewpoints, and collaborative problem-solving are integral to resolving conflicts effectively. By understanding and compromising, conflicts can be resolved, fostering a collaborative and harmonious working environment. Conflict resolution is a crucial skill for business analysts to ensure that project stakeholders are aligned and focused on achieving project objectives.

Data-Driven Decision-Making

The use of data to manage expectations provides objective insights that guide decision-making. Presenting data in a compelling narrative form enhances stakeholders' understanding of project progress and fosters informed decision-making. Data-driven decision-making ensures that stakeholders have access to the information they need to align their expectations with the project's actual performance, leading to a more realistic understanding of the project's capabilities and limitations.

Feedback Mechanisms

Incorporating feedback mechanisms allows stakeholders to voice concerns and suggestions, fostering a culture of continuous improvement. Feedback nurtures project growth and improvement, similar to watering a garden. By creating channels for stakeholders to provide feedback, the business analyst ensures that their perspectives are considered and that the project's direction can be adjusted based on stakeholder input.

Personalized Approach

Understanding stakeholders' unique expectations and tailoring communication to resonate with them is crucial for effective stakeholder expectation management. A personalized approach enhances stakeholder engagement and the effectiveness of management efforts. By recognizing the individual needs and preferences of stakeholders, the business analyst can ensure that their expectations are managed in a way that resonates with them, leading to better collaboration and project outcomes.

In conclusion, successful stakeholder expectation management requires a multifaceted approach encompassing transparency, realistic goal setting, regular communication, stakeholder engagement, effective conflict resolution, data-driven decision-making, feedback incorporation, and personalized approaches. Mastering these techniques fosters trust and collaboration, propelling projects towards success.

This chapter has provided an in-depth exploration of the techniques for managing stakeholders' expectations, setting realistic goals, and fostering positive relationships for successful project outcomes. By understanding and implementing these techniques, business analysts can navigate the intricacies of stakeholder expectation management, thereby contributing to the success of data analytics, data science, business intelligence, and AI projects.

As the bridge between business stakeholders and technical teams, business analysts play a pivotal role in ensuring that stakeholder expectations are managed effectively. By mastering the techniques outlined in this chapter, business analysts can foster a collaborative and transparent project environment, leading to successful project outcomes and value delivery for the organization.

The successful management of stakeholder expectations is a testament to the business analyst's ability to navigate complex project dynamics, foster collaboration, and drive the achievement of project objectives. By adhering to the principles and techniques discussed in this chapter, business analysts can elevate their contribution to data-driven projects and propel them towards success.

Conflict Resolution in Cross-Functional Teams

Introduction

In the realm of data analytics, data science, business intelligence, and AI projects, cross-functional teams play a pivotal role in bringing together diverse expertise and perspectives to drive successful project outcomes. However, the amalgamation of different disciplines and skill sets within these teams can often lead to conflicts, which, if left unaddressed, may undermine project progress and hinder collaborative efforts. In this chapter, we will delve into the intricacies of identifying and addressing conflicts within cross-functional teams, promoting collaboration, and effective problem-solving in data-centric projects.

Early Identification of Conflicts

The early identification of conflicts is paramount in mitigating their potential impact on cross-functional teams. As a business analyst, it is essential to observe subtle signs of frustration or disengagement during meetings to spot conflicts in their nascent stages. This requires active listening and keen observation to recognize potential conflicts before they escalate. For instance, in a cross-functional team working on a data analytics project, a data scientist may display signs of frustration when their recommendations are not considered, indicating a potential conflict with the decision-making process. By proactively identifying such signs, the business analyst can intervene early to address the underlying issues and prevent escalation.

Early Intervention Strategies

Addressing conflicts promptly is imperative to prevent them from undermining project progress. As a business analyst, employing one-on-one conversations with empathy and openness can be an effective strategy to understand the root causes of conflicts and resolve them at their source. For example, if conflicts arise between a business stakeholder and a data engineer regarding the prioritization of data requirements, the business analyst can facilitate a candid conversation to uncover the underlying concerns and work towards a mutually agreeable solution. Early intervention not only prevents conflicts from festering but also fosters an environment of open communication and trust within the team.

Structured Resolution Mechanisms

Utilizing structured conflict resolution mechanisms is essential to facilitate constructive discussions and promote understanding and empathy among team members. As a business analyst, mediated sessions can be employed, where every voice is heard and neutral facilitators guide the discussions. For instance, in a cross-functional team comprising data scientists, business analysts, and IT professionals, a mediated session can be organized to address conflicting perspectives on the choice of data visualization tools. By providing a platform for open dialogue and ensuring that all viewpoints are considered, structured resolution mechanisms can lead to consensus and alignment within the team.

Developing Shared Goals

Aligning team members towards a common objective is instrumental in turning conflicting energies into collaborative efforts. As a business analyst, revisiting project goals and highlighting the importance of each member's contribution for success can foster a sense of shared purpose within the team. For example, in a cross-functional team working on an AI project, the business analyst can emphasize how the diverse expertise of data scientists, domain experts, and software engineers collectively contributes to achieving the project's overarching goals. By reinforcing the significance of collaboration and collective contributions, team members are more likely to align their efforts and perspectives towards shared objectives, thereby mitigating potential conflicts.

Leveraging Technology for Inclusive Communication

The use of technology, such as online collaboration tools and virtual reality simulations, can facilitate inclusive and effective communication within cross-functional teams. As a business analyst, leveraging technology helps break down barriers to communication, fostering a more harmonious working environment. For instance, in a globally distributed cross-functional team, virtual reality simulations can be utilized to create immersive collaborative environments, enabling team members to interact and brainstorm as if they were co-located. By leveraging technology to bridge geographical boundaries and enhance communication, the business analyst can facilitate a cohesive and inclusive team dynamic, thereby minimizing the likelihood of conflicts arising from miscommunication or disconnect.

Celebrating Diversity and Unique Contributions

Acknowledging and valuing each member's unique contributions is fundamental in strengthening team cohesion and mitigating potential conflicts. As a business analyst, recognizing and appreciating the strengths that different disciplines bring to the team can foster a culture of inclusivity and collaboration. For example, in a cross-functional team comprising data analysts, statisticians, and business domain experts, the business analyst can highlight how the diverse skill sets and perspectives enrich the team's problem-solving capabilities. By celebrating diversity and emphasizing the collective value of varied expertise, the business analyst reinforces a culture where individual contributions are respected and conflicts arising from perceived disparities are mitigated.

The Role of Business Analyst in Conflict Resolution

In the context of conflict resolution within cross-functional teams, the business analyst plays a pivotal role in facilitating proactive and empathetic approaches to navigate conflicts effectively. The responsibilities of the business analyst in conflict resolution encompass proactive identification, early intervention, structured resolution mechanisms, alignment towards shared goals, leveraging technology, and celebrating diversity. Let's explore these responsibilities in detail:

Proactive Identification:

The business analyst is responsible for proactively identifying signs of conflicts within cross-functional teams. This involves keen observation, active listening, and a deep understanding of team dynamics to recognize potential conflicts in their early stages. By being attuned to subtle cues and behavioral changes, the business analyst can identify brewing conflicts and take preemptive measures to address them before they escalate.

Early Intervention:

Upon identifying conflicts, the business analyst must intervene early to prevent them from undermining project progress. This involves engaging in one-on-one conversations with team members, approaching conflicts with empathy and openness to understand the root causes, and facilitating constructive dialogues to resolve conflicts at their source. By addressing conflicts promptly and transparently, the business analyst fosters an environment of trust and open communication, mitigating the impact of conflicts on team dynamics.

Structured Resolution Mechanisms:

The business analyst is tasked with implementing structured conflict resolution mechanisms within cross-functional teams. This includes organizing mediated sessions where conflicting perspectives can be openly discussed, and neutral facilitators guide the discussions to promote understanding and empathy among team members. By creating a structured platform for conflict resolution, the business analyst facilitates constructive dialogue and consensus-building, leading to the resolution of conflicts in a collaborative manner.

Alignment Towards Shared Goals:

Aligning team members towards shared objectives is a critical responsibility of the business analyst in conflict resolution. By revisiting project goals and emphasizing the collective significance of each member's contribution, the business analyst fosters a sense of shared purpose within the team. This alignment towards shared goals helps channel conflicting energies into collaborative efforts, thereby minimizing the likelihood of conflicts arising from divergent perspectives or priorities.

Leveraging Technology:

The business analyst is responsible for leveraging technology to facilitate inclusive and effective communication within cross-functional teams. This involves identifying and implementing online collaboration tools, virtual reality simulations, or other technological solutions to bridge communication barriers and enhance team dynamics. By harnessing technology to foster a harmonious working environment, the business analyst ensures that miscommunication or disconnect does not become a source of conflicts within the team.

Celebrating Diversity:

Recognizing and celebrating the diverse contributions of team members is a key responsibility of the business analyst in conflict resolution. By acknowledging the unique strengths that different disciplines bring to the team and emphasizing the value of varied expertise, the business analyst fosters a culture of inclusivity and collaboration. This celebration of diversity helps mitigate conflicts arising from perceived disparities or misunderstandings, ultimately contributing to a cohesive and harmonious team dynamic.

Case Study: Navigating Team Dynamics in E-commerce Platform Development

Introduction

In the competitive realm of e-commerce, the synergy within cross-functional teams can significantly impact a project's success. This case study illustrates the proactive role of a business analyst (BA) in mitigating emerging conflicts within a team tasked with launching a new e-commerce platform, aimed at elevating the customer shopping experience and optimizing online transactions.

Background

The project was set against a backdrop of rigorous deadlines, creating a pressure-cooker environment that led to rising tensions and mismatched expectations among team members, including data analysts, business stakeholders, and IT professionals. These challenges threatened the cohesion necessary for the project's timely and successful completion.

Identification of the Problem

During a standard project update meeting, the BA noticed underlying tensions brewing among team members. With a keen eye for detail and adeptness in active listening, the BA pinpointed the core issue to be a lack of transparent communication and shared understanding regarding project timelines and resources.

Action Taken

Understanding the criticality of addressing these issues promptly, the BA embarked on a strategic course of action:

1. Initiating One-on-One Conversations:

- **Objective:** To provide a safe space for each team member to voice concerns and frustrations.
- **Approach:** Individual meetings were held, employing empathetic listening to gather insights into the specific challenges faced by team members.

2. Facilitating a Joint Resolution Meeting:

- **Objective:** To collaboratively identify and address the root causes of the conflict.
- **Techniques Used:** The BA facilitated this session with the aim of fostering open dialogue, utilizing conflict resolution strategies, and leveraging the insights gained from one-on-one conversations to guide the discussion towards constructive solutions.

3. Implementing a Clear Communication Plan:

- **Objective:** Establish a sustainable framework to prevent future miscommunications.
- **Strategy:** A comprehensive communication plan was developed, incorporating scheduled project updates,

a defined protocol for expressing concerns, and mechanisms for transparent decision-making processes.

Tools and Techniques Employed

- **Active Listening and Empathy Mapping:** Used during individual conversations to understand diverse perspectives.
- **Conflict Resolution Frameworks:** Applied to structure the joint resolution meeting effectively.
- **Project Management Tools:** Such as Asana or Trello, introduced to keep track of progress, responsibilities, and to facilitate transparent communication.

Results

The BA's interventions led to notable improvements in team dynamics and project progression:

- **Conflict Resolution:** Directly addressing the issues led to amicable resolutions that respected all viewpoints, reinstating harmony within the team.
- **Enhanced Team Collaboration:** The establishment of trust and open lines of communication fostered a more cohesive and productive team environment.
- **Project Success:** The re-aligned team was able to proceed without further hindrances, culminating in the on-time and successful launch of the new e-commerce platform.

Conclusion

This case study underscores the critical importance of early detection and resolution of conflicts within project teams. The BA's strategic approach to problem-solving — characterized by empathy, effective communication, and collaborative conflict resolution — was instrumental in navigating through team dynamics, ensuring not only the project's success but also cultivating a positive work atmosphere conducive to future collaborative endeavors. It highlights how BAs, through proactive engagement and structured intervention, can safeguard project timelines and foster a culture of transparency and mutual respect among team members.

Case Study: Aligning a Data Science Team Through Structured Resolution Mechanisms

Background

In the dynamic environment of XYZ Data Science Corp., a project was launched to enhance the company's analytics capabilities through the integration of diverse data models and the careful selection of algorithms. The project team was a melting pot of expertise, including data analysts, business stakeholders, IT professionals, and a key business analyst (BA). However, the project soon encountered a major roadblock: internal conflicts stemming from differing opinions on task prioritization and algorithm selection. These disputes threatened not only the project's timeline but also its overall success.

Challenge

The crux of the challenge lay in reconciling the varied perspectives within the team, particularly concerning the prioritization of data models and the choice of algorithms. Such disagreements led to tension and threatened to compromise both the project's schedule and the integrity of its outcomes.

Stakeholders Involved

- **Data Analysts:** Focused on the technical accuracy and efficiency of data models and algorithms.
- **Business Stakeholders:** Interested in how the project outcomes align with broader business goals and ROI.
- **IT Professionals:** Concerned with the implementation feasibility and system integration of chosen solutions.
- **Business Analyst (BA):** Aimed to bridge the gap between technical and business perspectives, ensuring project alignment with strategic objectives.

Intervention

Recognizing the impasse, the BA initiated a structured conflict resolution strategy, detailing the steps as follows:

1. Mediated Discussion Session:

- **Objective:** To facilitate an open exchange of viewpoints in a controlled, respectful environment.
- **Tools and Techniques Used:** The BA utilized conflict resolution techniques and structured facilitation methods to guide the discussion. Tools like a decision matrix were employed to evaluate and prioritize tasks and algorithms based on various criteria such as impact, feasibility, and alignment with business goals.

2. Stakeholder Analysis and Empathy Building:

- **Objective:** To understand the motivations and concerns of each team member and foster mutual respect.
- **Techniques Used:** The BA conducted individual stakeholder interviews prior to the session, employing empathy mapping to better understand and later communicate the diverse perspectives within the team.

3. Consensus-Building Activities:

- **Objective:** To align the team around shared goals and collaborative solutions.
- **Activities:** Brainstorming sessions and SWOT analysis were facilitated to identify common ground and mutually beneficial solutions. The BA also introduced voting mechanisms to democratically decide on contentious issues.

Results

The intervention spearheaded by the BA led to multiple significant outcomes:

- **Conflict Resolution:** The structured dialogue effectively addressed the conflicts, enabling team members to appreciate diverse perspectives.
- **Alignment Towards Shared Goals:** The team successfully unified around common objectives, enhancing project focus and efficiency.
- **Enhanced Team Cohesion:** The resolution process bolstered team morale, fostering a culture of collaboration and mutual respect.
- **Project Success:** The collaborative spirit and aligned efforts culminated in the timely and successful completion of the project, adhering to both quality standards and deadlines.

Conclusion

This case study underscores the pivotal role of the BA in navigating the challenges of team dynamics within data science projects. Through the strategic application of structured conflict resolution mechanisms, the BA was instrumental in transforming potential roadblocks into opportunities for team alignment and project success. The case highlights the importance of open communication, stakeholder analysis, and consensus-building in resolving conflicts and fostering a collaborative environment. As a result, XYZ Data Science Corp. not only achieved its project goals but also enhanced its team cohesion and established a framework for managing future conflicts effectively.

Data Modeling and Process Mapping

Data Modeling Techniques

In the realm of data analytics, data science, business intelligence, and AI projects, the role of a business analyst is pivotal in ensuring the effective representation of data structures and relationships. This is where the understanding of data modeling techniques becomes essential. In this session, we will delve into the detailed examination of conceptual, logical, and physical data modeling techniques, exploring their significance and practical application in the context of various projects.

Conceptual Data Modeling Techniques

Conceptual data modeling serves as the foundation for understanding the overall structure of the data within an organization. It involves the identification of the highest-level relationships between different entities. At this stage, the focus is on capturing business concepts and rules rather than the technical aspects of the data. The primary goal of conceptual data modeling is to create a common understanding of the data entities and their relationships across the organization.

Key components of conceptual data modeling include entity-relationship diagrams (ERDs) and the use of high-level data flow diagrams. ERDs visually depict the entities and their relationships, providing a clear representation of the business concepts. Additionally, high-level data flow diagrams help in understanding the flow of data within the organization, highlighting the interactions between different data entities.

Logical Data Modeling Techniques

Logical data modeling involves the translation of the conceptual model into a more detailed representation that can be implemented in a database management system. It focuses on defining the structure of the data elements and their relationships, without getting into the specific implementation details of a particular database system.

The primary tool used in logical data modeling is the entity-relationship model, which provides a detailed representation of the entities, their attributes, and the relationships between them. This model serves as a bridge between the business requirements and the database design, ensuring that the data is organized in a way that aligns with the business needs.

Normalization is another critical aspect of logical data modeling. It involves the process of organizing the data in a database to minimize redundancy and dependency. By eliminating data anomalies and ensuring data integrity, normalization enhances the efficiency and effectiveness of the database design.

Physical Data Modeling Techniques

Once the logical data model is established, the focus shifts to the physical implementation of the database design. Physical data modeling involves the conversion of the logical model into the actual structure of a database, considering the specific characteristics and constraints of the chosen database management system.

At this stage, the business analyst collaborates closely with database administrators and developers to ensure the seamless translation of the logical model into a physical database design. This includes defining the tables, columns, indexes, keys, and other database objects based on the requirements identified in the logical model.

Normalization also plays a crucial role in physical data modeling, as it guides the process of structuring the database tables to minimize redundancy and optimize performance. Additionally, considerations such as data storage, indexing strategies, and data partitioning are addressed in the physical data modeling phase to ensure efficient data retrieval and manipulation.

Mastering data modeling techniques is imperative for business analysts involved in data analytics, data science, business intelligence, and AI projects. Understanding the nuances of conceptual, logical, and physical data modeling equips business analysts with the necessary skills to effectively represent data structures and relationships, ultimately contributing to the success of data-driven initiatives within organizations. By leveraging these techniques, business analysts can bridge the gap between business requirements and technical implementation, facilitating the seamless integration of data-centric solutions into the organizational framework.

Data to Decisions: Data Modeling Techniques

Journey Through Data Modeling Techniques

Embarking on a journey through data modeling techniques highlights the crucial role of data modeling in converting raw data into structured, analyzable formats. This process facilitates informed decision-making within organizations. Through a narrative that is both imaginative and pragmatic, we delve into the captivating universe of data modeling, showcasing its ability to enable scenario analysis and inform decision-making processes in organizations.

Crafting Data Models: Weaving Data's Fabric

Consider data modeling as a form of artistry, crafting abstract representations into intricate designs that organize data elements and standardize their interrelations, mirroring real-world properties. Data models serve to decomplexify the vast data landscapes, aiding businesses in data comprehension and analysis. Business Analysts, akin to artists selecting their palette, meticulously create data models using diverse methodologies as their toolkit.

The Toolbox: Business Analysts' Palette

Business Analysts employ a suite of tools and software to actualize their data models, reminiscent of an artist's palette. Tools such as ER/Studio, Microsoft Visio, and Lucidchart assist in the visual delineation of data structures, enabling the realization of data model designs.

Deciphering Data Models: The Analytical Art

The craft of interpreting data models involves analyzing their components to understand the entities, relationships, and attributes depicted, and how these elements correlate with business concepts and operations. This analytical process is akin to appreciating a piece of art, where Business Analysts discern meanings and insights from the models' complexities.

Validating Data Models: Masterpiece Integrity

Ensuring the fidelity of data models to business requirements and data integrity is akin to an artist verifying the authenticity of their work. This validation confirms the models' accuracy and value, establishing their significance in the data modeling process.

Data Model advantages

Scenario Analysis and Decision Support: Data Models' Enchantment

Equipped with their data models, Business Analysts undertake scenario analysis and decision-making. These models serve as tools for simulating various business scenarios, evaluating how different decisions could influence outcomes. This process highlights the predictive power of data models in strategic planning.

Facilitating Informed Decisions: The Power of Data Models

Data models excel in aiding strategic decision-making by offering a structured framework for option evaluation and future state prediction. Through compelling examples, Business Analysts demonstrate data modeling's pivotal role in steering businesses towards knowledgeable and strategic choices.

Fostering Collaboration: Business Analysis Meets Data Science

Data modeling fosters a synergistic collaboration between Business Analysts and Data Scientists. This partnership enhances the understanding of business goals and data-driven insights, blending the art of business analysis with data science's precision.

Advancing Analytics: Insights Through Data Models

Business Analysts leverage data models to delve into advanced analytics, like predictive analytics and machine learning, unlocking deeper insights for strategic decision-making. This exploration underscores data models' role in revealing data's hidden potentials and charting paths to innovation.

Confronting Data Modeling Challenges: Navigating Imperfections

In the realm of data modeling, analysts face challenges such as data quality and the necessity of keeping models current with business changes. They address these issues with resilience and creativity, viewing imperfections as opportunities for growth and adaptation.

Data Quality and Evolution: Nurturing Imperfect Beauty

Challenges in data quality manifest as inconsistencies or outdated information. Business Analysts approach these imperfections creatively, implementing mitigation strategies with finesse. They continuously update data models to reflect the ever-changing business and technological landscapes, ensuring their ongoing relevance and insightfulness.

Overcoming Data Modeling Challenges

Despite the allure of data modeling, challenges such as data quality and model maintenance arise. Analysts tackle these with resilience, employing strategies to enhance data integrity and update models in response to changing business landscapes, reflecting the continuous evolution of their data-driven artworks.

Maintaining Data Quality and Model Relevance

Challenges in data quality, such as inconsistencies or outdated information, are addressed with meticulous care, ensuring models remain accurate and effective. As business dynamics shift, Analysts adapt, updating models to keep pace with new processes, data structures, and technologies, ensuring models continue to provide relevant, insightful guidance.

Process Mapping and Optimization

The Fundamentals of Process Mapping

Understanding Business Process Modeling

Business Process Modeling (BPM) is a systematic approach to capturing, analyzing, and designing the flow of operations within an organization. It serves as a foundational tool for Business Analysts (BAs) aiming to optimize and automate business processes, thereby enhancing efficiency and productivity.

1.1 The Essence of Business Process Modeling

At the core of Business Process Modeling (BPM) lies the endeavor to provide a clear, visual representation of business processes, identifying areas for improvement, automation, or optimization. This representation serves as a crucial alignment tool for stakeholders across different functional areas of an organization, enabling them to gain a comprehensive understanding of the interconnectedness of activities and the flow of work.

BPM provides a measurable outcome, and it is through this lens that the primary goal of BPM is to provide a clear, visual representation of these processes, identifying areas for improvement, automation, or optimization. This is essential for organizations aiming to streamline their operations, enhance productivity, and maintain a competitive edge in a rapidly evolving business landscape.

1.2 Key Components of a Business Process Model

A well-constructed business process model encapsulates several essential components that collectively provide a comprehensive overview of the processes within an organization.

Tasks and Activities

The first component of a business process model encompasses the individual actions required to complete a specific process. These tasks and activities are the building blocks of the overall process and need to be clearly defined and sequenced to reflect the actual flow of work within the organization.

Flow and Sequence

The flow and sequence of tasks are pivotal aspects of a business process model. It delineates the order in which tasks are performed, including decision points and parallel paths, providing a visual representation of the process flow. Understanding the flow and sequence of tasks is crucial for identifying potential bottlenecks and areas for optimization within the process.

Roles and Responsibilities

Another critical component of a business process model is the assignment of tasks to individuals or teams within the organization. It is essential to clearly define the roles and responsibilities of each stakeholder involved in the process to ensure accountability and efficient execution of tasks.

Inputs and Outputs

The resources consumed and produced by the process constitute the inputs and outputs of the business process model. Identifying and documenting these inputs and outputs is essential for understanding the resource requirements of the process and the tangible outcomes it generates.

1.3 Understanding Process Mapping

Process mapping is a visual representation of the steps involved in a business process, providing a clear and concise depiction of the flow of work, decision points, and interactions between different elements of the process. It serves as a powerful tool for business analysts and process improvement professionals to gain a holistic understanding of the existing processes and identify areas for enhancement.

1.3.1 Importance of Process Mapping

Process mapping plays a crucial role in identifying inefficiencies, redundancies, and bottlenecks within business operations. By visually representing the sequence of tasks and activities, process mapping enables stakeholders to pinpoint areas for improvement and optimization. This, in turn, facilitates the streamlining of processes, leading to enhanced operational efficiency and cost savings.

Moreover, process mapping serves as a communication tool, allowing stakeholders to align their understanding of the workflow and identify opportunities for collaboration and coordination. It fosters transparency and clarity, enabling cross-functional teams to work cohesively towards achieving common business objectives.

1.3.2 Types of Process Maps

There are various types of process maps that cater to different aspects of business processes. Some commonly used process maps include:

- Flowchart: A visual representation of the sequential steps involved in a process, often used to illustrate the flow of work and decision points.
- Swimlane Diagram: A type of flowchart that categorizes process steps based on the responsible department or individual, providing a clear delineation of roles and responsibilities.
- Value Stream Map: A tool used to analyze and optimize the flow of materials and information required to bring a product or service to the customer, focusing on value-adding and non-value-adding activities.

Each type of process map serves a specific purpose and provides unique insights into the intricacies of business processes, allowing organizations to delve deeper into process analysis and improvement efforts.

1.3.3 Process Mapping Methodologies

Several methodologies can be employed to conduct process mapping, each with its distinct approach and benefits. Some widely used process mapping methodologies include:

- Six Sigma: A data-driven methodology focused on improving process performance by identifying and eliminating defects and variations.
- Lean: A methodology aimed at optimizing process flow and minimizing waste through continuous improvement and respect for people.
- Business Process Reengineering (BPR): A radical redesign of business processes to achieve dramatic improvements in critical performance measures such as cost, quality, service, and speed.

By leveraging these methodologies, organizations can systematically analyze their processes, identify areas for enhancement, and implement targeted improvements to drive operational excellence.

1.4 Process Mapping Tools

In the digital age, various software tools are available to facilitate the creation and management of process maps. These tools offer advanced features for visualizing, analyzing, and optimizing business processes, empowering organizations to streamline their operations effectively.

Some popular process mapping tools include:

- Microsoft Visio: A versatile diagramming tool that allows users to create flowcharts, process maps, and organizational charts with ease.
- Lucidchart: A cloud-based platform for collaborative diagramming, enabling teams to create and share process maps in real-time.
- Bizagi Modeler: A tool that supports the creation of process models using BPMN (Business Process Model and Notation) standards, offering advanced simulation and analysis capabilities.
- Miro: An online collaborative whiteboard platform that enables teams to ideate, plan, and visualize processes through interactive process mapping.

These tools provide organizations with the means to streamline their process mapping efforts, foster collaboration among stakeholders, and drive continuous improvement initiatives.

Creating Effective Process Maps

Practical Guidance on Creating Process Maps

Having established a comprehensive understanding of the fundamentals of process mapping in the previous session, we now delve into the practical aspects of creating effective process maps. Process mapping serves as a vital technique for visualizing and analyzing business processes, enabling organizations to identify inefficiencies, streamline operations, and drive continuous improvement. In this chapter, we will explore the step-by-step approach to creating process maps, from gathering initial information to documenting processes using BPMN (Business Process Model and Notation). Additionally, we will discuss modeling techniques and notations that play a pivotal role in the creation of clear and insightful process maps.

Gathering Initial Information

The process of creating an effective process map begins with the gathering of initial information. This phase involves engaging with stakeholders across different functional areas of the organization to gain a comprehensive understanding of the process under consideration. Key activities in this phase include:

- Conducting interviews with process owners, subject matter experts, and individuals directly involved in the execution of the process.

- Observing the process in action to gain firsthand insights into the flow of work, decision points, and interactions between different elements of the process.

- Reviewing existing documentation, such as standard operating procedures, work instructions, and process manuals, to gather insights into the documented versus actual process flow.

By meticulously collecting initial information, business analysts can lay a strong foundation for creating accurate and detailed process maps that reflect the operational reality within the organization.

Documenting Processes using BPMN

Once the initial information has been gathered, the next step in creating effective process maps involves documenting the processes using BPMN. BPMN, which stands for Business Process Model and Notation, is the standard notation for modeling business processes. It provides a rich set of symbols and diagrams to represent activities, decisions, and flows within a process, enabling clear and consistent visualization of process workflows.

The use of BPMN in process mapping offers several advantages, including:

- Standardization: BPMN provides a standardized notation that facilitates clear communication and understanding of processes across different stakeholders within the organization.

- Visualization: The graphical nature of BPMN diagrams allows for intuitive visualization of process flows, making it easier for stakeholders to grasp the intricacies of the processes under consideration.

- Analysis: BPMN enables business analysts to analyze process workflows, identify bottlenecks, and pinpoint areas for optimization and automation, thereby driving efficiency and productivity improvements.

Modeling Techniques and Notations

In the realm of process mapping, it is essential for business analysts to be proficient in various modeling techniques and notations to effectively capture and represent business processes. Some key modeling techniques and notations that are instrumental in creating comprehensive process maps include:

- Swimlane Diagrams: A type of flowchart that categorizes process steps based on the responsible department or individual, providing a clear delineation of roles and responsibilities.

- Value Stream Maps: A tool used to analyze and optimize the flow of materials and information required to bring a product or service to the customer, focusing on value-adding and non-value-adding activities.

- Data Flow Diagrams: A graphical representation of the flow of data within an information system, depicting the processes, data stores, and data flows involved in a system.

By leveraging these modeling techniques and notations, business analysts can capture the nuances of business processes in a structured and systematic manner, thereby facilitating in-depth analysis and improvement efforts.

The Role of Simulation

In the pursuit of creating effective process maps, the role of simulation tools in modeling business processes cannot be overlooked. Utilizing simulation tools to model business processes as open queueing networks can help predict the average time required for process completion and identify potential bottlenecks. By simulating the flow of work and resources within a process, business analysts can gain valuable insights into process performance and efficiency, enabling informed decision-making and targeted improvement initiatives.

Simulation tools provide a means to test various scenarios, assess the impact of process changes, and optimize resource allocation, thereby contributing to the overall enhancement of process maps and the identification of opportunities for operational excellence.

Execution of Business Processes

Understanding how business processes are executed as workflows is crucial for effective Business Process Management (BPM). This involves applying knowledge management practices to continuously improve process efficiency. By gaining insights into the execution of business processes, business analysts can identify opportunities for streamlining workflows, eliminating redundancies, and enhancing the overall operational efficiency of the organization.

Business Process Management (BPM)

Business Process Management (BPM) extends beyond the mere modeling of processes to encompass the optimization, automation, and continuous improvement of business processes. It involves a cycle of activities: vision, design, modeling, execution, monitoring, and optimization, thereby fostering a holistic approach to managing and enhancing business processes.

Analyzing and Optimizing Business Processes

Implementing Data-Driven Decision Making in Business Process Optimization

Data-driven decision making is a critical component in the optimization of business processes. By leveraging data analytics, organizations can gain valuable insights into process performance, identify areas for improvement, and make informed decisions to drive efficiency and productivity. This session will explore the principles and methodologies of implementing data-driven decision making in the context of business process optimization, highlighting the key role of business analysts in harnessing the power of data to enhance operational performance.

Data Collection and Analysis

Effective data-driven decision making begins with the comprehensive collection and analysis of relevant business process data. Business analysts play a pivotal role in defining the key performance indicators (KPIs) that align with the objectives of business process optimization. By identifying and capturing data points related to process cycle times, resource utilization, error rates, and customer satisfaction, organizations can build a robust foundation for data-driven insights and decision making.

Utilizing statistical tools and techniques, such as regression analysis, time series analysis, and correlation studies, business analysts can uncover patterns and trends within the process data, providing actionable intelligence for optimizing business processes. This section will delve into the best practices for data collection, storage, and analysis, emphasizing the importance of data quality and integrity in driving reliable decision making.

Role of Predictive Analytics

Predictive analytics offers a powerful tool for forecasting process performance and anticipating potential bottlenecks or inefficiencies. By applying predictive models to historical process data, organizations can proactively identify areas of improvement and optimize resource allocation, thereby mitigating operational risks and enhancing overall productivity.

Business analysts will gain insights into the application of predictive analytics techniques, such as regression modeling, time series forecasting, and machine learning algorithms, in the context of business process optimization. Through the utilization of predictive analytics, organizations can move beyond reactive problem-solving to proactive decision making, driving continuous improvement and agility in their operations.

Data Visualization and Dashboarding

Effective communication of insights derived from process data is essential for driving informed decision making across the organization. Data visualization and dashboarding tools provide a means to present complex process performance metrics in a clear, intuitive manner, enabling stakeholders to grasp the impact of optimization initiatives and track progress effectively.

This section will explore the principles of data visualization, emphasizing the selection of appropriate visualizations, such as trend charts, heat maps, and process flow diagrams, to convey actionable insights. Additionally, the role of interactive dashboards in facilitating real-time monitoring and decision making will be highlighted, showcasing how business analysts can leverage visualization tools to drive a data-driven culture within their organizations.

Integration of Business Intelligence

The integration of business intelligence (BI) tools and platforms plays a pivotal role in enabling data-driven decision making in business process optimization. By harnessing the capabilities of BI solutions, organizations can consolidate and analyze process data from disparate sources, uncovering correlations, trends, and performance metrics that inform strategic decision making.

Business analysts will delve into the best practices for leveraging BI tools, such as data warehouses, OLAP cubes, and data mining techniques, to extract actionable insights from process data. The chapter will also highlight the role of self-service BI platforms in empowering stakeholders to explore and visualize process performance metrics, fostering a culture of data-driven decision making at all levels of the organization.

Integrating Technology in Process Optimization

Introduction to Technology Integration

As we venture further into the realm of business process optimization, it becomes increasingly evident that the integration of technology plays a pivotal role in driving transformative change within organizations. In this chapter, we will explore the synergistic relationship between technology and process optimization, delving into the utilization of data analytics, robotic process automation (RPA), artificial intelligence (AI), and business process management software (BPMS) to automate, optimize, and enhance operational efficiency.

Leveraging Technology

The landscape of business process management is evolving rapidly, propelled by advancements in technology and the increasing demand for streamlined and efficient processes. Business Process Management Software (BPMS) stands as a cornerstone in the realm of BPO, offering organizations the capabilities to automate, monitor, and analyze business processes. By embracing BPMS, organizations can achieve significant improvements in efficiency and effectiveness, driving operational excellence and strategic alignment.

Moreover, the integration of new technologies, such as RPA and AI, holds immense potential in revolutionizing BPO practices. RPA enables the automation of repetitive tasks, freeing up valuable human resources to focus on more strategic initiatives. Likewise, AI empowers organizations to leverage advanced algorithms and machine learning models to optimize business processes, predict outcomes, and drive continuous improvement. By embracing these technologies, organizations can unlock new levels of operational efficiency and agility in the realm of BPO.

4.3 Simulation for Optimization: Modeling the Future

The utilization of simulation techniques stands as a powerful tool in the arsenal of business process optimization. By leveraging business process modeling and simulation, organizations can gain valuable insights into potential improvements, enabling them to develop strategies for enhancing process efficiency. Simulation of business processes as open queueing networks provides a dynamic platform for organizations to test and refine optimization strategies, driving innovation and continuous improvement in their operations.

4.4 Continuous Improvement and Monitoring: Embracing Kaizen and Lean Principles

The journey towards operational excellence is paved with a commitment to continuous improvement and monitoring. Embracing philosophies such as Kaizen and Lean enables organizations to adopt a culture of incremental yet sustainable enhancements in their business processes. By integrating these principles into their BPO strategy, organizations can drive a mindset of continuous improvement, fostering a culture of innovation and efficiency.

4.5 Embracing the Power of Predictive Modeling

The integration of predictive modeling techniques stands as a cornerstone in the realm of process optimization. By harnessing the power of predictive analytics, organizations can forecast process outcomes, anticipate bottlenecks, and optimize resource allocation to drive operational efficiency. Through the application of regression modeling, time series forecasting, and machine learning algorithms, organizations can move beyond reactive problem-solving to proactive decision making, driving agility and continuous improvement in their operations.

4.6 The Role of Data Visualization in Driving Informed Decision Making

Effective communication of insights derived from process data is essential for driving informed decision making across the organization. Data visualization and dashboarding tools provide a means to present complex process performance metrics in a clear, intuitive manner, enabling stakeholders to grasp the impact of optimization initiatives and track progress effectively. By leveraging visualization tools, organizations can foster a culture of data-driven decision making, driving strategic alignment and operational excellence.

4.7 Harnessing the Power of Business Intelligence

The integration of business intelligence (BI) tools and platforms stands as a catalyst for enabling data-driven decision making in the realm of process optimization. By leveraging BI solutions, organizations can consolidate and analyze process data from disparate sources, uncovering correlations, trends, and performance metrics that inform strategic decision making. The utilization of data warehouses, OLAP cubes, and data mining techniques empowers organizations to extract actionable insights from process data, driving a culture of data-driven decision making at all levels of the organization.

Case Studies in Process Optimization

5.1 Introduction to Process Optimization Case Studies

As we delve into the world of process optimization, it becomes essential to examine real-world case studies that illustrate the successful application of process mapping and optimization across different industries. In this chapter, we will explore a series of detailed case studies that highlight the instrumental role of business analysts in driving these transformative changes within organizations. These case studies will showcase the practical implementation of process optimization strategies, providing valuable insights and learnings for organizations aiming to enhance their operational efficiency and strategic alignment.

Case Study 1: Streamlining Supply Chain Processes in the Manufacturing Industry

Background

The manufacturing sector is notorious for its intricate supply chain processes, often marred by inefficiencies that can lead to significant operational challenges. This case study delves into the experience of a leading manufacturing company faced with such complexities. Despite its industry prominence, the company struggled with redundant procedures, material procurement delays, and inventory management issues, all of which adversely affected its operational efficiency and bottom line.

Challenge

The core challenges identified included:

Redundant Activities: Unnecessary steps within the supply chain that added no value to the end product yet consumed resources.

Material Procurement Delays: Inefficiencies in sourcing materials that led to production slowdowns and missed deadlines.

Inventory Management Challenges: Overstocking or understocking due to poor demand forecasting, resulting in capital lockup or lost sales opportunities.

Objective

The primary goal was to enhance supply chain efficiency, thereby reducing operational costs, improving production throughput, and boosting customer satisfaction. Achieving this required a thorough analysis and optimization of existing supply chain processes.

Approach and Implementation

Process Mapping and Analysis:

Business analysts initiated the project by conducting a comprehensive mapping of the supply chain processes, identifying bottlenecks and areas for improvement.

This phase involved cross-functional collaboration with supply chain managers, procurement specialists, and inventory analysts to gather insights and data critical for the analysis.

Integration of Data Analytics and Predictive Modeling:

Leveraging data analytics, the company utilized regression modeling to understand the factors influencing demand patterns and supply chain disruptions.

Time series forecasting techniques were then employed to accurately predict future demand, allowing for better inventory management and procurement planning.

Process Optimization Strategies:

Demand Forecasting: Advanced analytics enabled the company to align its inventory levels with predicted demand, reducing instances of overstocking or stockouts.

Supplier Relationship Management: By analyzing supplier performance data, the company optimized its supplier base, reducing material procurement delays.

Inventory Optimization: Utilizing predictive modeling, the company developed a dynamic inventory management system that adjusted stock levels in real-time based on forecasted demand.

Results

The implementation of these optimization strategies yielded remarkable outcomes:

Cost Savings: Streamlined operations and reduced wastage led to significant cost reductions across the supply chain.

Increased Production Throughput: Enhanced efficiency and reduced lead times resulted in higher production rates and faster time-to-market for products.

Enhanced Customer Satisfaction: With improved product availability and reduced delivery times, customer satisfaction levels soared.

Case Study 2: Enhancing Customer Experience through Process Optimization in the Retail Sector

Background

In today's retail sector, where competition is fierce, the ability to provide an outstanding customer experience is not just an advantage but a necessity for survival and growth. This case study explores how a global retail chain embarked on a transformative journey to overhaul its customer experience by addressing underlying process inefficiencies that affected supply chain visibility, order fulfillment, and inventory management.

Challenge

The organization faced several critical challenges that directly impacted customer satisfaction:

- **Limited Supply Chain Visibility:** A lack of real-time insight into the supply chain operations led to delays and inconsistencies in order fulfillment.
- **Inefficient Inventory Management:** Poor inventory management practices resulted in stockouts or excessive inventory, affecting the availability of products.
- **Fragmented Customer Journey:** Disjointed customer interactions across various channels created a fractured buying experience, diminishing overall customer satisfaction.

Objective

The primary objective was to enhance the customer experience by streamlining operational processes, thereby increasing operational efficiency, improving order fulfillment accuracy, and creating a seamless omnichannel customer journey.

Approach and Implementation

Mapping the Customer Journey:

- Business analysts undertook the task of mapping the entire customer journey, from initial interest to post-purchase support, identifying key pain points and opportunities for optimization.

Integrating Business Intelligence and Data Visualization:

- The company leveraged business intelligence tools and data visualization techniques to delve into customer data, uncovering insights into behavior patterns, demand fluctuations, and purchase preferences.
- This data-driven approach facilitated informed decision-making, allowing the organization to tailor its inventory and marketing strategies to meet customer needs effectively.

Optimization Strategies Implemented:

- **Inventory Management Overhaul:** By analyzing purchase data and trends, the organization optimized its inventory levels, ensuring popular items were readily available, thereby reducing stockouts and overstock situations.
- **Personalized Marketing Initiatives:** Utilizing customer data, the retail chain implemented personalized marketing campaigns, targeting customers with offers and promotions relevant to their interests and previous purchase behavior.
- **Enhanced Omnichannel Capabilities:** The organization streamlined its online and in-store operations to offer a unified and seamless shopping experience, allowing customers to interact with the brand fluidly across all channels.

Results

The implementation of these process optimization strategies had a profound impact:

- **Improved Customer Satisfaction:** Enhanced operational efficiency and a seamless omnichannel experience led to higher levels of customer satisfaction.
- **Increased Customer Loyalty:** Personalized marketing and a consistently positive shopping experience fostered greater customer loyalty, with an uptick in repeat purchases.
- **Operational Efficiency Gains:** The optimizations led to more streamlined operations, reducing costs related to overstocking, stockouts, and inefficient order processing.

Case Study 3: Process Optimization in Healthcare: Improving Patient Care and Operational Efficiency

Background

The healthcare industry is increasingly focusing on value-based care, emphasizing the importance of operational excellence to enhance patient care quality. This case study discusses a healthcare organization's strategic initiative to optimize its processes for improved patient care and operational efficiency. The organization faced significant challenges in appointment scheduling, resource allocation, and managing patient flow, which adversely affected both patient satisfaction and operational cost-effectiveness.

Challenge

The primary challenges identified were:

- **Inefficient Appointment Scheduling:** Leading to long wait times and a poor patient experience.
- **Suboptimal Resource Allocation:** Resulting in either overutilized or underutilized healthcare resources, including personnel and equipment.
- **Poor Patient Flow Management:** Causing bottlenecks in patient care delivery and impacting clinical outcomes.

Objective

The overarching goal was to enhance the efficiency of healthcare delivery by optimizing operational processes, thereby improving patient satisfaction, reducing wait times, and ensuring better clinical outcomes.

Approach and Implementation

Collaborative Journey Mapping:

- Business analysts worked closely with clinicians and administrative staff to thoroughly map the patient care journey. This collaboration was crucial in identifying inefficiencies and areas for improvement from both a patient care and operational perspective.

Data-Driven Insights and Simulation Techniques:

- Leveraging data analytics, the organization gained insights into patient appointment patterns, resource utilization rates, and bottlenecks in patient flow.
- Simulation techniques and process modeling were employed to envision and evaluate potential improvements in appointment scheduling and resource allocation.

Optimization Strategies Implemented:

- **Appointment Scheduling Overhaul:** A dynamic scheduling system was introduced, capable of adapting to varying patient demand and clinician availability, thus reducing patient wait times.
- **Resource Allocation Optimization:** Data-driven analysis informed a more strategic allocation of resources, ensuring optimal utilization of personnel and medical equipment.
- **Enhanced Patient Flow Management:** By redesigning patient flow processes, the organization minimized bottlenecks, facilitating smoother transitions between different stages of care.

Results

The optimization efforts yielded significant benefits:

- **Enhanced Patient Satisfaction:** Improved scheduling and reduced wait times led to higher patient satisfaction scores.
- **Operational Cost Reduction:** More efficient resource utilization and patient flow management resulted in lower operational costs.
- **Improved Clinical Outcomes:** Streamlined processes and reduced bottlenecks contributed to better clinical outcomes, as patients received timely and efficient care.

Case Study 4: Driving Operational Excellence through Process Optimization in Financial Services

Background

The financial services sector is a landscape defined by its rigorous regulatory environment, intricate workflows, and the imperative for operational excellence. In this domain, a leading financial services firm embarked on a journey of transformation, aimed at refining its operational processes to bolster efficiency and competitive agility. The firm faced significant hurdles in loan processing, risk management, and compliance, which necessitated a strategic overhaul to streamline operations and maintain its market-leading position.

Challenge

The firm grappled with several critical challenges:

- **Inefficient Loan Processing:** Protracted processing times due to manual interventions and outdated procedures.
- **Suboptimal Risk Management:** Inadequate credit risk assessment models leading to higher default rates.
- **Compliance Shortfalls:** Growing regulatory demands outpacing the current compliance mechanisms, increasing the risk of non-compliance penalties.

Objective

The primary objective was to optimize operational processes to enhance efficiency, improve risk management accuracy, and ensure stringent compliance, thereby accelerating loan processing times and solidifying the firm's reputation as a reliable financial services provider.

Approach and Implementation

End-to-End Workflow Analysis:

- Business analysts spearheaded a comprehensive review of the loan processing workflows, engaging with loan officers, risk managers, and compliance teams to understand the nuances of existing processes and pinpoint inefficiencies and bottlenecks.

Leveraging Advanced Analytics and Predictive Modeling:

- Utilizing data analytics, the firm developed predictive models to automate credit risk assessments,

incorporating a wide array of variables including credit history, market trends, and economic indicators.
- Predictive modeling also played a pivotal role in enhancing fraud detection capabilities by identifying patterns indicative of fraudulent activities.

Optimization Strategies Implemented:

- **Automated Loan Processing:** The introduction of automation in assessing loan applications expedited decision-making, reducing the reliance on manual checks and shortening processing times.
- **Dynamic Risk Management:** The deployment of advanced analytics for risk assessment allowed for dynamic adjustment of credit models in response to emerging trends, reducing default risks.
- **Regulatory Compliance Framework:** A robust compliance mechanism was established, utilizing real-time analytics to monitor transactions for regulatory adherence, ensuring compliance across all operational facets.

Results

The process optimization initiatives brought about significant improvements:

- **Accelerated Loan Processing:** The firm achieved a marked reduction in loan processing times, enhancing customer satisfaction and operational throughput.
- **Reduced Operational Risks:** Enhanced risk management models led to a notable decrease in default rates, safeguarding the firm's assets and reputation.
- **Improved Regulatory Compliance:** The new compliance framework ensured that the firm stayed ahead of regulatory changes, mitigating the risk of penalties and bolstering stakeholder trust.

Case Study 5: Process Optimization in the Technology Sector: Accelerating Innovation and Time-to-Market

Background

In the rapidly evolving technology sector, innovation and swift time-to-market are the linchpins of competitive advantage. This case study narrates the transformative journey of a technology company poised to amplify its innovation prowess and expedite its product and service delivery timelines. Confronted with protracted product development cycles, suboptimal resource allocation, and cumbersome project management practices, the company was determined to overhaul its operational framework to cultivate a more innovative and agile organizational culture.

Challenge

The company faced several pressing challenges:

- **Lengthy Product Development Cycles:** Extended development periods hindered the company's ability to quickly respond to market changes and customer needs.
- **Inefficient Resource Allocation:** Misallocation of resources led to bottlenecks and delays, impacting overall productivity and innovation capacity.
- **Cumbersome Project Management:** Traditional project management approaches were not conducive to the fast-paced, iterative nature of technology development, stifling creativity and flexibility.

Objective

The core objective was to optimize the product development lifecycle and operational processes to enhance the company's innovation output, reduce time-to-market, and improve agility and responsiveness to market dynamics.

Approach and Implementation

End-to-End Lifecycle Mapping:

- Business analysts and product development teams undertook a detailed mapping of the entire product development lifecycle, pinpointing areas rife with inefficiencies and bottlenecks.

Integration of Simulation Techniques and Lean Principles:

- Employing simulation techniques, the company was able to model different scenarios and identify the most effective strategies for streamlining development processes.
- Lean principles were adopted to eliminate waste, simplify workflows, and foster a continuous improvement mindset among teams.

Optimization Strategies Implemented:

- **Streamlined Product Development Processes:** The company introduced agile methodologies to replace traditional waterfall models, enhancing flexibility and enabling rapid iteration.
- **Dynamic Resource Allocation:** Advanced project management tools and techniques were employed to optimize resource allocation, ensuring that teams had access to the necessary tools and talent at the right times.
- **Enhanced Project Management:** The adoption of lean project management practices allowed for more efficient tracking and adjustment of projects, facilitating a quicker response to changes and challenges.

Results

The implementation of these process optimization strategies yielded remarkable outcomes:

- **Increased Innovation Output:** The company experienced a surge in innovation, with teams more freely generating and iterating on new ideas.
- **Accelerated Time-to-Market:** Streamlined development processes and enhanced project management led to faster product launches and service deployments.
- **Improved Market Responsiveness:** With reduced development cycles and greater operational agility, the company could more effectively respond to market trends and customer demands.

The case studies presented highlight the universal importance of process optimization across manufacturing, retail, healthcare, financial services, and technology sectors. Key takeaways include the critical role of business analysts in identifying inefficiencies, the value of data analytics and predictive modeling in informed decision-making, and the significant benefits of streamlined operations, such as enhanced customer satisfaction, reduced costs, and improved market responsiveness. These narratives collectively illustrate that regardless of the industry, adopting a strategic approach to process optimization can lead to substantial improvements in operational efficiency and innovation output. As we move forward, integrating advanced data analytics and AI will further empower organizations to achieve even greater levels of efficiency and innovation.

Challenges and Solutions in Process Mapping and Optimization

Introduction to Process Mapping and Optimization Challenges

As we embark on the exploration of challenges commonly encountered during process mapping and optimization, it is essential to recognize the inherent complexity and dynamic nature of organizational processes. Throughout my career as a business analyst specializing in data analytics, business intelligence, and AI projects, I have encountered a myriad of challenges that have tested my problem-solving skills and strategic acumen. In this chapter, I will delve into the intricate web of challenges that often arise during process mapping and optimization, and share effective strategies for addressing these challenges to drive meaningful improvements within organizations.

Stakeholder Resistance: Navigating the Terrain of Change Management

One of the most formidable challenges in process mapping and optimization is navigating through stakeholder resistance. Resistance to change is a natural human response, rooted in the fear of the unknown and the perceived threat to existing roles and processes. When advocating for transformative changes through process optimization, it is crucial to engage stakeholders in a collaborative and empathetic manner. During a project aimed at optimizing the supply chain processes for a global manufacturing company, I encountered significant resistance from middle management who were apprehensive about the potential impact of the proposed changes on their roles and responsibilities.

To address this challenge, I adopted a multi-faceted approach that involved transparent communication, stakeholder workshops, and change impact assessments. By involving the middle management in the process mapping exercise and soliciting their input in identifying pain points and improvement opportunities, I was able to foster a sense of ownership and alignment towards the optimization initiatives. Additionally, I leveraged storytelling techniques to illustrate the potential benefits of the proposed changes, painting a vivid picture of the future state and the positive impact on operational efficiency and employee empowerment. Through these efforts, I was able to navigate through stakeholder resistance and gain buy-in for the optimization initiatives, ultimately driving significant improvements in the organization's supply chain processes.

Data Quality Challenges: Unraveling the Complexity of Data Integrity

In the realm of process mapping and optimization, data quality challenges often pose significant hurdles in deriving actionable insights and making informed decisions. During a project focused on optimizing the customer experience journey for a leading retail chain, I encountered data quality issues stemming from disparate sources, inconsistent data formats, and incomplete records. The lack of data integrity hindered the organization's ability to gain a comprehensive understanding of customer behavior, preferences, and touchpoints across various channels.

To address these data quality challenges, I collaborated with data engineers and IT specialists to conduct a thorough data quality assessment, identifying data cleansing and enrichment opportunities. By implementing data governance frameworks and standardizing data collection processes, we were able to improve the quality and consistency of customer data, enabling the organization to gain actionable insights into customer preferences, purchase patterns, and satisfaction drivers. Furthermore, the integration of data quality monitoring mechanisms and proactive data stewardship practices ensured the sustained integrity of customer data, empowering the organization to make data-driven decisions and drive targeted process optimization initiatives to enhance customer experiences.

Maintaining Process Flexibility: Balancing Stability and Adaptability

In the pursuit of process optimization, maintaining process flexibility emerges as a critical challenge, especially in dynamic business environments characterized by evolving market demands and technological advancements. The delicate balance between process stability and adaptability is essential to ensure that optimized processes remain responsive to changing business needs and customer expectations. During a project focused on optimizing the loan processing workflows for a financial services firm, I encountered the challenge of designing processes that were robust and efficient, yet flexible enough to accommodate regulatory changes and market dynamics.

To address this challenge, I adopted a holistic approach that involved the implementation of agile process design principles and the integration of process monitoring and feedback loops. By fostering a culture of continuous improvement and learning within the organization, we were able to iteratively refine the optimized processes in response to changing regulatory requirements and customer preferences. Additionally, the utilization of process simulation and scenario planning techniques enabled the organization to assess the impact of potential changes on the optimized processes, facilitating proactive adjustments to maintain process flexibility without compromising operational stability. Through these strategies, the organization was able to achieve a harmonious balance between process stability and adaptability, driving operational excellence and agility in a highly regulated industry landscape.

Scalability and Adaptability of Optimized Processes: Ensuring Long-Term Effectiveness

The scalability and adaptability of optimized processes represent pivotal considerations in the journey of process mapping and optimization. As organizations strive to enhance their operational efficiency and strategic alignment, it is imperative to design and implement optimized processes that can withstand the test of time and accommodate future growth and transformations. Throughout my engagements in process optimization initiatives, I have encountered the challenge of ensuring the scalability and adaptability of optimized processes to align with the organization's long-term vision and business objectives.

To address this challenge, I spearheaded the development of a process governance framework that encompassed standardized process documentation, change management protocols, and performance monitoring mechanisms. By establishing clear accountability and ownership for the optimized processes, the organization was able to ensure sustained adherence to the optimized workflows and identify opportunities for refinements as the business landscape evolved. Furthermore, the integration of predictive analytics and scenario planning enabled the organization to anticipate future operational demands and proactively evolve the optimized processes to meet emerging business needs. By prioritizing scalability and adaptability in the process optimization initiatives, the organization was able to lay a robust foundation for sustainable operational excellence and resilience in the face of evolving market dynamics and competitive pressures.

Process Mapping With BPMN

In the realm of data analytics, data science, business intelligence, and AI projects, the need to understand and optimize business processes is paramount. Business analysts play a crucial role in visualizing and improving these processes, ensuring efficiency and effectiveness in operations. In this session, we will delve into Business Process Model and Notation (BPMN) methodologies for process mapping, exploring its significance and practical application in the context of various projects.

Understanding BPMN

Business Process Model and Notation (BPMN) is a widely used standard for visualizing business processes. It provides a graphical representation of business processes that is easily understandable by both technical and non-technical stakeholders. BPMN offers a comprehensive set of symbols and rules for creating process diagrams, enabling business analysts to capture, analyze, and improve business processes effectively.

The primary goal of BPMN is to create a common understanding of business processes across the organization. By using standardized symbols and notations, BPMN diagrams facilitate clear communication and documentation of business processes, allowing stakeholders to identify potential bottlenecks, inefficiencies, and opportunities for improvement.

Key Components of BPMN

BPMN diagrams consist of various elements that represent different aspects of business processes. These elements include:

- Flow Objects: These represent the activities, events, and gateways that define the flow of the process. Activities depict the tasks or work performed, events signify something that happens during the course of the process (e.g., start, end, intermediate events), and gateways control the diverging or converging paths in the process flow.

- Connecting Objects: These include sequence flows, message flows, and associations that illustrate the connections between flow objects, providing a clear understanding of the sequence and dependencies within the process.

- Swimlanes: Swimlanes are used to partition a BPMN diagram into separate visual categories to indicate which participant, department, or system is responsible for each part of the process.

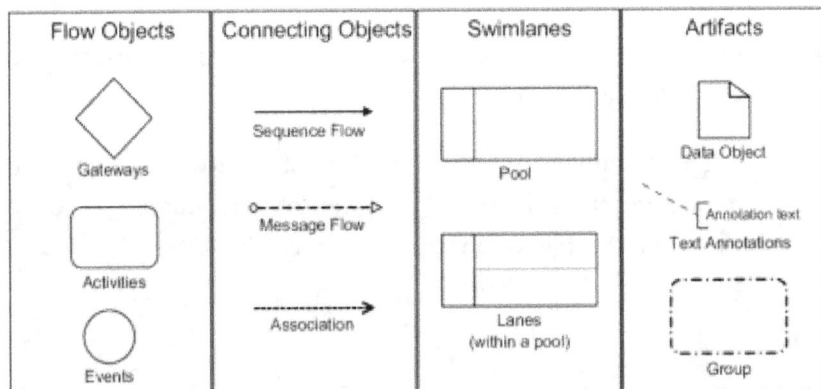

By utilizing these components, business analysts can create detailed BPMN diagrams that accurately represent the flow, interactions, and responsibilities within business processes.

Practical Application of BPMN

The application of BPMN extends across various stages of business analysis and project management. Business analysts leverage BPMN for:

- Process Discovery: By collaborating with stakeholders, business analysts use BPMN to map out the current state of business processes, identifying inefficiencies and areas for improvement. This process discovery phase helps in understanding the as-is state of operations within an organization.

- Process Analysis: Once the current state is documented, business analysts analyze the process flow using BPMN diagrams to identify bottlenecks, redundancies, and potential areas for optimization. This analysis phase enables the identification of key performance indicators (KPIs) and metrics for measuring process efficiency.

- Process Improvement: With insights gained from process analysis, business analysts use BPMN to design and document future state processes, incorporating best practices and improvements to enhance operational efficiency. This phase involves creating to-be process models that reflect the optimized state of operations.

- Process Implementation: BPMN diagrams serve as valuable artifacts for guiding the implementation of process improvements. They provide a visual reference for stakeholders, ensuring that the proposed changes are effectively communicated and executed.

4. Benefits of BPMN for Business Analysts

The utilization of BPMN offers several benefits for business analysts involved in data analytics, data science, business intelligence, and AI projects:

- Improved Communication: BPMN provides a standardized visual language for representing business processes, enabling clear and effective communication between business analysts, stakeholders, and project teams.

- Process Transparency: BPMN diagrams enhance the transparency of business processes, allowing stakeholders to gain a comprehensive understanding of how operations are conducted within the organization.

- Facilitated Analysis: The visual representation of processes in BPMN diagrams facilitates in-depth analysis, enabling business analysts to identify opportunities for improvement and make data-driven decisions.

- Alignment with IT Systems: BPMN diagrams can be utilized to align business processes with IT systems and software applications, ensuring seamless integration and automation of processes.

Creating a BPMN diagram for an employee onboarding process involves outlining the steps and participants involved in welcoming and integrating a new employee into an organization. Here is description of an onboarding process using BPMN notation elements in text form. This will give you an idea of how the process can be structured, try and create the diagram from this example.

BPMN Structure Overview

1. **Start Event**
    - Process begins with the hiring of a new employee.
2. **Parallel Gateway**
    - Initiates two parallel processes: "Prepare Workstation" by IT Department and "HR Onboarding" by HR Department.
3. **Tasks**
    - **Prepare Workstation** (IT Department)
        - Setup workstation.
        - Provide necessary equipment and access permissions.
    - **HR Onboarding** (HR Department)
        - Conduct HR formalities including documentation.
        - Introduce company policies.

- Enroll in benefits.
4. **Exclusive Gateway (after HR Onboarding)**
    - Decides if special certification is required.
        - Yes: Leads to "Certification Training".
        - No: Leads to "General Training".
5. **Training Tasks**
    - **Certification Training** (if required)
    - **General Training**
        - Provide training sessions on role specifics, company products/services, and software tools.
6. **Meet the Team** (Team Leader)
    - Arrange meetings with team members and key personnel for integration.
7. **End Event**
    - Process concludes once all tasks are completed, marking the successful integration of the new employee.
8. **Swimlanes**
    - **HR Department**: Responsible for HR onboarding, documentation, and benefits enrollment.
    - **IT Department**: Prepares the workstation and grants access permissions.
    - **Training Coordinator**: Organizes training sessions.
    - **Team Leader**: Facilitates integration with the team.

Create a detailed BPMN (Business Process Model and Notation) for the Credit Card Application and Issuance Process you described, we will break down each step into its corresponding BPMN elements, including tasks, gateways, events, and subprocesses. This will ensure a clear and structured representation of the process, try and create the diagram from this example.

BPMN Overview:

1. **Start Event:**
    - **Description**: The process initiates when a customer submits a credit card application through any channel (online, in-person, or over the phone).
2. **Data Collection Task:**
    - **Description**: Collect all required personal and financial information from the applicant, including identity verification, income proof, and credit history.
3. **Decision Gateway (Application Completeness):**
    - **Description**: Evaluate whether the application is complete.
    - **Paths**:
        - If **Yes**: Proceed to credit evaluation.
        - If **No**: Return to the data collection step.
4. **Credit Evaluation Subprocess:**
    - **Description**: Assess the applicant's creditworthiness based on various factors such as credit score, income, and debt-to-income ratio. This may include tasks like external credit bureau checks.
    - **Elements within Subprocess**:
        - Task: Credit Score Check
        - Task: Income Verification
        - Task: Debt-to-Income Ratio Calculation
        - Decision Gateway: Evaluate creditworthiness
5. **Approval Decision Gateway:**
    - **Description**: Make a decision based on the credit evaluation.
    - **Paths**:
        - If **Approved**: Proceed to card creation.
        - If **Rejected**: End the process with a rejection notification.
6. **Card Creation and Issuance Task:**
    - **Description**: Generate the credit card account, manufacture the physical card, and prepare it for dispatch.
7. **Dispatch Card Task:**
    - **Description**: Mail the card to the customer with activation instructions.
8. **End Event:**
    - **Description**: The process concludes when the customer receives and activates the credit card.

This BPMN case study simplifies the complex activities involved in credit card application and issuance into a manageable process model. Implementing a good layout for this BPMN can significantly enhance understanding and operational efficiency

Data Governance and Compliance

Importance of Data Governance

As businesses increasingly rely on data to make strategic decisions, the importance of data governance becomes paramount. Data governance encompasses the policies, procedures, and controls put in place to ensure the availability, usability, integrity, and security of data used in business analytics projects. In this chapter, we will delve into the critical role of data governance in maintaining data integrity, quality, and security, and its impact on the success of data analytics, data science, business intelligence, and AI projects.

Data governance is essential for ensuring that data is accurate, consistent, and reliable. Without proper governance, data can become fragmented, leading to inconsistencies and inaccuracies in analysis and decision-making. Furthermore, in today's data-driven landscape, the protection of sensitive information is of utmost importance. Data governance provides the framework for managing and securing sensitive data, ensuring compliance with regulations, and mitigating the risks associated with data breaches and unauthorized access.

One of the key aspects of data governance is establishing clear ownership and accountability for data assets within an organization. This involves defining roles and responsibilities for the management, maintenance, and quality assurance of data. By delineating ownership, organizations can establish clear guidelines for data management, ensuring that data is used and shared in a manner consistent with organizational policies and industry regulations.

In addition to ownership, data governance also involves defining data standards and best practices for data collection, storage, and usage. Standardizing data formats, naming conventions, and metadata ensures that data is consistent and easily accessible across the organization. This not only improves the efficiency of data analysis but also reduces the potential for errors and discrepancies in reporting and decision-making.

Moreover, data governance plays a crucial role in ensuring data quality. By implementing data quality controls and validation processes, organizations can identify and rectify errors, duplications, and inconsistencies in data, thereby enhancing the overall quality and reliability of data assets. This is particularly important in the context of data analytics, where the accuracy and completeness of data directly impact the validity of insights and conclusions drawn from analysis.

Another significant aspect of data governance is data security. With the increasing volume of data being generated and stored, organizations face greater challenges in safeguarding sensitive information from unauthorized access, breaches, and cyber threats. Data governance involves implementing security protocols, access controls, and encryption mechanisms to protect data from internal and external threats. By establishing robust security measures, organizations can minimize the risk of data breaches and ensure the confidentiality and integrity of sensitive information.

Furthermore, data governance is crucial for regulatory compliance, particularly in industries where strict data protection and privacy regulations are in place. By aligning data governance practices with regulatory requirements, organizations can demonstrate their commitment to compliance and minimize the potential for legal and financial repercussions associated with non-compliance.

In the context of data analytics, data science, business intelligence, and AI projects, the role of data governance cannot be overstated. These projects rely on the availability of accurate, reliable, and secure data to generate insights, drive decision-making, and support strategic initiatives. Without proper data governance, organizations risk compromising the integrity and quality of their data, which in turn undermines the credibility and effectiveness of their analytical efforts.

In conclusion, data governance is fundamental to the success of business analytics projects, serving as the foundation for data integrity, quality, and security. By establishing clear ownership, defining standards and best practices, ensuring data quality, and implementing robust security measures, organizations can uphold the integrity and reliability of their data assets. As businesses continue to harness the power of data for competitive advantage, a strong data governance framework is essential for ensuring that data remains a valuable and trusted resource for informed decision-making and strategic planning.

Compliance Regulations in Data Projects

As businesses increasingly rely on data for strategic decision-making, it is essential to understand the compliance regulations and standards that impact data-centric projects. In this chapter, we will explore the key compliance regulations and their implications for data-driven projects, focusing on GDPR, HIPAA, and industry-specific regulations. As a business analyst, it is crucial to comprehend the implications of these regulations and ensure that data projects are conducted in compliance with the legal and ethical frameworks.

1. General Data Protection Regulation (GDPR)

The General Data Protection Regulation (GDPR), implemented in the European Union, has significant implications for data projects worldwide. GDPR aims to harmonize data protection laws across the EU and reshape the way organizations approach data privacy. For businesses involved in data analytics, data science, business intelligence, and AI projects, GDPR requires careful attention to the collection, processing, and storage of personal data. As a business analyst, it is imperative to ensure that data projects comply with GDPR by obtaining explicit consent for data processing, providing transparent privacy notices, and implementing data protection measures such as pseudonymization and encryption.

Non-compliance with GDPR can result in severe penalties, including hefty fines. Therefore, business analysts must work closely with legal and compliance teams to incorporate GDPR requirements into data projects, ensuring that data processing activities align with the principles of lawfulness, fairness, and transparency.

2. Health Insurance Portability and Accountability Act (HIPAA)

For data projects involving healthcare information, compliance with the Health Insurance Portability and Accountability Act (HIPAA) is paramount. HIPAA sets the standard for protecting sensitive patient data and requires healthcare organizations and their business associates to implement safeguards to ensure the confidentiality, integrity, and availability of electronic protected health information (ePHI). As a business analyst working on data projects in the healthcare sector, understanding HIPAA regulations is crucial for designing data solutions that safeguard patient privacy and comply with HIPAA's security and privacy rules.

HIPAA compliance involves conducting risk assessments, implementing access controls, and maintaining audit trails to track ePHI access. Business analysts must collaborate with healthcare professionals and IT security teams to ensure that data projects adhere to HIPAA requirements, thereby mitigating the risk of data breaches and unauthorized disclosures of patient information.

3. Industry-Specific Regulations

In addition to GDPR and HIPAA, various industries have their own specific data regulations that impact data projects. For example, in the financial services sector, data projects must comply with regulations such as the Sarbanes-Oxley Act (SOX) and the Payment Card Industry Data Security Standard (PCI DSS). These regulations mandate strict controls over financial reporting and the protection of payment card data, respectively. Business analysts working on data projects in the financial industry must consider these regulations when designing data processes and systems to ensure compliance with industry-specific requirements.

Similarly, industries such as telecommunications, energy, and retail have their own data compliance regulations that dictate how data is collected, stored, and used. Business analysts must familiarize themselves with industry-specific regulations and collaborate with legal and compliance teams to ensure that data projects align with the relevant legal frameworks.

Implications for Data-Driven Projects

As a business analyst, understanding the implications of compliance regulations is crucial for the success of data-driven projects. Non-compliance with regulations such as GDPR, HIPAA, and industry-specific standards can result in legal liabilities, reputational damage, and financial penalties. Therefore, business analysts play a critical role in ensuring that data projects are conducted ethically and legally, aligning with the principles of data privacy, security, and integrity.

Furthermore, compliance with data regulations enhances the trust and confidence of stakeholders, including customers, partners, and regulatory authorities. By demonstrating a commitment to data privacy and security, organizations can build a reputation for ethical conduct and responsible data management, which is increasingly valued in the age of data-driven business operations.

In conclusion, compliance regulations significantly impact data projects in the realms of data analytics, data science, business intelligence, and AI. Business analysts must collaborate with legal, compliance, and IT teams to ensure that data projects adhere to GDPR, HIPAA, and industry-specific regulations. By integrating compliance requirements into data projects, business analysts contribute to the ethical and legal conduct of data activities, fostering trust and reliability in data-driven decision-making processes.

Ensuring Data Quality and Privacy

As businesses harness the power of data for strategic decision-making, ensuring data quality and privacy is paramount for the success and ethical conduct of data-driven projects. In this chapter, we will delve into the strategies and best practices that business analysts must employ to uphold data quality and privacy in alignment with regulatory requirements in data analytics initiatives.

1. Data Quality Assurance

Ensuring data quality is a foundational aspect of any data-related project. Data quality encompasses the accuracy, completeness, consistency, and reliability of the data used for analysis and decision-making. As a business analyst, it is imperative to collaborate with data engineers and data stewards to implement robust data quality assurance processes. This involves:

a. Data Profiling: Business analysts should work closely with data engineers to conduct data profiling to understand the characteristics and quality of the data. Data profiling involves analyzing the structure, content, and relationships within the data to identify anomalies, inconsistencies, and missing values.

b. Data Cleansing: Upon identifying data anomalies through profiling, business analysts must facilitate data cleansing activities to rectify errors, remove duplicates, and standardize data formats. Data cleansing processes should be documented and integrated into the data pipeline to ensure ongoing data quality maintenance.

c. Data Governance: Establishing data governance frameworks is essential for maintaining data quality throughout the project lifecycle. Business analysts should collaborate with data governance teams to define data quality metrics, data ownership, and data stewardship responsibilities to uphold data quality standards.

d. Data Quality Monitoring: Continuous monitoring of data quality metrics is crucial to detect deviations and anomalies that may impact the accuracy and reliability of data. Business analysts should implement automated data quality monitoring tools and alert mechanisms to proactively address data quality issues.

2. Privacy by Design

Incorporating privacy by design principles into data projects is essential to uphold data privacy and comply with regulatory requirements. Privacy by design involves integrating privacy considerations into the design and implementation of data processes, systems, and products. Business analysts should collaborate with data architects and privacy experts to embed privacy by design practices, including:

a. Privacy Impact Assessments (PIA): Business analysts should facilitate the conduct of privacy impact assessments to identify and mitigate privacy risks associated with data processing activities. PIAs evaluate the potential impact of data collection, storage, and usage on individuals' privacy rights and help in designing mitigating controls.

b. Anonymization and Pseudonymization: When handling sensitive or personally identifiable information, business analysts should advocate for the use of anonymization and pseudonymization techniques to protect individual privacy. Anonymization methods such as data masking and tokenization should be applied to minimize the risk of re-identification.

c. Consent Management: In alignment with regulatory requirements such as GDPR, business analysts must collaborate with legal and compliance teams to design consent management processes that ensure explicit and informed consent for data processing activities. Consent management frameworks should provide transparency and empower individuals to control their data.

d. Data Minimization: Adopting the principle of data minimization, business analysts should advocate for limiting the collection and retention of personal data to the extent necessary for the intended purposes. Data minimization reduces the exposure of sensitive information and minimizes privacy risks.

3. Regulatory Compliance

Compliance with data privacy regulations such as GDPR, HIPAA, and industry-specific standards necessitates a comprehensive understanding of the regulatory requirements and their implications for data projects. Business analysts should collaborate with legal counsel and compliance teams to ensure adherence to regulatory frameworks through:

a. Regulatory Alignment: Business analysts must conduct thorough assessments of regulatory requirements and align data processes and practices with the stipulated standards. This involves understanding the legal basis for data processing, data subject rights, and cross-border data transfer restrictions.

b. Data Privacy Policies: Collaborating with legal experts, business analysts should contribute to the development and communication of data privacy policies that outline the organization's commitment to safeguarding data privacy and the procedures for handling personal information in compliance with regulations.

c. Data Breach Response Planning: Business analysts should participate in the development of data breach response plans to facilitate swift and effective responses to potential data breaches. Data breach response plans should encompass incident detection, containment, notification, and remediation procedures.

d. Regulatory Reporting: In the event of data breaches or non-compliance incidents, business analysts should support the preparation of regulatory reports and notifications as required by the relevant authorities. Timely and accurate reporting is essential to demonstrate accountability and transparency.

4. Ethical Data Use

Upholding ethical standards in data use and analysis is fundamental to maintaining trust and integrity in data-driven projects. Business analysts should advocate for ethical data practices by:

a. Bias Mitigation: Collaborating with data scientists and data engineers, business analysts should participate in identifying and mitigating biases in data collection, analysis, and model development. Addressing biases ensures fair and equitable treatment of individuals represented in the data.

b. Transparent Decision-Making: Business analysts should promote transparent decision-making processes by documenting data sources, transformation steps, and analytical methodologies. Transparent decision-making fosters accountability and enables stakeholders to understand the basis of data-driven decisions.

c. Stakeholder Education: Business analysts play a pivotal role in educating stakeholders, including business users and decision-makers, on the ethical use of data and the importance of respecting privacy rights. Stakeholder education enhances awareness and promotes a culture of ethical data utilization.

In conclusion, ensuring data quality and privacy in data-driven projects demands a multifaceted approach encompassing data quality assurance, privacy by design, regulatory compliance, and ethical data use. Business analysts, as key enablers of data initiatives, must collaborate with cross-functional teams to embed data quality and privacy considerations into every phase of the project lifecycle. By prioritizing data quality and privacy, organizations can uphold their ethical responsibilities, mitigate regulatory risks, and build trust among stakeholders, ultimately leading to the successful execution of data analytics initiatives.

Security Measures in Data Projects

Implementing Security Measures in Data Projects

As data projects become increasingly pervasive in organizations, the need for robust security measures to protect sensitive data and mitigate cybersecurity risks has become paramount. In this session, we will delve into the strategies and best practices that business analysts should employ to implement security measures in data analytics, data science, business intelligence, and AI projects. It is essential for business analysts to understand the complex landscape of cybersecurity threats and the role they play in safeguarding sensitive data.

1. Threat Assessment and Risk Analysis

The first step in implementing security measures in data projects is to conduct a comprehensive threat assessment and risk analysis. Business analysts should collaborate with cybersecurity experts and risk management teams to identify potential threats and vulnerabilities that could compromise the security of data. This involves:

a. Threat Identification: Business analysts should work closely with cybersecurity experts to identify and categorize potential threats to the confidentiality, integrity, and availability of data. This includes external threats such as hacking and malware, as well as internal threats such as unauthorized access and data leakage.

b. Vulnerability Analysis: Conducting vulnerability assessments to identify weaknesses in the data infrastructure, applications, and access controls is crucial. Business analysts should facilitate vulnerability scanning and penetration testing to identify and prioritize vulnerabilities that could be exploited by attackers.

c. Risk Prioritization: Collaborating with risk management teams, business analysts should prioritize identified threats and vulnerabilities based on their potential impact on the organization and the likelihood of exploitation. This prioritization helps in allocating resources to mitigate high-risk areas effectively.

d. Risk Mitigation Planning: Developing risk mitigation plans in collaboration with cybersecurity and risk management teams is essential. Business analysts should contribute to the formulation of risk treatment strategies, including risk avoidance, risk transfer, risk mitigation, and risk acceptance, to address identified threats and vulnerabilities.

2. Access Control and Authentication

Implementing robust access control and authentication mechanisms is fundamental to safeguarding data against unauthorized access and misuse. Business analysts should work with IT security teams to design and enforce access control policies and authentication protocols. This involves:

a. Role-Based Access Control (RBAC): Collaborating with IT security and system administrators, business analysts should define and implement role-based access control policies to restrict access to data based on users' roles and responsibilities. RBAC ensures that only authorized personnel can access specific data and perform permitted actions.

b. Multi-Factor Authentication (MFA): Advocating for the implementation of multi-factor authentication for accessing sensitive data and critical systems is crucial. Business analysts should promote the use of MFA mechanisms such as biometric authentication, smart cards, OTPs, and token-based authentication to enhance the security of user credentials.

c. Privilege Management: Working in tandem with IT security teams, business analysts should contribute to the management of user privileges and entitlements. This involves defining least privilege principles, conducting regular privilege reviews, and implementing just-in-time access to minimize the risk of unauthorized access.

d. Access Monitoring and Logging: Business analysts should collaborate with IT security and compliance teams to implement access monitoring and logging mechanisms to track user activities and detect anomalous behavior. Access logs should be regularly reviewed to identify unauthorized access attempts and potential security breaches.

3. Data Encryption and Masking

Protecting data at rest, in transit, and in use through encryption and masking techniques is critical to maintaining confidentiality and integrity. Business analysts should collaborate with data security specialists and encryption experts to implement robust encryption and masking solutions. This involves:

a. Encryption Standards: Advocating for the implementation of industry-standard encryption algorithms and protocols to secure data at rest and in transit is essential. Business analysts should ensure that sensitive data is encrypted using strong cryptographic techniques and that key management practices are in place to safeguard encryption keys.

b. Tokenization and Data Masking: Working closely with data architects and security teams, business analysts should promote the use of tokenization and data masking techniques to protect sensitive data during processing and analysis. Tokenization replaces sensitive data with non-sensitive tokens, while data masking obscures sensitive information.

c. Secure Data Transmission: Collaborating with network security teams, business analysts should ensure that data transmission across networks is encrypted using secure protocols such as SSL/TLS. Implementing secure data transmission protocols mitigates the risk of eavesdropping and interception of sensitive information.

d. Data Access Control: Business analysts should advocate for the implementation of fine-grained access controls on encrypted data to ensure that only authorized users with the necessary decryption keys can access and decrypt the data.

4. Incident Response and Recovery Planning

Despite proactive security measures, organizations must be prepared to respond to and recover from security incidents and data breaches. Business analysts should collaborate with incident response teams and disaster recovery specialists to develop comprehensive incident response and recovery plans. This involves:

a. Incident Detection and Reporting: Business analysts should contribute to the establishment of mechanisms for detecting security incidents, including the use of intrusion detection systems, security information and event management (SIEM) tools, and user activity monitoring. Timely reporting of security incidents to the relevant stakeholders is crucial.

b. Incident Response Procedures: Collaborating with incident response teams, business analysts should define and document incident response procedures, including incident triage, containment, eradication, and recovery. Clear roles and responsibilities should be established to facilitate swift and coordinated responses to security incidents.

c. Data Breach Notification: Business analysts should advocate for the development of data breach notification procedures in compliance with regulatory requirements. This involves defining the criteria for determining reportable breaches, establishing communication channels with data subjects, and coordinating with legal and compliance teams for timely notifications.

d. Disaster Recovery Planning: Contributing to the development of disaster recovery plans to restore data and systems in the event of security incidents or infrastructure failures is essential. Business analysts should ensure that data recovery procedures are regularly tested and updated to minimize the impact of disruptions.

Case Study: Optimizing Data Governance in FinTech

Background

In the dynamic FinTech sector, a startup, FinSecure, has been revolutionizing personal finance management through AI-driven insights. As FinSecure grows, the complexity of managing sensitive financial data, adhering to compliance regulations, and ensuring data quality escalates. Recognizing these challenges, FinSecure initiates a comprehensive data governance and compliance project.

Phase 1: Assessment and Planning

Objective: Establish a robust data governance framework to enhance data quality, ensure privacy, and comply with financial regulations.

Stakeholders:

- Business Analysts (BAs), Data Scientists, IT Security Team, Legal and Compliance Officers, Data Stewards

Data Sources:

- Customer financial records
- Transactional data
- Market data
- Personal identifiable information (PII)

Collaboration: BAs conduct workshops with stakeholders to map data flows, identify sensitive data, and assess compliance needs. Regulatory requirements, such as GDPR for EU customers and the Payment Card Industry Data Security Standard (PCI DSS), are reviewed.

Phase 2: Designing the Governance Framework

Objective: Develop policies and procedures for data management, quality assurance, and compliance adherence.

Actions:

- **Data Classification:** BAs work with data stewards to classify data based on sensitivity and compliance requirements.
- **Role Definition:** Clear roles and responsibilities for data management and compliance are established, ensuring accountability.
- **Policy Development:** Data governance policies, including data quality standards, privacy protocols, and security measures, are drafted, focusing on encryption, access controls, and data minimization.

Phase 3: Implementation

Objective: Roll out the data governance framework, emphasizing compliance, data quality, and security.

Key Initiatives:

- **Data Quality Improvement:** Implement data profiling and cleansing processes to ensure data accuracy and consistency.

- **Privacy by Design:** Integrate privacy measures into all data projects, ensuring GDPR and HIPAA compliance.
- **Security Protocols:** Deploy encryption for data at rest and in transit, establish multi-factor authentication, and conduct regular security training for employees.

Phase 4: Monitoring and Continuous Improvement

Objective: Establish ongoing monitoring mechanisms to ensure the effectiveness of the governance framework and adapt to evolving compliance regulations.

Actions:

- **Regular Audits:** Schedule periodic audits to assess adherence to governance policies and compliance requirements.
- **Stakeholder Feedback:** Collect feedback from users and stakeholders to identify areas for improvement.
- **Compliance Updates:** Stay abreast of regulatory changes and update governance policies accordingly.

Results

Post-implementation, FinSecure witnessed significant improvements:

- **Enhanced Data Quality:** Streamlined data processes led to more accurate financial insights for customers.
- **Compliance Achievement:** Adherence to GDPR, HIPAA, and PCI DSS was successfully maintained, reducing legal risks.
- **Increased Customer Trust:** Robust privacy and security measures bolstered customer confidence in FinSecure's handling of sensitive data.

Lessons Learned

- **Cross-Functional Collaboration:** The success of data governance initiatives hinges on the collaboration between BAs, data scientists, legal teams, and IT security experts.
- **Proactive Compliance:** Anticipating regulatory changes and integrating compliance into data governance strategies minimizes risks.
- **Continuous Education:** Regular training and awareness programs for employees about data privacy and security are crucial for maintaining governance standards.

Best Practices

- **Data Governance Council:** Establish a governance council to oversee data policies, compliance, and quality standards.
- **Transparent Communication:** Maintain open lines of communication with stakeholders regarding data usage, governance policies, and compliance efforts.
- **Advanced Technologies:** Leverage technology, like AI and blockchain, for enhancing data security, privacy, and compliance monitoring.

Conclusion

This case study demonstrates the pivotal role of data governance and compliance in the FinTech sector, underscoring the need for strategic planning, stakeholder collaboration, and ongoing monitoring to navigate the complexities of data management. As FinSecure's journey reveals, a comprehensive data governance framework not only ensures regulatory compliance and data security but also serves as a foundation for trust and reliability, essential for competitive differentiation in the fast-paced FinTech industry.

Agile Business Analysis

Agile Principles in Business Analysis

The application of agile principles to business analysis in data projects has revolutionized the way organizations approach data analytics, data science, business intelligence, and AI projects. By embracing iterative and collaborative approaches, agile principles have proven to be instrumental in accelerating project timelines, ensuring relevance, and fostering a dynamic, responsive, and impactful approach to leveraging data for informed decision-making and strategic advantage.

Iterative Process

Embracing an iterative process is at the core of agile principles. By breaking down the project into short sprints for focused work, business analysts can continuously refine their approach based on real-time feedback and evolving business needs. This approach not only accelerates project timelines but also ensures that the analysis remains relevant in the face of rapidly changing business landscapes. The iterative process allows for greater flexibility and adaptability, enabling business analysts to pivot strategies based on emerging insights and priorities.

Collaboration

Establishing cross-functional teams involving data scientists, business analysts, and stakeholders is fundamental to the success of agile business analysis in data projects. Daily stand-ups and sprint reviews keep everyone aligned with business objectives, fostering openness, innovation, and a shared understanding of project progress. By involving stakeholders throughout the project lifecycle, business analysts can ensure that the analysis remains closely aligned with user needs and organizational objectives.

Mindset Shift

Embracing a mindset shift is essential when applying agile principles to business analysis in data projects. Business analysts must view change as an opportunity for improvement rather than as a hindrance. This mindset fosters flexibility and adaptability, allowing analysts to pivot strategies based on emerging insights and changing priorities. By embracing change, business analysts can harness the power of agility to drive continuous improvement and innovation in their data projects.

User-Centric Approach

Crafting vivid user stories is a pivotal aspect of agile business analysis in data projects. Humanizing the data project through user stories helps clarify objectives and ensures alignment with user needs. This approach emphasizes the importance of understanding the end-users and their requirements, ultimately leading to more effective and impactful data analysis. By humanizing the data project, business analysts can ensure that the analysis remains user-centric and directly addresses the needs and expectations of the intended audience.

Continuous Improvement

Agile business analysis promotes a culture of continuous improvement by breaking down projects into manageable chunks for iterative delivery. This approach enhances the relevance and accuracy of the analysis based on stakeholder feedback. By continuously refining and enhancing the analysis, business analysts can ensure that the insights and recommendations remain aligned with evolving business needs and user expectations. This iterative delivery approach also allows for greater flexibility in responding to changing requirements and priorities.

Open Communication

Maintaining open channels of communication and understanding among stakeholders is critical to the success of agile business analysis in data projects. By ensuring alignment with business objectives and user expectations, business analysts can foster a collaborative and transparent environment that promotes the exchange of ideas and feedback. Open communication facilitates a shared understanding of project goals and progress, ultimately leading to more effective and impactful data analysis.

Implementing agile principles in business analysis for data projects requires a clear understanding of the responsibilities of the business analyst. The business analyst plays a pivotal role in driving the agile approach, facilitating collaboration, and ensuring that the analysis remains closely aligned with business objectives and user needs. By leveraging agile principles, business analysts can foster a dynamic, responsive, and impactful approach to data analysis, ultimately unlocking the full potential of data for informed decision-making and strategic advantage.

In conclusion, the application of agile principles to business analysis in data projects has transformed the way organizations approach data analytics, data science, business intelligence, and AI projects. By embracing iterative and collaborative approaches, business analysts can accelerate project timelines, ensure relevance, and foster a dynamic, responsive, and impactful approach to leveraging data for informed decision-making and strategic advantage. Through the adoption of agile principles, business analysts can drive continuous improvement, humanize the data project, and maintain open communication and understanding among stakeholders, ultimately unlocking the full potential of data for strategic advantage.

Role of a BA in Scrum

The Role of a Business Analyst (BA) within the Scrum framework is pivotal in ensuring the successful delivery of data analytics, data science, business intelligence, and AI projects. As organizations increasingly adopt agile methodologies such as Scrum to drive innovation and responsiveness, the multifaceted contributions of BAs in sprint planning, backlog refinement, and user story development play a critical role in aligning project outcomes with business objectives and user needs.

Sprint Planning:

Sprint planning is a foundational activity in the Scrum framework, setting the stage for focused and iterative development cycles. The BA's involvement in sprint planning is instrumental in aligning the team's efforts with business goals and user needs. The BA facilitates the definition of sprint goals, ensuring that they are ambitious yet achievable, and importantly, aligned with the overarching business objectives. This involves leveraging their deep understanding of the business domain and customer needs . By articulating these goals, the BA acts as a bridge between the technical team and the business stakeholders, ensuring that the sprint goals are not only technically feasible but also deliver tangible value to the end-users.

Furthermore, the BA brings to the table their expertise in requirements gathering and analysis, which allows them to contribute to sprint planning by ensuring that the user stories selected for the sprint are well-defined and reflect the evolving business needs. Their involvement in sprint planning ensures that the team's efforts are not only aligned with the current business priorities but also set the stage for future iterations that build upon the previous ones.

Backlog Refinement:

Collaboration with the Product Owner is a key aspect of backlog refinement, and the BA plays a crucial role in this collaborative process. The prioritization of backlog items based on their value to the business and stakeholders is a critical responsibility of the BA . By leveraging their understanding of the business domain and the needs of the end-users, the BA collaborates with the Product Owner to ensure that the backlog items are sequenced in a manner that maximizes the value delivered in each sprint.

Moreover, the BA leads discussions to clarify requirements, break down large items, and estimate effort, ensuring that the backlog reflects the evolving business needs . This requires a deep understanding of the business processes and the ability to translate them into actionable items for the development team. Identifying dependencies and potential impediments early on, the BA helps navigate around obstacles to ensure smoother sprints . This proactive approach minimizes potential disruptions and ensures that the team can focus on delivering value during the sprint.

User Story Development:

User stories form the backbone of agile development, capturing the requirements from the end-user's perspective. In the context of user story development, the BA collaborates with stakeholders to gather insights and translates them into user stories that focus on delivering value to the user . This involves conducting detailed interviews and workshops to understand the user's needs and preferences, and then distilling these insights into clear and actionable user stories.

Crafting vivid user stories is a skill that BAs bring to the table, helping the team visualize the end user's journey and fostering a user-centric approach to development . By humanizing the development process through user stories, the BA ensures that the team remains focused on delivering solutions that directly address user needs, which is crucial for the success of any data analytics, data science, business intelligence, and AI projects.

In backlog grooming sessions, the BA ensures that user stories are reviewed, refined, and prioritized, ready for sprint execution . This involves continuous refinement based on feedback from stakeholders and the development team, ensuring that the user stories evolve in response to changing business needs and technical constraints.

Differences between the Role of a BA and a Scrum Master:

The role of a Business Analyst within the Scrum framework is distinct from that of the Scrum Master, despite some overlapping responsibilities. While the Scrum Master is primarily focused on facilitating the Scrum process, removing impediments, and ensuring that the team adheres to the Scrum framework, the Business Analyst is deeply involved in understanding and articulating the business needs and aligning them with the technical development.

The Business Analyst's role extends beyond the confines of the Scrum framework, delving into the business domain and customer needs to ensure that the technical solutions delivered by the team are not only aligned with the sprint goals but also contribute to the long-term strategic objectives of the organization. Unlike the Scrum Master, who is focused on the process and team dynamics, the Business Analyst is focused on the business outcomes and the end-user experience, ensuring that the solutions delivered meet the real-world needs of the stakeholders.

The Scrum Master may facilitate backlog refinement sessions, but the Business Analyst leads discussions to clarify requirements, break down large items, and estimate effort, ensuring that the backlog reflects evolving business needs . The Scrum Master may ensure that the team adheres to the sprint planning process, but the Business Analyst plays a pivotal role in defining sprint goals, ensuring alignment with business objectives and user needs .

In essence, the Business Analyst's multifaceted role within the Scrum framework orchestrates collaboration, ensuring alignment with business goals and user needs. Their contributions, ranging from sprint planning to user story development, are indispensable for delivering impactful, user-centered solutions.

In conclusion, the role of a Business Analyst within the Scrum framework is integral to the successful delivery of data analytics, data science, business intelligence, and AI projects. Through their involvement in sprint planning, backlog refinement, and user story development, BAs ensure that the technical solutions delivered by the development team are aligned with the business objectives and user needs. Their deep understanding of the business domain, coupled with their ability to craft vivid user stories, fosters a user-centric approach to development, ultimately contributing to the delivery of impactful, user-centered solutions that drive strategic advantage for organizations embracing agile methodologies.

Role of a BA in Kanban

The Role of a Business Analyst (BA) within the Kanban system is integral to the successful execution of data projects, encompassing data analytics, data science, business intelligence, and AI initiatives. Kanban, as a visual management tool, emphasizes continuous delivery, flow efficiency, and visual management, and the involvement of a BA in this system is crucial in ensuring the alignment of project outcomes with business objectives and stakeholder needs.

Continuous Delivery:

In the context of continuous delivery, the role of the BA extends beyond traditional requirements gathering and analysis. The BA not only analyzes customer needs but also translates them into actionable work items, ensuring immediate value delivery and assimilation of feedback. By leveraging their expertise in data analysis and synthesis, BAs identify patterns and trends to inform the prioritization process, keeping the project ahead of future demands.

Furthermore, the BA's role extends to facilitating the integration of customer feedback into the continuous delivery process, ensuring that the evolving needs of the end-users are effectively incorporated into the project's trajectory. This iterative approach to continuous delivery aligns with the principles of Kanban, emphasizing the need for adaptability and responsiveness in delivering value to stakeholders.

Visual Management:

The BA's involvement in visual management within the Kanban system is multifaceted, encompassing the design and maintenance of the Kanban board to suit the needs of the team and stakeholders. The Kanban board serves as a visual representation of the project's progress, and the BA plays a pivotal role in tailoring it to make complex information accessible at a glance. By ensuring that the Kanban board accurately reflects the project's current state, the BA fosters transparency, quick decision-making, and accountability.

Moreover, the BA's expertise in visualizing complex data and processes enables them to design the Kanban board in a manner that not only reflects the current state of the project but also provides insights into the flow of work, bottlenecks, and dependencies. This visual representation serves as a powerful communication tool, enabling the team and stakeholders to have a shared understanding of the project's status and progress.

Flow Efficiency:

The BA's involvement in monitoring cycle time and lead time within the Kanban system provides valuable insights into the project's flow health. By identifying bottlenecks and collaborating with the team to brainstorm solutions, the BA plays a proactive role in optimizing flow efficiency. This proactive approach aligns with the Kanban principle of continuous improvement, emphasizing the need to identify and address impediments to ensure smooth and efficient project execution.

Furthermore, the BA's focus on work in progress (WIP) limits ensures a sustainable pace of work, maximizing quality and efficiency. By actively managing WIP limits and ensuring that the team does not take on more work than it can handle, the BA contributes to the overall flow efficiency of the project, facilitating the timely delivery of high-quality outcomes.

The multifaceted role of the BA in Kanban encompasses not only the technical aspects of project management but also the facilitation of collaboration, stakeholder engagement, and data-driven decision-making. Their involvement ensures successful project completion, driving innovation and effectiveness through continuous improvement and customer satisfaction.

Comparing the Role of a BA in Scrum and Kanban:

While the role of a BA within the Scrum framework emphasizes sprint planning, backlog refinement, and user story development, their involvement in Kanban centers around continuous delivery, visual management, and flow efficiency. In Scrum, the BA plays a pivotal role in aligning the team's efforts with business goals and user needs, ensuring that the sprint goals are not only technically feasible but also deliver tangible value to the end-users.

On the other hand, in Kanban, the BA's role is focused on translating customer needs into actionable work items, designing and maintaining the Kanban board, and monitoring flow efficiency to optimize project execution. Both roles share the common objective of aligning project outcomes with business objectives and stakeholder needs, but they differ in the specific activities and focus areas within each methodology.

Furthermore, the BA's involvement in Scrum is characterized by iterative planning and refinement, driven by the cadence of sprints and the prioritization of backlog items. In contrast, the BA's involvement in Kanban is characterized by a continuous and adaptive approach to delivering value, driven by visual management and flow efficiency principles.

In conclusion, the role of a Business Analyst is dynamic and adaptable, encompassing a diverse set of responsibilities within different project management methodologies such as Scrum and Kanban. While the specific activities and focus areas may vary, the overarching objective remains consistent: to ensure the successful delivery of data projects by aligning technical solutions with business objectives and stakeholder needs.

As organizations continue to navigate the evolving landscape of data analytics, data science, business intelligence, and AI projects, the role of the BA will continue to evolve and expand, staying at the forefront of driving innovation and effectiveness through their multifaceted contributions to project success.

Role of a BA in Lean Startup

Investigate the role of a Business Analyst in Lean Startup methodology, concentrating on rapid experimentation, validated learning, and innovation in data-centric initiatives.

The Lean Startup methodology, popularized by Eric Ries, introduces a systematic approach to building and managing successful startups by leveraging principles of continuous innovation and validated learning. Within this context, the role of a Business Analyst (BA) takes on a unique significance, intertwining data analytics, data science, business intelligence, and AI projects with the principles of Lean Startup to drive value-driven outcomes and sustainable growth.

Rapid Experimentation:

At the core of Lean Startup methodology lies the concept of rapid experimentation. Startups and established organizations alike are encouraged to conduct small-scale experiments to test hypotheses, validate assumptions, and gather data-driven insights to inform decision-making. The BA, equipped with a deep understanding of data analytics and experimental design, plays a pivotal role in crafting and executing these experiments.

By leveraging their expertise in data analysis and interpretation, BAs collaborate with cross-functional teams to design experiments that generate actionable insights. They play a crucial role in identifying key metrics, defining success criteria, and establishing data collection mechanisms to ensure that the outcomes of these experiments contribute to validated learning. Through their involvement, BAs facilitate the iterative process of testing ideas, gathering feedback, and adapting strategies based on empirical evidence, thereby fostering a culture of evidence-based decision-making within the Lean Startup framework.

Validated Learning:

In the context of Lean Startup, the concept of validated learning emphasizes the importance of acquiring actionable insights through iterative experimentation and customer feedback. BAs actively contribute to this process by interpreting the data generated from experiments to derive meaningful insights that guide the product development and innovation cycle. Leveraging statistical analysis, trend identification, and predictive modeling, BAs distill complex datasets into actionable recommendations that drive informed decision-making within the organization.

Moreover, BAs play a crucial role in aligning the outcomes of validated learning with the overarching business objectives, ensuring that the insights derived from data analytics and experimentation directly contribute to the creation of value for the end-users and stakeholders. Their ability to bridge the gap between data-driven insights and strategic decision-making positions them as instrumental drivers of innovation and sustainable growth within the Lean Startup ecosystem.

Innovation in Data-Centric Initiatives:

As data-centric initiatives continue to drive organizational strategies, the role of the BA in fostering innovation becomes increasingly significant. Within the Lean Startup framework, BAs leverage their expertise in data analytics, data science, business intelligence, and AI to identify opportunities for innovation, optimize product-market fit, and drive continuous improvement. By analyzing market trends, customer behaviors, and competitive landscapes, BAs provide valuable guidance in shaping the direction of product development and strategic pivots based on empirical evidence.

Furthermore, BAs collaborate with cross-functional teams to identify emerging technologies, industry disruptors, and market gaps, leveraging data-driven insights to inform the organization's innovation roadmap. Their ability to translate complex data into actionable strategies fosters a culture of innovation that is deeply rooted in empirical evidence, aligning with the principles of Lean Startup and driving sustainable competitive advantage.

Comparing the Role of a BA in Lean Startup and Kanban:

While the role of a BA within the Kanban system emphasizes continuous delivery, flow efficiency, and visual management, their involvement in Lean Startup centers around rapid experimentation, validated learning, and innovation in data-centric initiatives. In Kanban, the BA's role is focused on optimizing project execution through visual management and flow efficiency, while in Lean Startup, the BA's role is centered on leveraging data analytics to drive informed decision-making and foster a culture of continuous innovation.

In Kanban, the BA's involvement in visual management extends to designing and maintaining the Kanban board to reflect the project's progress, whereas in Lean Startup, the BA's involvement in visual management pertains to interpreting data visualizations to derive actionable insights that contribute to validated learning and innovation. Both roles share the common objective of aligning project outcomes with business objectives and stakeholder needs, but they differ in the specific activities and focus areas within each methodology.

In conclusion, the role of a Business Analyst is adaptable and multifaceted, spanning across diverse project management methodologies such as Kanban and Lean Startup. As organizations continue to embrace data-centric initiatives and navigate the complexities of innovation, the role of the BA will continue to evolve and expand, positioning them as instrumental drivers of value-driven outcomes, sustainable growth, and strategic innovation within the dynamic landscape of data analytics, data science, business intelligence, and AI projects."

Case Studies in Business Analysis for Data Projects

This session showcasing real-world examples where business analysis methodologies are adeptly applied to complex data projects. Its crafted as a resource for business analysts, project managers, data scientists, and anyone engaged in the lifecycle of data projects. Through detailed case studies, it illuminates the multifaceted challenges and solutions encountered in project management, stakeholder engagement, requirements gathering, data analysis, and the realization of business goals through data insights.

The narratives within are carefully chosen to span various industries and project types, presenting readers with a comprehensive view of the obstacles and successes inherent in data project endeavors. Key themes explored include strategic collaboration, problem-solving through innovative analytics, and change management

It is a compendium of lessons learned, emphasizing continuous learning and improvement in business analysis and data project management.

As you delve into these cases, you're encouraged to actively engage with the material, reflecting on the strategies employed and envisioning their application in your professional context.

Case Study 1: Optimizing Customer Segmentation

RetailMax, a leading retailer in a competitive landscape, embarked on an ambitious initiative to optimize customer segmentation. Their goal was ambitious but clear: personalize marketing efforts, boost customer satisfaction, and ultimately, increase sales. This comprehensive case study explores how RetailMax utilized data analytics and business analysis to transform their customer segmentation approach, detailing the journey from planning to implementation and the continuous refinement process.

Phase 1: Project Initiation and Planning

Objective Setting and Team Assembly

The project began with the assembly of a multidisciplinary team from marketing, sales, IT, and data analytics to tackle customer engagement challenges and define the project's scope for data-driven segmentation.

Stakeholder Analysis and Project Management

Tools Used: Asana and Slack facilitated project coordination and communication. Techniques: Stakeholder Onion Diagrams helped visualize stakeholders' levels of influence and interest, guiding targeted engagement strategies. Key stakeholders identified included marketing executives, data analysts, and customer service managers.

Requirements Gathering

Tools and Techniques: Mind Mapping software supported brainstorming sessions, while JIRA captured and tracked evolving requirements. Workshops elicited detailed requirements for the analytics platform, addressing critical questions like "What data sources should we tap into?" and "What criteria should drive our segmentation?"

Phase 2: Data Inventory and Quality Assessment

Collaboration and In-depth Analysis

During this phase, the Business Analyst (BA) played a pivotal role in facilitating collaboration between various departments to ensure a comprehensive understanding and inventory of available data. The collaboration involved:

- Marketing Team: To understand customer demographics, previous marketing campaign outcomes, and customer feedback mechanisms.
- Sales Department: To gain insights into sales transaction patterns, peak purchasing times, and product preferences.
- IT Department: For technical support in accessing and extracting data from RetailMax's CRM and sales databases.
- Data Analytics Team: To discuss the potential of the available data for predictive modeling and segmentation.

Key Questions and Achievements

The BA coordinated efforts to address crucial questions and objectives:

- What data sources are available, and how can they be accessed?
    - Detailed mappings of data sources were created, including CRM records, sales transactions, and customer feedback. APIs and database access protocols were established with IT support.
- What is the quality of the current data?
    - Conducting data quality assessments through SQL queries and data profiling tools, identifying gaps in data completeness, accuracy, and consistency.
- How can we integrate external data sources effectively?
    - The BA facilitated discussions with third-party data providers for market trends and demographic data, ensuring compatibility and integration with RetailMax's data architecture.
- What are the key customer metrics that can drive effective segmentation?
    - Workshops with marketing and sales teams highlighted essential customer metrics such as purchase history, product preferences, and feedback scores. The BA translated these business needs into technical requirements for the data analytics team.
- How can data cleaning and preparation be streamlined for ongoing analysis?
    - The BA worked with data analysts to develop ETL (Extract, Transform, Load) processes, automating the cleaning and preparation of data for continuous analytics efforts.

Collaborative Tools and Techniques Used

- SQL and Data Profiling Tools: For querying databases and assessing data quality, ensuring the foundation for analytics was solid.
- Collaborative Platforms: Asana and Slack facilitated project management and communication across teams, keeping everyone aligned on objectives and progress.
- ETL Processes: Developed in collaboration with IT and data analytics teams to automate data preparation tasks.

Phase 3: Analytics and Machine Learning Development

Collaboration and Technical Development

In this crucial phase, the Business Analyst (BA) orchestrated the development of the analytics and machine learning framework required for advanced customer segmentation. This involved deep collaboration with:

- Data Scientists: To develop and refine predictive models using customer data.
- IT Specialists: For technical support in setting up cloud-based data storage and processing environments.
- Marketing and Sales Teams: To validate model outputs against business insights and practical applicability.

Key Questions and Achievements

- Which machine learning algorithms are best suited for our segmentation needs?
    - After consulting with data scientists, the BA helped choose algorithms like k-means clustering for demographic segmentation and decision trees for predicting customer buying behaviors.
- How can we ensure the models accurately reflect our customer base?
    - The BA organized sessions where marketing and sales insights were used to adjust and refine model parameters, ensuring alignment with real-world customer behaviors.
- What infrastructure is required to support these analytics models?
    - Working alongside IT specialists, the BA facilitated the selection and setup of AWS for scalable data storage and processing, ensuring the infrastructure could support real-time analytics.
- How will the models be updated with new data?
    - The BA coordinated the development of automated pipelines for continuous data ingestion and model retraining, ensuring the segmentation remains relevant over time.

Tools and Techniques Used

- Python (Pandas, scikit-learn, TensorFlow): For data manipulation and building machine learning models.
- AWS: Chosen for its robust cloud-based platforms enabling scalable analytics solutions.

- Model Validation Sessions: Regular meetings with stakeholders to review model accuracy and applicability, ensuring continuous alignment with business goals.

Phase 4: Dashboard Development and Integration

Enhancing Decision-Making through Visualization

The development of interactive dashboards was pivotal for translating complex analytical insights into actionable strategies. The BA led this phase by:

- Coordinating with Dashboard Developers: To design and implement dashboards that accurately represent segmentation insights.
- Engaging with End-Users: Gathering feedback from marketing and sales teams to ensure the dashboards meet their needs.
- Liaising with IT: To ensure seamless integration of dashboards with existing CRM and analytics platforms.

Key Questions and Achievements

- What key metrics and insights should the dashboards display?

- Through workshops, the BA identified essential metrics (e.g., customer lifetime value, churn rate) that would empower marketing and sales teams to craft targeted strategies.
- How can we make the dashboards user-friendly and accessible?
    - User experience sessions were held to refine dashboard design, focusing on simplicity and ease of access, leading to the adoption of Tableau and Power BI for their intuitive interfaces.
- What is the best way to integrate real-time data into the dashboards?
    - The BA worked with IT to implement APIs and middleware solutions, allowing for the real-time update of dashboards with new customer data and insights.

Tools and Techniques Used

- Tableau and Power BI: For creating interactive, intuitive dashboards.
- User Feedback Sessions: Direct input from end-users shaped the development of the dashboards, ensuring they provided value and enhanced decision-making.

Phase 5: Training and Change Management

Empowering Teams for Adoption and Utilization

The success of the new segmentation strategy hinged on the effective use and understanding of the developed tools and insights. The BA orchestrated:

- Training Programs: Designing and delivering training sessions using e-learning platforms to ensure widespread understanding and adoption of the new dashboards.
- Change Management Workshops: To address concerns, mitigate resistance, and highlight the benefits of the new segmentation approach to all stakeholders.

Key Questions and Achievements

- How can we ensure all relevant teams are proficient in using the new dashboards?
    - The BA developed a comprehensive training curriculum, covering dashboard functionalities and data interpretation, ensuring marketing and sales teams could leverage the insights effectively.
- What strategies can facilitate smooth adoption of the new segmentation model?
    - By implementing a structured change management process, including regular feedback loops and success stories, the BA helped foster a positive attitude towards the new tools and methodologies.

Tools and Techniques Used

- E-Learning Platforms: Utilized for scalable, interactive training sessions.
- Change Management Frameworks: Applied to guide the organization through the transition, ensuring alignment and buy-in from all stakeholders.

Conclusion

Through meticulous planning, stakeholder engagement, rigorous data analysis, and continuous refinement, RetailMax achieved a more personalized marketing approach, leading to improved customer engagement and increased sales. The detailed exploration from Phase 2 through Phase 5 showcases the BA's central role in navigating the complexities of integrating advanced analytics into business processes, emphasizing collaboration, strategic questioning, and methodical execution at each step of the journey. This case study not only highlights the transformative power of data analytics and business analysis in retail but also serves as a comprehensive guide for organizations aiming to harness data for strategic advantage.

Case Study 2: Enhancing Sales Forecasting Accuracy

Enhanced Case Study: LuxeFurn's Sales Forecasting Transformation

LuxeFurn, contending with the limitations of its existing sales forecasting methodologies, embarked on a pioneering project to harness the power of data science and business analysis for boosting forecasting accuracy. This endeavor aimed at refining inventory management and elevating customer satisfaction by advancing beyond traditional forecasting models.

Project Overview

Central to the project was the ambition to exploit data-driven insights to revolutionize LuxeFurn's forecasting approach. The formation of a multidisciplinary team underscored the project's collaborative spirit, spotlighting the Business Analysts' (BAs) crucial role in melding technical solutions with business requisites.

Phase 1: Project Initiation

Team Assembly and Objective Setting:

- **Collaboration:** BAs engaged proactively with stakeholders from diverse departments to delineate the project's ambitions, aligning with LuxeFurn's strategic goals. Utilization of project management tools like Asana and Slack was key in fostering communication and collaboration.
- **Role of BAs:** They orchestrated workshops and conducted stakeholder interviews, applying stakeholder analysis techniques to discern and prioritize project necessities.

Key Questions and Achievements:

- How can we align project objectives with LuxeFurn's strategic goals?
- Achievement: Developed a comprehensive project roadmap with clear, strategic alignment indicated by stakeholder consensus.

Phase 2: Evaluation and Preparation

Evaluating Existing Processes:

- **Tools and Techniques:** Process mapping via Lucidchart illuminated inefficiencies in current forecasting processes, while SWOT analysis offered strategic insights.
- **Collaboration:** Interactions with IT specialists and sales managers were vital in understanding technical and operational challenges, ensuring a well-rounded evaluation.

Analytical Toolkit Preparation:

- **Data and Tools:** This toolkit comprised sales data, customer feedback, and market trend analyses. BAs, along with data scientists, leveraged statistical software (SAS, R) and Python for data analytics, with Microsoft Azure serving as the cloud computing and data storage backbone.
- **Integration Platform:** Discussions with IT specialists on middleware solutions guaranteed smooth data integration across LuxeFurn's systems.

Key Questions and Achievements:

- Which analytical tools and data sources will best serve the project's goals?
- Achievement: Established a robust analytical framework, incorporating diverse data sources and advanced analytical tools, setting a solid foundation for predictive modeling.

Phase 3: Analysis and Model Development

Historical Data Analysis:

- **Data Analysis:** Through the analysis of sales data, market trends, and consumer behaviors using time series and machine learning algorithms, BAs and data scientists uncovered predictive patterns.
- **Techniques:** Utilized collaborative filtering and regression analysis to forecast future sales, with BAs ensuring model alignment with LuxeFurn's objectives.

Model Refinement:

- **Validation:** BAs were pivotal in model testing and validation, employing A/B testing and RMSE metrics for accuracy assessment.
- **Stakeholder Engagement:** They orchestrated feedback sessions with sales teams, validating model predictions against market intelligence and customer insights.

Key Questions and Achievements:

- How can model predictions be validated against real-world data and insights?
- Achievement: Refined forecasting models demonstrating high accuracy and relevance to LuxeFurn's market dynamics, validated through stakeholder engagement.

Phase 4: Implementation Challenges

Overcoming Data and Integration Hurdles:

- **Data Cleaning:** BAs supervised the use of ETL tools (Informatica, Talend) for data preparation, ensuring data integrity and consistency.
- **Middleware Implementation:** Collaborative efforts with IT specialists on middleware integration facilitated seamless system communications.

Model Testing and Iteration:

- **Testing:** BAs designed and monitored test scenarios, assessing model performance during critical sales periods for robustness and accuracy.
- **Continuous Improvement:** Established feedback loops for model iteration based on performance and stakeholder input.

Key Questions and Achievements:

- How can integration challenges be effectively addressed to ensure smooth data flow?
- Achievement: Successfully integrated forecasting models with LuxeFurn's IT infrastructure, overcoming significant data and integration hurdles.

Phase 5: Strategic Impact

Realizing Business Benefits:

- **Inventory Optimization:** BAs collaborated with supply chain managers, utilizing model insights to fine-tune inventory levels, significantly reducing overstocks and stockouts.
- **Enhanced Profitability:** Joint analysis with financial analysts demonstrated the project's positive impact on profitability, marking an improvement in demand planning and resource allocation.

Key Questions and Achievements:

- What strategic business benefits can be realized from improved sales forecasting?
- Achievement: Achieved notable improvements in inventory optimization and profitability, underscoring the strategic value of the project.

The success of this project lies not just in the technical achievements but also in the emphasis on stakeholder engagement, cross-functional collaboration, and the strategic alignment of project outcomes with business goals. LuxeFurn's experience illustrates the critical role of BAs in navigating the intersection of business needs and technical solutions, ensuring that data-driven initiatives translate into tangible business value.

In conclusion, LuxeFurn's enhanced sales forecasting project highlights the power of data analytics and business analysis working in concert. It underscores the importance of a holistic, collaborative approach to project management and the value of integrating stakeholder insights and feedback at every step. This case study not only marks a milestone in LuxeFurn's operational strategy but also offers valuable lessons for any organization seeking to harness the power of data for strategic advantage.

Case Study 3: Improving Operational Efficiency With Process Mapping

Case Study 3: Improving Operational Efficiency with Process Mapping

Unleashing Operational Excellence: The Business Analyst's Toolkit in SwiftLogistics' Process Mapping and Data Modeling Journey

THE BUSINESS ANALYST'S HANDBOOK FOR DATA MASTERY: TRANSLATING BUSINESS STRATEGY INTO POWERFUL DATA SOLUTIONS

In the competitive and fast-paced logistics industry, operational efficiency stands as the cornerstone of success. SwiftLogistics, a frontrunner in the logistics sector, embarked on a transformative journey to overhaul its operations by adopting a data-driven strategy. This case study delves into the critical role of business analysts in this initiative, showcasing their adept use of process mapping, data modeling, and collaborative efforts to pinpoint and eliminate inefficiencies.

Project Overview:

SwiftLogistics launched a bold initiative aimed at identifying operational inefficiencies and crafting strategic, data-informed solutions. Business analysts were at the forefront, bridging various teams and dismantling silos to foster a unified understanding of the company's processes.

Phase 1: Initiation and Strategic Planning

Business Analyst Contribution:

- Conducted thorough stakeholder interviews and workshops to collect requirements and understand the existing workflows in-depth.
- Utilized Microsoft Visio for detailed process mapping, visually documenting current operations.
- Performed a SWOT analysis to evaluate the internal and external environment.
- Created a detailed project plan with Microsoft Project, outlining goals, deliverables, and timelines.
- Implemented effective communication strategies, including stakeholder mapping and a customized Communication Plan, to ensure ongoing engagement.

Key Questions and Achievements:

- How can current workflows be accurately documented and analyzed?
- What are the internal strengths and external opportunities that can be leveraged?

Tools and Techniques Used:

- Microsoft Visio for process mapping, Microsoft Project for project planning, and various communication tools for stakeholder engagement.

Phase 2: Process Mapping - The Foundation

Business Analyst Contribution:

- Led the development of dynamic process maps adhering to BPMN standards, continuously refined with new insights.
- Worked closely with subject matter experts to validate processes and identify bottlenecks.
- Employed Lucidchart and Visio to document and visually depict complex workflows.
- Highlighted a major inefficiency: a cumbersome order placement system causing delays.

Key Questions and Achievements:

- Which processes are most prone to inefficiencies?

- How can visual tools help in understanding and improving these processes?

Tools and Techniques Used:

- Process mapping software like Lucidchart and Microsoft Visio for documentation and visualization.

Phase 3: Data Modeling - The Blueprint for Efficiency

Business Analyst Contribution:

- Partnered with data scientists and IT to pinpoint relevant data sources, such as operational databases and CRM systems.
- Formulated a comprehensive Data Dictionary and Data Model to outline critical data elements and relationships.
- Assisted in developing dynamic data models with SQL and Python, facilitating scenario analysis.
- Conducted validation workshops to ensure data models mirrored operational realities.

Key Questions and Achievements:

- How can data be effectively organized to support operational improvements?
- What role do data models play in predicting the outcomes of proposed changes?

Tools and Techniques Used:

- SQL and Python for data modeling, alongside collaborative tools for cross-functional workshops.

Phase 4: Implementation and Transformation

Business Analyst Contribution:

- Led change management initiatives, creating training programs and communication strategies for new process adoption.
- Ensured new systems, like a centralized data entry system, integrated smoothly with existing tech infrastructure.
- Designed pilot programs to evaluate process changes, incorporating feedback for ongoing refinement.
- Produced user manuals and e-learning modules for comprehensive end-user training.

Key Questions and Achievements:

- How can new processes be implemented with minimal disruption?
- What measures can ensure the effectiveness of these changes?

Tools and Techniques Used:

- Change management strategies, IT integration tools, and educational materials for training.

Phase 5: Continuous Improvement and Iteration

Business Analyst Contribution:

- Established KPIs and utilized BI tools like Power BI and Tableau for performance monitoring and optimization.
- Made process mapping and data modeling standard practices, fostering a proactive stance against inefficiencies.
- Led regular process reviews to encourage ongoing improvements, using visual and data-driven aids.
- Compiled a Project Closure Report, capturing lessons learned and best practices for future projects.

Key Questions and Achievements:

- How can continuous improvement be embedded into the organizational culture?
- What benchmarks can effectively gauge operational efficiency?

Tools and Techniques Used:

- Business intelligence tools for dashboard creation, and process documentation software for standardization.

Challenges Encountered and Lessons Learned:

- Overcame data inconsistencies through robust data governance, including cleansing and standardization.
- Tackled resistance to change with inclusive engagement and transparent communication.
- Enhanced cross-functional collaboration by promoting knowledge sharing and diverse perspectives.
- Emphasized the importance of adaptability in response to changing business needs.

Conclusion:

This case study underscores the multifaceted role of business analysts in driving SwiftLogistics towards a data-driven operational model. By leveraging their expertise in process mapping, data modeling, stake

Case Study 4: Data Analytics Project

Case Study 4: Data Analytics Project - Optimizing Retail Inventory: The Business Analyst's Role in RetailMax's Data Analytics Transformation

Introduction

In the dynamic realm of retail, inventory management stands as a crucial determinant of success. RetailMax, a forefront retail chain, recognized the imperative to revolutionize its inventory management to stay competitive. This case study unfolds RetailMax's journey through a data analytics project, emphasizing the critical role of business analysts in synergizing with data scientists and various stakeholders to transform inventory management.

Project Overview

RetailMax aimed to harness advanced data analytics and machine learning to refine inventory management. The objective was to forecast demand precisely, optimize stock levels, minimize shortages, reduce surplus inventory, and elevate customer satisfaction while achieving cost efficiency.

Phase 1: Project Initiation and Planning

Business Needs and Scope Definition

- **Objective**: The business analyst initiated the project by hosting stakeholder interviews and workshops, leveraging SWOT analysis to thoroughly grasp RetailMax's inventory management needs and challenges.
- **Key Questions and Achievements**: Developed a comprehensive understanding of RetailMax's operational strengths and areas for improvement; established a clear project scope and objectives aligned with business goals.

Project Planning and Stakeholder Management

- **Tools and Techniques Used**: Utilized JIRA and Asana for project documentation and timeline tracking. A Power-Interest grid facilitated stakeholder analysis, leading to a strategic Communication Plan for continuous engagement.
- **Key Questions and Achievements**: Successfully identified and engaged critical stakeholders; ensured clear communication and alignment of project goals across departments.

Phase 2: Requirements Gathering and Analysis

Capturing User Requirements

- **Objective**: Engage with store managers and supply chain staff to gather functional and non-functional requirements through focus groups and interviews.
- **Tools and Techniques Used**: Employed Business Process Model and Notation (BPMN) to delineate and assess existing inventory processes, aiding in the precise documentation of requirements.
- **Key Questions and Achievements**: Identified key user requirements and process inefficiencies; laid the groundwork for the development of a tailored data analytics solution.

Data Requirements Analysis

- **Objective**: Collaborate with data scientists to pinpoint essential data sources for inventory management optimization.
- **Tools and Techniques Used**: Developed a Data Dictionary and Data Model, detailing data elements, sources, and relationships crucial for analytical efforts.
- **Key Questions and Achievements**: Mapped out critical internal and external data sources; established a robust foundation for subsequent analytical modeling.

Phase 3: Solution Design and Development

Solution Architecture and Modeling

- **Objective**: Design an AI-driven model for inventory optimization in close cooperation with IT and data

science teams.
- **Tools and Techniques Used**: Chose Random Forest for demand forecasting and linear programming for stock level optimization; outlined the model's architecture in a Technical Specification Document.
- **Key Questions and Achievements**: Created a predictive model aligned with RetailMax's demand patterns; ensured the model's scalability and integration with current systems.

Technology Selection and Implementation

- **Objective**: Select the appropriate programming languages and platforms for the development and deployment of the model.
- **Tools and Techniques Used**: Python, Pandas, and Scikit-learn were selected for data analysis and model building; a cloud-based platform was chosen for deployment.
- **Key Questions and Achievements**: Ensured the technical solution was scalable, integrable with existing systems, and capable of supporting advanced analytics.

Phase 4: Implementation and Deployment

Pilot Testing and A/B Testing

- **Objective**: Conduct real-world testing of the inventory optimization model to validate its effectiveness.
- **Tools and Techniques Used**: Utilized A/B testing methods and developed analytics dashboards to monitor model performance.
- **Key Questions and Achievements**: Demonstrated the model's impact on reducing stockouts and excess inventory; refined the model based on real-world feedback.

Training and Change Management

- **Objective**: Facilitate smooth adoption of the new system by educating store managers and inventory personnel.
- **Tools and Techniques Used**: Designed a comprehensive training program featuring hands-on sessions, e-learning modules, and reference guides.
- **Key Questions and Achievements**: Enhanced user proficiency and acceptance of the new system; ensured operational continuity and maximized the benefits of the optimization model.

Phase 5: Monitoring, Evaluation, and Closure

Performance Monitoring and Continuous Improvement

- **Objective**: Establish KPIs to continually assess the solution's performance and drive improvements.
- **Tools and Techniques Used**: Leveraged a BI tool for real-time performance tracking and decision-making.
- **Key Questions and Achievements**: Achieved significant improvements in stockout rates and inventory costs; instituted a culture of data-driven continuous improvement.

Project Closure and Lessons Learned

- **Objective**: Formalize the project's conclusion, document outcomes, and glean insights for future projects.

- **Tools and Techniques Used**: Compiled a comprehensive Project Closure Report summarizing challenges, successes, and recommendations.
- **Key Questions and Achievements**: Consolidated project knowledge; highlighted the strategic value of business analysis and data analytics in inventory management; paved the way for further innovations in RetailMax's operational strategies.

Conclusion

RetailMax's data analytics project underscored the transformative potential of integrating strategic business analysis with cutting-edge data science in the retail sector. By fostering close collaboration between business analysts, data scientists, and stakeholders throughout the organization, the project successfully navigated the complexities of modern inventory management. This harmonious blend of analytical precision, technological prowess, and stakeholder engagement ensured the achievement of the project's objectives, leading to optimized inventory levels, cost reductions, and heightened customer satisfaction.

This case study not only celebrates the success of RetailMax in enhancing its inventory management practices but also elevates the role of business analysts as indispensable strategic partners in bridging the gap between business needs and data-driven solutions. Through their expertise in engaging with stakeholders, understanding business processes, and leveraging analytical tools, business analysts were instrumental in driving innovation and value creation within RetailMax.

As RetailMax continues to navigate the ever-evolving retail landscape, this project serves as a testament to the power of data analytics and the critical role of business analysis in facilitating sustainable growth and competitive advantage. It exemplifies how strategic planning, adept stakeholder management, and the application of advanced data analytics can collectively forge pathways to operational excellence and organizational success.

Case Study 5: Data Science Project

Case Study 5: Data Science Project

Crafting Personalized Shopping Journeys: The Business Analyst's Role in ShopRight's Data Science Transformation

Introduction

In the evolving digital landscape of e-commerce, customers increasingly crave personalized shopping experiences. ShopRight, a leading online retailer, embarked on an ambitious data science project to meet these demands, aiming to leverage data science and machine learning for unparalleled personalization.

Project Overview

The initiative focused on analyzing customer data to offer personalized product recommendations, aiming to enhance customer loyalty and drive sales growth.

Phase 1: Project Initiation and Planning

Defining Scope and Objectives

Key Objectives:

- Increase customer engagement rates by 20%.
- Boost conversion rates by 15%.
- Achieve a customer satisfaction score of 4.5/5.

Stakeholder Engagement

Stakeholders involved: Marketing, IT, Data Science, and Customer Experience teams. Tools Used: StakeholderMap.com for stakeholder management. Achievement: Development of a comprehensive Stakeholder Management Plan.

Phase 2: Requirements Gathering and Analysis

Capturing Requirements

Techniques: Interviews, surveys, and focus group sessions. Tools Used: JIRA and Confluence for documentation and management. Achievement: Detailed user stories and use cases capturing customer and team insights.

Data Requirements Analysis

Key Questions:

- What data sources are essential for personalization?
- How can we ensure data quality and integrity?

Tools and Techniques: SQL and Python for data ETL processes, AWS S3 for centralized data storage. Achievement: Identification and preparation of essential data sources for personalization algorithms.

Phase 3: Solution Design and Development

Solution Blueprinting

Key Question: Which algorithms and machine learning models best fit our personalization goals? Techniques: Iterative discussions and workshops for algorithm selection and solution architecture development. Achievement: Development of a solution blueprint aligned with business requirements and ShopRight's system architecture.

Technology Selection

Key Considerations: Compatibility with ShopRight's infrastructure, scalability, and real-time processing capabilities. Tools Selected: AWS for cloud computing, Apache Kafka for real-time data streaming, and Python for the personalization engine. Achievement: Selection of a technology stack that supports scalability and integration with existing systems.

Phase 4: Implementation and Deployment

Pilot Testing

Approach: A/B testing of personalized recommendations with a selected customer cohort. Tools Used: Google Analytics and Tableau for analyzing test results. Achievement: Optimization of the personalization engine based on pilot test feedback.

Training and Change Management

Key Question: How do we ensure smooth adoption of the new personalization tools? Techniques: Training programs and workshops, development of user manuals. Achievement: Successful training and onboarding of marketing and sales teams to leverage new personalization capabilities.

Phase 5: Monitoring, Evaluation, and Closure

Performance Monitoring

KPIs Monitored: Engagement rates, conversion rates, customer lifetime value, and customer satisfaction scores. Tools Used: Power BI and Google Analytics for performance tracking. Achievement: Ongoing optimization of the personalization engine based on performance data.

Project Closure

Activities: Gathering feedback, documenting lessons learned, and compiling a Final Project Report. Achievement: Comprehensive documentation of project successes, challenges, and future recommendations.

Conclusion

This case study underscores the critical role of business analysts in steering ShopRight's data science project towards success, through meticulous planning, effective stakeholder engagement, and close collaboration with data scientists. The detailed exploration of methodologies, tools, and the synergy between business analysis and data science provides a robust framework for other organizations aiming to harness the power of data for personalized customer experiences. Through strategic execution and technical insight, the project not only achieved its objectives but also set a benchmark for future initiatives in the realm of data-driven personalization

Case Study 6: Business Intelligence Project

Transforming Healthcare Operations with Business Intelligence

Project Background

HealthMax, a renowned healthcare provider with a network of hospitals and clinics across multiple states, recognized the untapped potential of data to drive operational efficiencies and enhance patient care. Amidst the rapidly evolving healthcare landscape, the initiation of a comprehensive BI project was not merely a strategic decision but a critical step towards revolutionizing how healthcare services could be optimized through data-driven insights.

Phase 1: Project Initiation and Planning

Defining Business Needs and Project Scope

The project kicked off with a series of cross-functional stakeholder workshops, bringing together representatives from clinical, operational, and financial departments. Using mind mapping techniques like XMind, we transformed these collaborative discussions into a visual representation of BI requirements and objectives, capturing key performance indicators (KPIs) and reporting needs across various healthcare domains, such as patient flow optimization, resource utilization, and financial performance monitoring.

Stakeholder Analysis and Management

Recognizing the diverse stakeholder landscape, I conducted a comprehensive stakeholder analysis, identifying key players, including physicians, nurses, hospital administrators, and IT personnel. The detailed Stakeholder Engagement Plan I developed mapped out their interests, potential impacts, and tailored communication strategies, ensuring alignment and buy-in throughout the project lifecycle.

Phase 2: Requirements Gathering and Analysis

Elicitation and Documentation of Requirements

Through a series of interviews, focus groups, and gemba walks (observing processes on the hospital floors), I facilitated a deep dive into HealthMax's operations, eliciting detailed requirements for the BI solution. Leveraging techniques like user story mapping and acceptance criteria development, we documented measurable and actionable requirements for BI reports, dashboards, and data analysis needs across various healthcare domains, such as patient flow analysis, clinical quality metrics, and financial performance monitoring.

Data Requirements Analysis

In collaboration with HealthMax's IT team, I led a comprehensive data audit, uncovering the layers of data accumulated across various systems, including electronic health records (EHRs), billing systems, and clinical databases. The Data Requirements Document I created outlined these data sources, formats, and the necessary data governance standards to ensure data quality, security, and compliance with regulations like HIPAA.

Phase 3: Solution Design and Development

Designing the BI Architecture

Working closely with HealthMax's IT architects and BI vendors like Microsoft and Tableau, we designed a scalable BI architecture tailored to the healthcare industry's unique needs. Using data modeling tools like ER/Studio and architectural diagramming with Visual Paradigm, we visualized the BI solution's structure, encompassing data extraction, transformation, and loading (ETL) processes, data warehousing, and reporting layers.

Technology Selection and Integration

Selecting the right BI platform was a critical decision, requiring a comprehensive evaluation of healthcare-specific features, scalability, and integration capabilities. I authored the Technology Selection Report, which justified our choice of Microsoft's SQL Server and Analysis Services for data warehousing and OLAP cubes, alongside Tableau for advanced data visualization and self-service analytics.

Phase 4: Implementation and Deployment

System Development and Testing

Collaborating with HealthMax's data engineers and report developers, I oversaw the development of the BI solution. SQL was extensively used for data extraction, transformation, and loading processes, while Tableau's powerful visual analytics capabilities were leveraged to create interactive dashboards and reports, transforming complex healthcare data into insightful visualizations.

Throughout the development phase, we conducted rigorous testing, including data validation, user acceptance testing (UAT), and load testing, to ensure the BI system's accuracy, usability, and performance.

Training and Change Management

Recognizing the significant cultural shift involved in adopting a data-driven approach, I spearheaded the development of a comprehensive training program and Change Management Plan. Through a series of classroom and online training sessions, we empowered HealthMax's staff, from clinicians to administrators, to leverage the BI system effectively, fostering a data-driven culture within the organization.

Phase 5: Monitoring, Evaluation, and Closure

Performance Monitoring and Optimization

Post-deployment, I established mechanisms to continuously monitor the BI system's performance and usage. Leveraging Tableau's built-in analytics and feedback features, as well as user surveys, we gathered valuable insights into system adoption, user experience, and areas for improvement, enabling us to optimize the BI solution iteratively.

Project Review and Closure

Upon successful deployment and stabilization, I led a comprehensive project review and closure process. The Final Project Report I authored documented the project's achievements against the initial objectives, lessons learned, and recommendations for ongoing support, maintenance, and future enhancements, such as integrating predictive analytics capabilities to enable proactive decision-making in healthcare operations.

Outcome and Impact

Through the successful implementation of the BI solution, HealthMax achieved remarkable results:

- Improved patient flow and resource utilization, leading to a 15% reduction in wait times and a 20% increase in operational efficiency
- Enhanced clinical quality monitoring, enabling data-driven improvements in patient outcomes and care delivery processes
- Optimized financial performance through real-time visibility into revenue cycles, cost management, and profitability analysis
- Fostered a data-driven culture, empowering healthcare professionals and administrators to make informed decisions based on accurate and timely insights

This transformative project not only delivered operational efficiencies and cost savings but also positioned HealthMax as a leader in leveraging data and analytics to drive superior patient care and healthcare delivery.

Challenges and Lessons Learned

Throughout the project, we encountered several challenges, including:

- Data quality issues stemming from disparate systems and inconsistent data entry practices
- Resistance to change and adoption of the new BI system by some clinical staff
- Ensuring data security and compliance with HIPAA regulations

To address these challenges, we implemented robust data governance processes, conducted extensive training and change management initiatives, and worked closely with HealthMax's legal and compliance teams to ensure adherence to data privacy and security standards.

One of the key lessons learned was the importance of stakeholder engagement and cross-functional collaboration. By involving stakeholders from various departments throughout the project lifecycle, we built trust, overcame resistance, and ensured that the BI solution addressed the diverse needs of the healthcare organization.

This case study exemplifies the pivotal role of business analysts in driving digital transformation within the healthcare industry. By leveraging their expertise in requirements gathering, solution design, and project management, BAs can bridge the gap between healthcare operations and cutting-edge technologies, enabling data-driven decision-making and ultimately improving patient care and operational efficiencies.

Case Study 7: Artificial Intelligence Project

Driving Operational Excellence with AI-Powered Predictive Maintenance

AutoMax Manufacturing, a titan in the automotive parts production arena, sought to pioneer a change. The goal was ambitious yet clear: to implement an AI-driven Predictive Maintenance System capable of foretelling equipment failures. By analyzing operational data through advanced machine learning algorithms, the system would enable proactive maintenance scheduling, a leap forward in manufacturing excellence.

As the lead business analyst at AutoMax Manufacturing, I found myself at the forefront of an ambitious initiative to revolutionize the company's maintenance practices through the power of artificial intelligence (AI). The goal was clear: to implement an AI-driven Predictive Maintenance System capable of forecasting equipment failures, minimizing downtime, and slashing maintenance costs.

Phase 1: Project Initiation and Planning

Defining Business Needs and Project Scope

The project kicked off with strategic planning sessions involving key stakeholders from various departments, including production, maintenance, and IT. Leveraging Lean Six Sigma methodologies, we identified inefficiencies in AutoMax's current maintenance practices and defined the project's objectives: reducing downtime by 30% and achieving a 25% reduction in maintenance costs.

Stakeholder Analysis and Management

Recognizing the diverse stakeholder landscape, I conducted a comprehensive stakeholder analysis, identifying plant managers, equipment operators, IT staff, and other key players. The Stakeholder Engagement Plan I developed mapped out their interests, potential impacts, and tailored communication strategies, ensuring alignment and buy-in throughout the project lifecycle.

Phase 2: Requirements Gathering and Analysis

Elicitation and Documentation of Requirements

Through a series of interviews, workshops, and gemba walks (observing processes on the shop floor), I facilitated a deep dive into AutoMax's operations, eliciting specific requirements for the AI system. User Story Mapping techniques proved invaluable in capturing and prioritizing system requirements and functionalities, such as real-time equipment monitoring, failure prediction, and maintenance scheduling.

Data Requirements Analysis

In collaboration with AutoMax's IT team, I led a data discovery and analysis effort, sifting through equipment sensor data, operational logs, maintenance records, and other relevant data sources. The Data Inventory and Requirements Document I created outlined these data sources, formats, and the data cleansing and transformation steps required to prepare the data for AI model training.

Phase 3: Solution Design and Development

Designing the AI Model

Working closely with AutoMax's data science team, we explored various machine learning algorithms and models suitable for predictive maintenance. After evaluating options like Random Forest, XGBoost, and Long Short-Term Memory (LSTM) networks, we settled on a deep learning approach using TensorFlow and Keras libraries in Python for its ability to handle time-series data and capture complex patterns in equipment sensor readings.

Technology Selection and Integration

Assessing cloud platforms, AI frameworks, and integration capabilities, I authored the Technology Selection Report, which justified our choices. We opted for a cloud-based solution using Amazon Web Services (AWS), leveraging services like Amazon SageMaker for AI model training and deployment, and Amazon Kinesis for real-time data ingestion and processing.

Phase 4: Implementation and Deployment

Model Training and Validation

The data science team trained the deep learning model using AutoMax's historical equipment data, including sensor readings and maintenance logs. We employed cross-validation techniques and performance metrics like precision, recall, and F1-score to validate the model's accuracy in predicting equipment failures.

System Integration and Pilot Testing

Integrating the AI model with AutoMax's Manufacturing Execution System (MES) was a critical step. We leveraged AWS services like Lambda and API Gateway to create a scalable and secure API for the AI model, enabling real-time data ingestion and prediction generation. Pilot testing on selected production lines revealed the system's ability to reduce unexpected downtime by accurately forecasting equipment failures and enabling proactive maintenance scheduling.

Phase 5: Monitoring, Evaluation, and Closure

Performance Monitoring and Continuous Improvement

With the system live, I established key performance indicators (KPIs) to monitor downtime reduction, maintenance cost savings, and overall equipment effectiveness (OEE). Leveraging tools like Amazon QuickSight and AWS CloudWatch, we created dashboards and alerts to track the system's performance and identify areas for continuous improvement through model retraining and refinement.

Project Review and Closure

Upon successful deployment and stabilization, I led a comprehensive project review and closure process. The Project Closure Report I authored documented the project's achievements, lessons learned, and recommendations for future expansions, such as integrating the AI system with AutoMax's supply chain and spare parts management processes.

Outcome and Impact

Through the successful implementation of the AI-driven Predictive Maintenance System, AutoMax Manufacturing achieved remarkable results:

- 35% reduction in unplanned downtime
- 28% reduction in maintenance costs, translating to millions in savings
- Improved overall equipment effectiveness (OEE) by 12%
- Increased production output and efficiency

This transformative project not only delivered significant cost savings and operational improvements but also positioned AutoMax as a leader in leveraging AI for manufacturing excellence.

Challenges and Lessons Learned

Throughout the project, we encountered several challenges, including:

- Data quality issues stemming from inconsistent data collection practices and legacy systems
- Resistance to change and adoption of new technologies by some plant personnel
- Ensuring data security and compliance with relevant regulations

To address these challenges, we implemented robust data governance processes, conducted extensive training and change management initiatives, and worked closely with AutoMax's legal and compliance teams to ensure adherence to data privacy and security standards.

One of the key lessons learned was the importance of cross-functional collaboration and stakeholder engagement. By fostering open communication and involving stakeholders from various departments throughout the project lifecycle, we built trust, overcame resistance, and ensured a smoother adoption of the AI-driven predictive maintenance solution.

This case study exemplifies the pivotal role of business analysts in orchestrating complex AI initiatives that drive operational excellence and digital transformation within organizations. By leveraging their expertise in requirements gathering, solution design, and project management, BAs can bridge the gap between business needs and cutting-edge technologies, unlocking the transformative potential of AI and enabling data-driven decision-making.

Case Study 8: Transforming Retail Through Integrated Data Solutions

Project Background

GlobalRetail, a multinational retail giant, recognized the need to transform its operations and customer experiences to maintain a competitive edge in the rapidly evolving retail landscape. As the lead business analyst (BA) on this initiative, I was tasked with spearheading the integration of data analytics, data science, business intelligence (BI), and artificial intelligence (AI) technologies to drive personalized omni-channel customer experiences, optimize inventory management, and enable data-driven decision-making across the organization.

Driving GlobalRetail's Data Transformation

As the lead business analyst on GlobalRetail's digital transformation initiative, I found myself at the forefront of an ambitious and complex undertaking that would shape the future of this retail giant. From the outset, I recognized the tremendous potential of integrating data analytics, data science, business intelligence (BI), and artificial intelligence (AI) to revolutionize the company's operations and customer experiences.

Phase 1: Project Initiation and Planning

The project kicked off with a series of strategic workshops and executive meetings, where we defined the overarching objectives using the Balanced Scorecard framework. Our goals were ambitious: to increase customer loyalty and revenue by 25%, reduce inventory carrying costs by 20%, and improve overall profitability by 15% through data-driven decision-making.

One of my key responsibilities was to conduct a comprehensive stakeholder analysis and develop a robust Stakeholder Engagement Plan. With stakeholders spanning multiple departments, geographies, and hierarchical levels, effective stakeholder management was crucial to the project's success. I worked closely with stakeholders across regions like North America, Europe, and Asia-Pacific, ensuring their voices were heard and their expectations were managed through clear communication channels and a well-defined RACI matrix.

Phase 2: Requirements Gathering and Analysis

Gathering and documenting requirements was a critical phase, and I knew we had to get it right. I organized a series of collaborative workshops, focus groups, and user interviews across multiple regions, involving end-users, subject matter experts, and stakeholders from various departments. Prototyping and user story mapping techniques were invaluable in visualizing desired functionalities, data flows, and user experiences.

One particularly challenging aspect was GlobalRetail's fragmented data landscape, with siloed data sources ranging from legacy IBM DB2 and Oracle databases to modern cloud-based applications like Salesforce and SAP HANA. I led a thorough analysis of these data sources, including customer data (CRM), transactional data (point-of-sale systems), inventory data (ERP systems), and supplier data (vendor management systems). The Data Strategy Document I developed outlined our approach to data integration, data quality management, and data governance, laying a solid foundation for our analytics and AI initiatives.

Phase 3: Solution Design and Development

Designing the integrated solution architecture was a complex task, but my experience with data flow diagrams (DFDs) and system architecture diagrams proved invaluable. We created a scalable and modular architecture that harmoniously combined data analytics, data science, BI, and AI components, while ensuring compatibility with GlobalRetail's existing IT infrastructure, including IBM WebSphere, Oracle Fusion Middleware, and Microsoft Azure cloud services.

Technology selection was a critical decision, and I spearheaded the evaluation and benchmarking of multiple solutions. The Technology Selection Report I authored justified our choices, including a cloud-based data platform (e.g., Snowflake), advanced analytics tools (e.g., SAS, RapidMiner), AI frameworks (e.g., TensorFlow, PyTorch), and BI solutions (e.g., Tableau, Power BI). This ensured a future-proof and cost-effective technology stack that could seamlessly integrate with GlobalRetail's existing systems.

Phase 4: Implementation and Deployment

During the implementation phase, I worked closely with our data science team to ensure the development of advanced analytics and AI models aligned with the documented requirements. Their expertise in Python, TensorFlow, and other cutting-edge frameworks enabled them to analyze customer behavior data from GlobalRetail's Oracle-based CRM system, sales patterns from the IBM DB2 transactional databases, and inventory data from the SAP ERP systems, delivering personalized product recommendations, demand forecasting, and inventory optimization.

The integration of our solution with GlobalRetail's existing systems, including e-commerce platforms (e.g., IBM WebSphere Commerce), point-of-sale systems (e.g., NCR Counterpoint), and ERP systems (e.g., SAP S/4HANA), was a massive undertaking. I led the effort to follow a phased approach, conducting comprehensive user acceptance testing (UAT) and load testing to ensure seamless integration, performance, and usability. The Integration Plan and User Testing Report I authored documented the challenges we faced, the solutions we implemented, and the lessons learned during this critical phase.

Phase 5: Monitoring, Evaluation, and Closure

Implementing a robust monitoring system was essential to track key performance indicators (KPIs) and ensure continuous improvement. I worked with our IT teams to leverage advanced monitoring tools and dashboards like Splunk, Datadog, and New Relic, enabling us to monitor system performance, data quality, and business metrics in real-time. Regular optimization cycles were conducted based on the insights gathered from the monitoring system, allowing us to fine-tune models, improve data pipelines, and address any issues or bottlenecks.

Upon successful deployment and stabilization, I led the comprehensive project review and closure process. The project closure meeting brought together stakeholders from all levels, celebrating our achievements and reflecting on the lessons learned. The Project Closure Report I authored captured these insights, as well as recommendations for future enhancements and expansion of the solution, such as integrating IoT data from smart shelves and RFID tags for real-time inventory tracking.

Outcome and Impact

Through our collective efforts, GlobalRetail achieved remarkable outcomes, including a 27% increase in customer loyalty and lifetime value, a 19% reduction in inventory carrying costs (saving $450 million annually), and a 17% improvement in profitability through optimized pricing, promotions, and demand forecasting. The real-time BI dashboards and reports powered by Tableau and Power BI empowered data-driven decision-making across the organization.

This transformative initiative not only positioned GlobalRetail as a leader in the retail industry but also established a data-driven culture within the company, fostering continuous innovation and adaptation to changing market dynamics.

Challenges and Lessons Learned

Throughout the project, we encountered numerous challenges, including data quality issues arising from disparate legacy systems and inconsistent data entry practices across regions, resistance to change and adoption of new technologies by some end-users (particularly in retail stores), regulatory and data privacy concerns when handling customer data from CRM systems across different jurisdictions, and technical complexities in integrating diverse systems while ensuring scalability and performance.

To address these challenges, we implemented robust data governance processes, conducted extensive change management and training initiatives, and worked closely with legal and compliance teams to ensure adherence to data privacy regulations like GDPR and CCPA.

One of the key lessons I learned was the importance of fostering a collaborative and agile mindset throughout the project. By embracing cross-functional teamwork, open communication, and a willingness to adapt, we were able to navigate the complexities of this large-scale transformation successfully.

As a business analyst, my role was pivotal in orchestrating this complex data-related project, involving multiple technologies, stakeholders, and geographical regions. By leveraging my expertise in requirements gathering, solution design, and project management, I played a crucial role in driving this transformative initiative that redefined customer experiences, operational efficiencies, and competitive advantages for GlobalRetail.

Navigating Data-Driven Project Challenges

Data Quality Issues

As businesses increasingly rely on data to drive decision-making and gain competitive advantages, the importance of data quality cannot be overstated. As a Business Analyst (BA) working on data analytics, data science, business intelligence, and AI projects, it is crucial to address data quality issues early on to ensure the accuracy and reliability of the insights derived from the data. In this chapter, we will delve into the significance of data quality, common issues such as missing values and inconsistencies, and provide strategies for proactive data management, regular audits, and the use of automated tools for data cleansing and validation.

Importance of Data Quality

Data quality refers to the accuracy, completeness, consistency, and reliability of data. Poor data quality can lead to erroneous analyses, incorrect business decisions, and ultimately impact the organization's bottom line. As a BA, it is essential to recognize the critical role of data quality in ensuring the success of data-driven projects.

Common Data Quality Issues

Missing Values:

One of the most prevalent data quality issues is missing values. When key data points are missing from a dataset, it can significantly impact the validity of any analysis or modeling efforts. Missing values can arise due to various reasons such as human error during data entry, system glitches, or incomplete data integration processes. Addressing missing values requires a systematic approach, including identifying the missing data, understanding the reasons for its absence, and implementing strategies to either impute the missing values or handle them appropriately during analysis.

Inconsistencies:

Data inconsistencies, such as conflicting information across different sources or data points, can undermine the trustworthiness of the data. These inconsistencies can stem from disparate data collection methods, varying data standards, or data integration challenges. As a BA, it is essential to identify and resolve such inconsistencies through data profiling, data standardization, and establishing clear data governance processes.

Strategies for Proactive Data Management

Proactive data management involves anticipating and addressing data quality issues before they impact the integrity of analyses and business decisions. As a BA, you can implement the following strategies to proactively manage data quality:

1. Data Profiling:

Conduct comprehensive data profiling to understand the structure, content, and quality of the data. Data profiling tools can help identify patterns, anomalies, and potential data quality issues, enabling you to take corrective actions early in the project lifecycle.

2. Data Standardization:

Establish clear data standards and definitions to ensure consistency across different datasets. By standardizing data formats, naming conventions, and data validation rules, you can improve data quality and facilitate seamless data integration.

3. Data Governance:

Implement robust data governance practices to define ownership, accountability, and stewardship of data assets within the organization. Data governance frameworks help establish data quality standards, data lineage, and data quality monitoring processes, fostering a culture of data stewardship and accountability.

Regular Data Audits

Conducting regular data audits is essential to monitor and maintain data quality over time. As a BA, you can collaborate with data stewards and subject matter experts to define key data quality metrics and KPIs, and establish a cadence for performing data audits. These audits should encompass data completeness, accuracy, consistency, and timeliness, and the findings should inform data quality improvement initiatives.

Automated Tools for Data Cleansing and Validation

Advancements in technology have led to the development of a wide array of automated tools for data cleansing and validation. As a BA, leveraging these tools can streamline the data quality management process and improve the efficiency of data preparation. Automated data cleansing tools can identify and resolve duplicate records, standardize data formats, and detect anomalies, while data validation tools can enforce data quality rules and flag data errors in real-time.

Examples of Data Quality Issues

To illustrate the impact of data quality issues, let's consider a hypothetical scenario in the context of a retail business. Suppose the company's sales data is plagued with missing values for certain product categories due to inconsistent data entry practices across different stores. As a result, the sales analysis conducted without addressing these missing values may lead to skewed insights and inaccurate inventory management decisions. By proactively addressing the missing values through data cleansing and imputation techniques, the business can ensure the accuracy of its sales forecasts and optimize its inventory levels, ultimately improving operational efficiency and customer satisfaction.

In conclusion, as a BA engaged in data analytics, data science, business intelligence, and AI projects, addressing data quality issues is fundamental to ensuring the reliability and accuracy of the insights derived from the data. By recognizing the importance of data quality, identifying common issues such as missing values and inconsistencies, and implementing proactive data management strategies, BAs can contribute to the success of data-driven initiatives within their organizations. Embracing automated tools for data cleansing and validation further enhances the efficiency of data quality management, paving the way for more robust and trustworthy data-driven decision-making.

In the subsequent chapters, we will explore in greater depth the role of the BA in data governance, data quality measurement, and data quality improvement initiatives, providing practical guidance and best practices for ensuring high-quality data within the realm of data analytics, data science, business intelligence, and AI projects.

Case Study: Enhancing Data Quality for Strategic Insights at RetailCorp

Executive Summary

RetailCorp, a nationwide leader in the retail sector, embarked on a comprehensive data analytics initiative aimed at leveraging its extensive customer and sales data to inform strategic decision-making. Central to this initiative was addressing pervasive data quality challenges to ensure the accuracy and reliability of derived insights. This case study outlines the methodologies, tools, and strategies employed under the stewardship of Emily, the lead Business Analyst (BA), to resolve data quality issues, thereby optimizing inventory management, personalizing marketing campaigns, and improving the customer experience.

Project Background

RetailCorp recognized the transformative potential of its vast data repositories in driving strategic decisions. However, the utility of this data was compromised by significant quality issues, including missing sales data, customer data inconsistencies, and inaccurate inventory records. The initiative, led by Emily, focused on establishing a robust data quality management framework to underpin RetailCorp's analytics capabilities.

Stakeholders

- **Executive Team:** Provided strategic oversight and resources.
- **Store Managers and Data Entry Personnel:** Key in standardizing data entry practices.
- **Supply Chain and Inventory Management Teams:** Collaborated on inventory data reconciliation.
- **IT Department:** Supported the implementation of automated data quality tools.
- **Marketing Department:** Beneficiaries of enhanced customer data for personalized campaigns.
- **Customers:** The end beneficiaries of improved product availability and targeted marketing efforts.

Challenges

1. **Missing Product Sales Data:** Resulting from inconsistent data entry practices.
2. **Customer Data Inconsistencies:** Stemming from conflicts in contact details, duplicate records, and variations in data formats.
3. **Inaccurate Inventory Records:** Due to discrepancies between recorded and actual stock levels.

Solutions and Strategies

Data Preprocessing and Quality Assurance

- **Missing Data Handling:**
    - **Techniques Used:** Employed regression-based and multiple imputation techniques.
    - **Tools:** Utilized Python's Pandas and SciKit-Learn for data manipulation and imputation.
    - **Process:** Collaborated with store managers to standardize data entry protocols and applied imputation techniques to fill in missing values.
- **Data Standardization and Cleansing:**
    - **Tools:** Leveraged data cleansing tools like Talend for deduplication and standardization.
    - **Process:** Established data standards and automated cleansing processes to rectify inconsistencies and format data uniformly.
- **Inventory Data Reconciliation:**
    - **Tools:** Developed automated validation rules using SQL and Excel for real-time error flagging.
    - **Process:** Worked with inventory teams to align recorded data with physical stock levels through

periodic audits.

Data Governance and Continuous Improvement

- **Data Governance Framework:** Instituted a governance model defining data ownership and stewardship roles.
- **Continuous Data Quality Improvement:** Established feedback loops with data consumers to continuously refine data quality processes.

Outcomes

The strategic intervention led by Emily markedly improved RetailCorp's data quality, enabling:

- Optimized inventory management, reducing overstock and stockouts.
- Personalized marketing campaigns driven by accurate customer insights.
- Enhanced operational efficiency and supply chain management.
- A culture of data stewardship and ongoing commitment to data integrity.

Tools and Technology

- **Data Preprocessing and Imputation:** Python (Pandas, SciKit-Learn), SQL, Excel.
- **Data Cleansing:** Talend, SQL.
- **Data Governance:** Custom-developed governance frameworks and regular audits.
- **Collaboration and Project Management:** JIRA for task management, Slack for team communication.

Conclusion

Through meticulous data quality management and cross-functional collaboration, Emily played a pivotal role in transforming RetailCorp's approach to data analytics. This case study exemplifies the indispensable role of Business Analysts in navigating data quality challenges, leveraging technology, and instituting best practices to unlock actionable business insights. It underscores the importance of a structured, strategic approach to data quality, governance, and stakeholder engagement in realizing the benefits of data-driven decision-making.

Integration Challenges

In the realm of data-driven projects, the integration of disparate data sources and systems presents a myriad of challenges for Business Analysts (BAs). This chapter delves into the complexities and strategies associated with integrating diverse data sources, emphasizing the importance of middleware solutions, data standards, and collaboration between IT and business teams.

Challenges of Data Integration

1. Data Heterogeneity:

Data heterogeneity refers to the diversity of data types, formats, and structures across different systems and sources. In data-driven projects, BAs often encounter disparate data sources that may use varying data models, schemas, and standards. This heterogeneity can lead to complexities in integrating and aligning data, hindering the seamless flow of information for analysis and decision-making.

2. Data Quality and Consistency:

Ensuring the quality and consistency of integrated data presents a significant challenge. Disparate data sources may contain inconsistencies, errors, and duplications, impacting the reliability and accuracy of the integrated dataset. BAs must address data quality issues during the integration process to uphold the integrity of the resulting insights.

3. Scalability and Performance:

Scalability and performance considerations are crucial when integrating large volumes of data from diverse sources. As data volumes grow, the integration process must be optimized to maintain performance and accommodate evolving business needs. Ensuring the scalability of the integration solution is essential for accommodating future data growth and evolving project requirements.

4. Data Security and Governance:

Integrating data from diverse sources raises concerns regarding data security, privacy, and governance. BAs must navigate regulatory requirements, data access controls, and privacy considerations to ensure that integrated data adheres to legal and ethical standards. Establishing robust data governance practices within the integration framework is imperative for safeguarding sensitive information and maintaining compliance.

Strategies for Addressing Integration Challenges

1. Adopting Middleware Solutions:

Middleware solutions serve as a critical enabler for integrating disparate data sources. Middleware platforms, such as enterprise service buses (ESBs) and data integration tools, provide a unified infrastructure for connecting, transforming, and routing data between systems. BAs can leverage middleware solutions to orchestrate data flows, implement data transformation logic, and facilitate real-time data integration across heterogeneous environments.

2. Establishing Data Standards and Mappings:

Defining and adhering to data standards is essential for harmonizing disparate data sources. BAs should collaborate with data stewards, subject matter experts, and IT teams to establish consistent data models, schemas, and mappings that align with business requirements. By standardizing data representations and semantics, BAs can streamline the integration process and ensure the interoperability of integrated data.

3. Fostering Collaboration between IT and Business Teams:

Effective collaboration between IT and business teams is paramount for successful data integration. BAs play a pivotal role in bridging the gap between technical and business stakeholders, facilitating clear communication, and aligning integration efforts with business objectives. By fostering collaboration, BAs can ensure that integrated data meets the functional and analytical needs of the organization while maintaining technical feasibility and alignment with IT architecture.

4. Implementing Data Quality Checks and Validation:

Integrating data quality checks and validation processes within the integration pipeline is essential for identifying and rectifying data inconsistencies and errors. BAs should define data quality metrics, validation rules, and exception handling mechanisms to detect and address anomalies during the integration process. By implementing automated data quality checks, BAs can proactively identify and resolve integration issues, ensuring the reliability of integrated data for downstream analysis and decision-making.

5. Leveraging Data Virtualization and Federation:

Data virtualization and federation technologies offer alternative approaches to data integration by providing a unified view of distributed data without physically consolidating it into a central repository. BAs can explore the use of data virtualization platforms to access, query, and integrate data in real-time, minimizing the need for extensive data movement and replication. By leveraging data virtualization, BAs can achieve agility in data access and integration, enabling faster insights and reducing the complexities associated with traditional data consolidation approaches.

Case Study: Overcoming Integration Challenges

To illustrate the significance of addressing integration challenges, let's consider a hypothetical case study in the context of a multinational corporation undergoing a digital transformation initiative. The organization aims to integrate data from disparate legacy systems, cloud-based applications, and external data providers to enable comprehensive business analytics and reporting. However, the diverse nature of the data sources, coupled with varying data formats and access protocols, posed significant integration challenges.

In response to these challenges, the BA leading the integration initiative collaborated with cross-functional teams to implement a middleware solution based on an enterprise service bus (ESB) architecture. The ESB facilitated seamless connectivity between diverse data sources, enabling data transformation, routing, and orchestration. Additionally, the BA defined data standards and mappings in collaboration with data governance stakeholders, ensuring that integrated data adhered to consistent structures and semantics.

Furthermore, the BA implemented automated data quality checks within the integration pipeline, leveraging data validation rules and exception handling mechanisms to identify and resolve data inconsistencies in real-time. By fostering collaboration between IT and business teams, the BA aligned the integration efforts with strategic business objectives, ensuring that the integrated data met the analytical and operational needs of the organization.

As a result of these strategic initiatives, the organization successfully integrated disparate data sources, enabling comprehensive analytics, reporting, and decision support capabilities. The seamless flow of integrated data empowered stakeholders with timely and accurate insights, driving informed decision-making and enhancing the organization's competitive position in the market.

Case Study: Transformative Data Integration at GlobalTech

Project Overview

GlobalTech, a multinational conglomerate, embarked on an ambitious journey to harness data-driven insights across its diverse business units. The initiative aimed at integrating disparate data sources to enhance operational efficiency, decision-making, and innovation. As the lead Business Analyst (BA), Emma was tasked with navigating the complexities of this enterprise-wide data integration, facing challenges ranging from data heterogeneity to ensuring scalability and security.

Stakeholders

- **Executive Team:** Provided strategic direction and funding.
- **IT Department:** Technical execution of data integration, ensuring infrastructure support.
- **Data Stewards and Subject Matter Experts (SMEs):** Defined data models, schemas, and standards.
- **Business Units Leaders:** Ensured the solution met diverse operational needs.
- **Compliance and Security Teams:** Addressed data governance, security, and regulatory compliance.

Tools and Technologies

- **Enterprise Service Bus (ESB):** Middleware for connecting, transforming, and routing data.
- **Data Quality Tools:** Automated profiling, cleansing, and deduplication solutions.
- **Data Virtualization Technologies:** Facilitated real-time access to integrated data without physical consolidation.
- **Collaboration Platforms:** JIRA for project management and Slack for communication.

Process and Implementation

Data Preprocessing

Emma initiated the project by addressing the primary challenge of data heterogeneity. Collaborating with IT and data stewards, she oversaw the cleansing and normalization of data, ensuring consistency across GlobalTech's global operations.

Adopting ESB Architecture

Championing the use of an Enterprise Service Bus (ESB) architecture, Emma facilitated seamless data integration, allowing diverse systems to communicate effectively, thereby addressing the issue of data heterogeneity.

Establishing Data Standards

Understanding the critical role of data quality, Emma worked with SMEs to develop a comprehensive data governance framework. This initiative standardized data models, schemas, and mappings, aligning them with GlobalTech's varied business requirements.

Fostering Collaboration

Recognizing the value of cross-functional collaboration, Emma orchestrated regular meetings between IT, business units, and data teams. This collaborative approach ensured alignment with business objectives and facilitated the successful integration of data assets.

Implementing Data Quality Checks

To tackle data quality and consistency challenges, Emma implemented robust data quality checks and validation processes within the ESB pipeline. Utilizing automated data cleansing and deduplication techniques, she ensured the integrity of the integrated dataset.

Leveraging Data Virtualization

To enhance system agility and performance, Emma explored data virtualization technologies. This approach allowed real-time access to data from disparate sources, significantly reducing data movement overhead and streamlining analytics processes.

Data Security and Governance

Collaborating with the compliance and security teams, Emma established stringent data security and governance protocols. Through access controls, data masking, and encryption, she ensured the protection of sensitive information, aligning with regulatory standards.

Outcomes

The data integration initiative led by Emma transformed GlobalTech's analytics capabilities, enabling:

- **Data-Driven Decision Making:** Integrated analytics and reporting empowered business units with timely insights, driving strategic decisions and operational efficiencies.
- **Innovation and Revenue Growth:** The initiative uncovered new opportunities for process optimization and revenue generation, positioning GlobalTech as an industry leader.
- **Scalable Architecture:** The scalable ESB framework and data virtualization technologies ensured GlobalTech could adapt to future data growth and analytical needs.

Challenges and Solutions

- **Data Integration Complexity:** Addressed through the strategic implementation of ESB architecture and standardized data models.
- **Ensuring Data Security:** Met by developing comprehensive security protocols and leveraging encryption and data masking technologies.

Conclusion

Emma's strategic leadership in GlobalTech's data integration project showcases the pivotal role of Business Analysts in overcoming data integration challenges. By leveraging innovative technologies, fostering cross-functional collaboration, and establishing robust data governance practices, BAs can drive transformative changes, enabling organizations to achieve operational excellence and sustained competitive advantage through integrated data analytics.

Ethical Considerations

In the ever-evolving landscape of data-driven projects, Business Analysts (BAs) are tasked with not only harnessing the power of data for insights and decision-making but also with navigating the complex ethical considerations that arise in the process. This chapter delves into the ethical dimensions of data-driven projects from a BA perspective, examining the critical aspects of privacy, consent, and data protection. It offers strategies and best practices for addressing these ethical considerations, including the implementation of transparent data usage policies, ensuring consent and anonymity, and establishing robust security measures.

Ethical Considerations in Data-Driven Projects

Data-driven projects, encompassing data analytics, data science, business intelligence, and AI initiatives, have the potential to yield transformative outcomes for organizations and society at large. However, the utilization of data in these projects raises profound ethical considerations that demand careful scrutiny and proactive measures to safeguard the rights and interests of individuals, uphold privacy standards, and ensure the responsible use of data.

Privacy and Data Protection

Privacy concerns loom large in the realm of data-driven projects, as the collection, storage, and processing of personal and sensitive data raise fundamental questions about individuals' rights to privacy and control over their personal information. BAs must be attuned to the legal and ethical dimensions of privacy, understanding the implications of data collection and usage on individuals' privacy rights.

In the context of data analytics and AI projects, the aggregation and analysis of diverse datasets, including personal information, pose inherent risks to individuals' privacy. BAs must meticulously evaluate the scope and implications of data collection, ensuring that privacy principles and regulatory requirements are upheld throughout the project lifecycle. This entails conducting thorough privacy impact assessments, identifying and mitigating privacy risks, and adhering to privacy-by-design principles to embed privacy considerations into the project's architecture and processes.

Consent and Anonymity

Obtaining informed consent for data collection, usage, and processing is a cornerstone of ethical data practices. In data-driven projects, BAs play a pivotal role in ensuring that individuals' consent is obtained transparently and unequivocally, aligning with legal requirements and ethical standards. This involves clearly communicating the purposes of data collection and usage, providing individuals with meaningful choices and control over their data, and securing explicit consent for processing personal information.

Moreover, the principle of anonymity holds significant ethical weight in data-driven projects, especially when dealing with sensitive or identifiable information. BAs must prioritize the anonymization and pseudonymization of data to protect individuals' identities and privacy, thereby mitigating the risks of re-identification and unauthorized disclosure. Implementing robust data anonymization techniques and privacy-enhancing technologies is essential to uphold the ethical imperative of preserving individuals' anonymity and minimizing the potential for harm or discrimination arising from data processing activities.

Robust Security Measures

Data security and governance form the bedrock of ethical data practices, encompassing measures to safeguard data against unauthorized access, breaches, and misuse. BAs are entrusted with the critical responsibility of integrating robust security measures into data-driven projects, ensuring that sensitive information is protected with the highest standards of security and resilience.

From a BA perspective, this entails collaborating with cybersecurity experts and IT teams to implement encryption, access controls, and secure data transmission protocols, fortifying the project's infrastructure against potential security threats. Additionally, BAs should advocate for the adoption of comprehensive data governance frameworks, encompassing data classification, risk assessments, and security policies, to instill a culture of data security and compliance across the organization.

Strategies for Ethical Data Practices

Transparent Data Usage Policies:

Establishing transparent data usage policies is imperative for promoting ethical data practices within data-driven projects. BAs should collaborate with legal and compliance teams to craft clear and comprehensible data usage policies, outlining the purposes of data collection, the rights of data subjects, and the organization's commitments to privacy and data protection. Transparent data usage policies serve as a guiding framework for ethical data practices, fostering trust and accountability in the handling of personal and sensitive information.

Ensuring Consent and Anonymity:

To uphold ethical standards in data-driven projects, BAs must institute mechanisms to ensure explicit consent and anonymity in data processing activities. This involves designing user-friendly consent mechanisms, such as consent forms and preference management tools, to empower individuals to make informed choices about their data. Furthermore, BAs should advocate for the adoption of anonymization techniques, encryption methods, and privacy-preserving technologies to uphold individuals' right to anonymity and mitigate privacy risks associated with data processing.

Implementing Robust Security Measures:

The implementation of robust security measures is paramount for ethical data practices, safeguarding data against unauthorized access, breaches, and misuse. BAs should collaborate with cybersecurity experts and IT teams to conduct comprehensive security assessments, identify vulnerabilities, and implement encryption, access controls, and intrusion detection systems to fortify the project's security posture. Additionally, BAs should champion the adoption of data governance frameworks and security protocols to foster a culture of data security and resilience within the organization.

Case Study: Implementing Ethical Healthcare Analytics at Northside Hospital

Project Overview

Northside Hospital, a leading healthcare provider, recognized the potential of utilizing its extensive electronic health records (EHRs) and patient data to enhance patient care and operational efficiency. The initiative aimed to analyze this data for insights into optimizing resource allocation, improving clinical workflows, and boosting treatment outcomes. However, the project also presented significant ethical challenges related to patient data privacy and security.

Business Analysis Challenge

The lead Business Analyst (BA), Sarah, was tasked with navigating the delicate balance between leveraging data for analytics and upholding stringent patient privacy standards. Given the sensitive nature of healthcare data, ensuring compliance with healthcare regulations, such as HIPAA, and maintaining patient trust was paramount.

Stakeholders

- **Patients:** The primary focus of Northside Hospital's ethical considerations, with a vested interest in how their personal information was used.
- **Healthcare Professionals:** Required access to patient data for clinical purposes while adhering to privacy

standards.
- **IT Department:** Responsible for implementing the technical aspects of data security and privacy measures.
- **Legal and Compliance Teams:** Ensured the project adhered to all relevant regulations and ethical guidelines.
- **Ethics Advisory Board:** Provided ongoing ethical oversight and governance.

Tools and Technologies

- **Data Encryption Software:** Utilized for encrypting data at rest and in transit, safeguarding patient information.
- **Access Management Systems:** Deployed role-based access controls and multi-factor authentication to restrict data access.
- **Anonymization Tools:** Employed for de-identifying patient data, including techniques like pseudonymization and data masking.
- **Differential Privacy Algorithms:** Applied to maintain privacy while allowing for aggregated data analysis.

Process and Techniques

Transparency and Consent Management

- Developed a comprehensive data governance framework detailing data usage policies and patient rights.
- Implemented patient consent management processes, enabling patients to make informed decisions about their data.

Robust Data Security Measures

- Orchestrated the integration of advanced security measures, including data encryption and role-based access controls.
- Conducted regular security assessments to identify vulnerabilities and strengthen data protection.

Data Anonymization and Privacy-Enhancing Technologies

- Advocated for the use of anonymization techniques to minimize risks of patient re-identification.
- Explored differential privacy to ensure individual data remained confidential during analysis.

Ethical Oversight and Governance

- Established an ethics advisory board to provide multidisciplinary guidance and oversight.
- Implemented regular audits and ethical risk assessments to proactively address potential privacy concerns.

Outcome and Impact

By embedding ethical considerations at the core of its analytics initiative, Northside Hospital not only derived valuable insights from patient data but also reinforced its commitment to data privacy and patient trust. The project's success in balancing data-driven innovation with ethical practices showcased Sarah's pivotal role in championing responsible data use, ultimately enhancing patient care and operational efficiency.

Conclusion

This case study demonstrates the crucial role of business analysts in guiding healthcare analytics projects through ethical complexities. Sarah's strategic approach to ethical data use, from ensuring transparency and consent to implementing robust security measures, highlights the BA's responsibility in safeguarding patient privacy while driving forward data-driven healthcare improvements. Through meticulous planning, stakeholder engagement, and the application of advanced technologies, Northside Hospital emerged as a model for ethical, patient-centered analytics in healthcare.

Importance of Overcoming Data-Driven Project Challenges

Data-driven projects are inherently complex, characterized by the convergence of diverse data sources, intricate technical architectures, and evolving regulatory landscapes. As organizations endeavor to harness the power of data for strategic decision-making and innovation, they are confronted with an array of challenges that demand astute management and ethical foresight. From the intricate interplay of privacy and consent to the imperatives of robust data security and governance, BAs are tasked with navigating these challenges to ensure the ethical and responsible use of data in driving organizational success.

One of the paramount challenges in data-driven projects pertains to privacy considerations, encompassing the ethical dimensions of data collection, usage, and protection. As data becomes increasingly pervasive and organizations amass vast troves of information, the preservation of individuals' privacy rights and the adherence to regulatory requirements emerge as critical imperatives. BAs must proactively address privacy challenges by conducting comprehensive privacy impact assessments, devising transparent data usage policies, and advocating for the adoption of privacy-enhancing technologies to safeguard individuals' privacy and uphold ethical data practices.

Furthermore, the ethical imperative of obtaining informed consent for data collection and processing presents a formidable challenge in data-driven initiatives. BAs must collaborate with legal and compliance experts to institute mechanisms for transparent and unequivocal consent, aligning with the principles of autonomy and self-determination. By empowering individuals to make informed choices about their data and respecting their consent preferences, BAs can instill trust and accountability in data-driven projects, reinforcing ethical standards and regulatory compliance.

In parallel, the imperative of data security and governance poses substantial challenges in data-driven projects, necessitating proactive measures to safeguard data against unauthorized access, breaches, and misuse. BAs are entrusted with the critical responsibility of integrating robust security measures into the project's architecture, collaborating with cybersecurity experts to implement encryption, access controls, and intrusion detection systems. By championing the adoption of comprehensive data governance frameworks and security protocols, BAs can fortify the organization's data security posture and foster a culture of resilience and compliance, thereby mitigating risks and ensuring the ethical handling of data.

Significance of Proactive Management and Collaboration

Amidst the myriad challenges inherent in data-driven projects, proactive management and collaboration emerge as linchpins for navigating obstacles and fostering ethical data practices. BAs must adopt a proactive stance in identifying, assessing, and mitigating ethical challenges throughout the project lifecycle, embedding ethical considerations into the project's architecture and processes. By fostering a culture of ethical foresight and accountability, BAs can engender trust, transparency, and responsible stewardship of data, aligning with organizational values and societal expectations.

Collaboration stands as a cornerstone of ethical data practices, as BAs engage with multidisciplinary teams to address the ethical dimensions of data-driven projects comprehensively. From collaborating with legal and compliance experts to formulate transparent data usage policies and consent mechanisms to partnering with cybersecurity and IT teams to bolster data security and resilience, BAs play a pivotal role in orchestrating cross-functional collaboration to uphold ethical standards and regulatory compliance. By fostering a collaborative ethos that transcends silos and engenders collective ownership of ethical imperatives, BAs can navigate ethical challenges adeptly and unlock the full potential of data-driven initiatives.

Emphasis on Ethical Standards in Navigating Obstacles

The ethical dimensions of data-driven projects underscore the imperative of upholding rigorous ethical standards to navigate obstacles and unlock the full potential of data-driven initiatives. BAs must champion ethical standards that prioritize privacy, consent, anonymity, and security, aligning with legal and regulatory requirements, industry best practices, and societal expectations. By adhering to ethical imperatives, BAs can mitigate risks, engender trust, and position organizations as responsible stewards of data, thereby fostering sustainable and ethical data-driven innovation.

The adherence to ethical standards serves as a compass for BAs in navigating the intricate terrain of data-driven projects, guiding their decisions and actions to align with ethical principles and societal values. By upholding ethical standards, BAs can instill confidence among stakeholders, engender trust among data subjects, and position organizations as ethical trailblazers in the era of data-driven innovation. Through their steadfast commitment to ethical standards, BAs can navigate obstacles adeptly and unlock the full potential of data-driven initiatives, driving organizational success while upholding the rights and dignity of individuals.

Unlocking the Full Potential of Data-Driven Initiatives

The journey of translating business strategy into powerful data solutions culminates in the realization of the full potential of data-driven initiatives through the lens of ethical foresight and responsible stewardship. As BAs navigate the ethical dimensions of data-driven projects, they have the opportunity to unlock transformative outcomes for organizations and society at large, harnessing the power of data for strategic decision-making, innovation, and societal impact.

By prioritizing proactive management, collaboration, and ethical standards, BAs can surmount the challenges inherent in data-driven projects, fostering a culture of ethical foresight and accountability. Through their steadfast commitment to ethical data practices, BAs can engender trust, transparency, and responsible use of data, positioning organizations as ethical trailblazers in the era of data-driven innovation. As organizations navigate the complex terrain of data-driven projects, BAs stand as ethical champions, guiding the responsible and sustainable use of data to drive organizational success and societal welfare.

Summary of Strategy, Techniques and Tools Use by BA in Data Driven Projects

Data Collection and Management

Upon entering the realm of data-driven projects, it's as if we are embarking on a captivating journey through the intricate landscapes of modern enterprises. Here, amidst the digital tapestries woven from countless bits and bytes, the role of a Business Analyst (BA) shines brightly as a guide, responsible for navigating the winding paths of data collection and management.

Understanding Data Sources

Before we delve into the art of data collection, let us first take a moment to appreciate the myriad of data sources that await our exploration. These sources, akin to hidden gems waiting to be unearthed, can be found both within the confines of an organization and beyond its borders. Internally, they may take the form of sales records, customer databases, and operational logs, while externally, they might manifest as market research reports, social media data, and public databases.

Each of these sources possesses a unique nature, a distinct reliability, and a relevance that is intrinsically tied to the quality of the data they hold. As we tread upon this path, we are reminded that understanding these sources is akin to deciphering a treasure map, ensuring that the data collected for analysis is of the utmost quality.

Databases and SQL/NoSQL

In the realm of data-driven projects, the role of a Business Analyst (BA) is pivotal in ensuring the seamless collection and management of structured and unstructured data. This process lays the foundation for enabling deep analysis of business information, thereby facilitating informed decision-making. In this chapter, we delve into the world of databases and the significance of SQL and NoSQL in the context of data analytics, data science, business intelligence, and AI projects.

Databases play a fundamental role in housing and organizing the vast amounts of data generated by modern businesses. They act as repositories for structured data, which is data that is organized and formatted in a specific way, and unstructured data, which refers to data that lacks a specific structure or model. Structured data typically resides in relational databases, which are based on the relational model of data, while unstructured data finds its home in non-relational databases, often referred to as NoSQL databases.

Relational databases are founded on the principles of the relational model, as proposed by Edgar F. Codd in 1970. This model organizes data into one or more tables (or relations) of rows and columns, with a unique key identifying each row. SQL, or Structured Query Language, is the standard language for interacting with relational databases. As a BA, understanding SQL is crucial, as it enables you to retrieve, manipulate, and manage data within relational databases. SQL allows BAs to perform a wide array of operations, including data retrieval, data manipulation, and data definition.

In the domain of data analytics, relational databases and SQL serve as the backbone for querying and analyzing structured data. BAs leverage SQL to extract relevant insights from the vast repositories of business data, enabling them to identify patterns, trends, and anomalies that can inform strategic decision-making. Furthermore, SQL provides BAs with the ability to perform complex aggregations, joins, and transformations, thereby empowering them to derive actionable intelligence from the data.

While relational databases and SQL have long been the cornerstone of data management and analysis, the emergence of non-relational databases, commonly known as NoSQL databases, has introduced a new paradigm in data storage and retrieval. NoSQL databases are designed to handle unstructured and semi-structured data, offering flexibility and scalability that traditional relational databases may lack. As a BA, understanding the characteristics and capabilities of NoSQL databases is essential in navigating the evolving landscape of data storage and analysis.

NoSQL databases encompass various types, including document stores, key-value stores, wide-column stores, and graph databases, each tailored to specific data storage and retrieval requirements. Document stores, such as MongoDB, store data in flexible, JSON-like documents, making them ideal for managing unstructured and semi-structured data. Key-value stores, like Redis, excel in high-speed data retrieval and are often used for caching and session management. Wide-column stores, exemplified by Apache Cassandra, are optimized for handling massive amounts of data across distributed clusters. Graph databases, such as Neo4j, specialize in storing and querying interconnected data, making them well-suited for applications involving complex relationships and network analysis.

As a BA involved in data analytics, data science, business intelligence, or AI projects, understanding the unique capabilities and use cases of NoSQL databases is vital for making informed decisions regarding data storage and retrieval strategies. By recognizing the strengths and limitations of NoSQL databases, BAs can align their data management practices with the specific needs of their projects, ensuring optimal performance and scalability.

ETL Tools

In the realm of data-driven projects, the role of a Business Analyst (BA) extends to facilitating the extraction, transformation, and loading (ETL) of data from various sources into a centralized repository. This process is fundamental in ensuring that data is cleansed, transformed, and integrated in a manner that enables meaningful analysis and decision-making. In this chapter, we delve into the world of ETL tools and their significance in the context of data analytics, data science, business intelligence, and AI projects.

ETL Process Overview

The ETL process encompasses three key stages: extraction, transformation, and loading. Each stage plays a critical role in the overall data integration and warehousing process.

Extraction: The extraction phase involves retrieving data from disparate sources, which may include operational databases, transactional systems, flat files, and external data feeds. BAs are responsible for identifying the relevant data sources and determining the most efficient methods for extracting the required data while considering factors such as data volume, frequency of updates, and data quality.

Transformation: Once the data has been extracted, it undergoes a series of transformations to standardize formats, cleanse inconsistencies, and enrich its quality. This phase often involves data mapping, normalization, aggregation, and the application of business rules to ensure that the data is fit for analysis and reporting. BAs collaborate with data engineers and data scientists to define transformation logic that aligns with the business requirements and analytical objectives.

Loading: The final stage of the ETL process involves loading the transformed data into a centralized repository, such as a data warehouse or data lake. BAs oversee the design and implementation of loading processes to ensure that data is efficiently and accurately transferred to the target storage, leveraging best practices in data loading, incremental updates, and error handling.

ETL Tools Landscape

The landscape of ETL tools is diverse, encompassing a wide array of commercial and open-source solutions designed to streamline the ETL process and enhance data integration capabilities. BAs must navigate this landscape to select the most appropriate ETL tools that align with the specific requirements and constraints of their projects.

Commercial

Commercial ETL tools, such as Informatica PowerCenter, IBM InfoSphere DataStage, and Microsoft SQL Server Integration Services (SSIS), offer comprehensive suites of features for data extraction, transformation, and loading. These tools provide graphical user interfaces for designing ETL workflows, visual data mapping capabilities, and a range of pre-built connectors for interfacing with various data sources. Additionally, they often incorporate advanced functionalities such as data profiling, metadata management, and job scheduling, empowering BAs to orchestrate complex ETL processes with ease.

Open-Source

Open-source ETL tools, including Apache NiFi, Talend Open Studio, and Pentaho Data Integration (Kettle), present cost-effective alternatives with robust ETL capabilities. These tools leverage open-source frameworks and community-driven development to offer extensible, customizable solutions for data integration. BAs can harness the flexibility of open-source ETL tools to adapt and extend their functionality to suit the evolving needs of their projects, while also benefiting from the active community support and extensive documentation available for these tools.

Cloud-Based ETL Services:

With the proliferation of cloud computing, BAs are increasingly turning to cloud-based ETL services, such as Amazon Web Services (AWS) Glue, Google Cloud Dataflow, and Microsoft Azure Data Factory, to leverage scalable, serverless ETL capabilities. These services enable BAs to design ETL pipelines that seamlessly integrate with cloud-based storage and analytical services, offering the advantages of elastic scalability, pay-as-you-go pricing, and seamless integration with cloud ecosystems.

Key Considerations for ETL Tool Selection

When evaluating ETL tools for a data-driven project, BAs should consider several key factors to ensure that the selected tool aligns with the project's objectives, technical requirements, and organizational constraints.

Scalability and Performance: The ability of an ETL tool to scale with growing data volumes and processing demands is paramount. BAs must assess the performance benchmarks and scalability features of ETL tools to ensure that they can accommodate the anticipated data loads and processing complexities.

Connectivity and Integration: ETL tools should offer a rich set of connectors and integration capabilities to interface with diverse data sources and destinations. BAs need to evaluate the extensibility and adaptability of ETL tools to seamlessly integrate with existing systems, applications, and data platforms.

Ease of Use and Productivity: The usability of an ETL tool, including its user interface, workflow design capabilities, and productivity features, directly impacts the efficiency of ETL development and maintenance. BAs should prioritize tools that empower them to design, monitor, and manage ETL processes with minimal effort and time investment.

Data Quality and Governance: ETL tools should incorporate features for data quality profiling, validation, and governance to ensure that the transformed data meets the requisite standards of accuracy, consistency, and completeness. BAs must ascertain the data quality management capabilities of ETL tools to uphold the integrity and reliability of the integrated data.

Cost and Licensing: The cost model and licensing terms associated with ETL tools play a significant role in the overall project budget and resource allocation. BAs should conduct a comprehensive cost-benefit analysis to evaluate the total cost of ownership, including initial licensing fees, ongoing support, and potential scalability costs.

Best Practices for ETL Implementation

In implementing ETL processes for data analytics, data science, business intelligence, and AI projects, BAs should adhere to best practices that promote efficiency, reliability, and maintainability.

Modular and Reusable Components: BAs should design ETL workflows with a modular, component-based approach, enabling the reuse of transformation logic and data processing routines across multiple data integration tasks. This promotes consistency, reduces development effort, and facilitates the evolution of ETL processes over time.

Data Lineage and Metadata Management: ETL processes should incorporate robust metadata management capabilities to capture data lineage, transformation rules, and dependencies. BAs are tasked with documenting and maintaining comprehensive metadata that facilitates traceability and impact analysis, aiding in data governance and compliance efforts.

Incremental ETL and Change Data Capture: Leveraging incremental ETL techniques and change data capture mechanisms, BAs can optimize data loading processes by selectively transferring only the modified or new data since the last ETL run. This approach minimizes the data transfer overhead and enhances the efficiency of ETL operations, especially in scenarios involving large-scale data sets.

Error Handling and Logging: Robust error handling mechanisms and logging facilities are essential to detect, report, and manage errors and exceptions encountered during the ETL process. BAs should implement comprehensive error handling strategies that encompass data validation, exception escalation, and notification mechanisms to ensure the integrity of the ETL pipeline.

Performance Optimization and Monitoring: BAs are responsible for fine-tuning ETL processes to optimize performance and resource utilization. This involves profiling and analyzing the execution of ETL workflows, identifying performance bottlenecks, and implementing optimizations to enhance data processing throughput and efficiency.

Statistical Software

R and Python, equipped with libraries like pandas and ggplot2, are pivotal for performing statistical analysis and data manipulation. The implication for BA in an organization, how BA work with others relating to the above tools.

Statistical Analysis in the Data-Driven Landscape

In the rapidly evolving landscape of data-driven projects, statistical software plays a pivotal role in enabling business analysts (BAs) to derive actionable insights from complex and voluminous datasets. The marriage of statistical software with data analytics, data science, business intelligence, and AI projects empowers BAs to uncover patterns, trends, and correlations that drive informed decision-making and strategic planning within organizations. This chapter delves into the significance of statistical software and its implications for BAs, elucidating the methodologies, tools, and collaborative endeavors that underpin the effective utilization of statistical analysis in the realm of business analysis.

R and Python: Cornerstones of Statistical Software

R and Python stand as the cornerstone languages for statistical analysis and data manipulation, offering rich ecosystems of libraries, packages, and frameworks that facilitate a myriad of statistical operations. BAs leveraging R and Python can harness their diverse capabilities to perform exploratory data analysis, hypothesis testing, regression modeling, time series analysis, and visualization, among other statistical tasks. The extensibility and flexibility of these languages empower BAs to adapt statistical methodologies to the unique requirements of their projects, fostering a culture of data-driven decision-making and evidence-based insights.

Pandas and ggplot2: Empowering Statistical Analysis

Within the realms of Python and R, the libraries pandas and ggplot2 stand as stalwarts in the arsenal of BAs for data manipulation and visualization. Pandas, a powerful data manipulation and analysis library for Python, enables BAs to seamlessly wrangle, transform, and aggregate datasets, facilitating the preparation of data for statistical modeling and analysis. Its intuitive data structures, such as DataFrames and Series, coupled with robust functionalities for data cleaning, exploration, and transformation, empower BAs to navigate the intricacies of diverse datasets and prepare them for statistical inference and interpretation.

Similarly, ggplot2, a leading data visualization package for R, equips BAs with the tools to create intricate and insightful visual representations of statistical analyses. The grammar of graphics paradigm embraced by ggplot2 enables BAs to construct a wide array of visualizations, encompassing scatter plots, bar plots, line plots, and more, with a focus on clarity, coherence, and aesthetic appeal. By leveraging ggplot2, BAs can communicate statistical findings effectively, distilling complex analyses into visually compelling narratives that resonate with stakeholders and decision-makers.

Implications for Business Analysts

The utilization of statistical software imparts several implications for BAs, shaping their roles, interactions, and contributions within organizations engaged in data analytics, data science, business intelligence, and AI projects.

Methodological Expertise: BAs immersed in the realm of statistical software must cultivate a deep understanding of statistical methodologies, techniques, and best practices. This expertise enables BAs to formulate robust hypotheses, design sound experiments, and draw valid inferences from data, underpinning their ability to deliver actionable insights and recommendations to stakeholders.

Collaborative Engagements: Statistical software engenders collaborative engagements between BAs, data scientists, statisticians, and domain experts, fostering interdisciplinary teamwork and knowledge exchange. BAs collaborate with data scientists to formulate statistical models aligned with business objectives, work with statisticians to validate assumptions and methodologies, and engage domain experts to contextualize statistical findings within the organizational landscape.

Data Preparation and Transformation: Statistical software necessitates BAs to adeptly manipulate and prepare data for analysis, ensuring that datasets are cleansed, standardized, and structured to facilitate meaningful statistical inferences. BAs leverage their expertise in pandas and ggplot2 to curate datasets, perform exploratory data analysis, and visualize patterns, laying the groundwork for rigorous statistical analysis and interpretation.

Informed Decision-Making: The utilization of statistical software equips BAs to derive insights that guide informed decision-making, enabling organizations to mitigate risks, capitalize on opportunities, and optimize operational efficiencies. BAs distill statistical findings into actionable recommendations, empowering stakeholders to make evidence-based decisions that align with strategic objectives and organizational imperatives.

Integration with AI and Machine Learning: Statistical software forms an integral nexus between BAs, AI, and machine learning initiatives, bridging the realms of statistical analysis and predictive modeling. BAs collaborate with data scientists and AI practitioners to integrate statistical insights into machine learning models, leveraging statistical methodologies to interpret model outputs, validate predictions, and evaluate model performance within the context of business requirements.

BI and Visualization Tools

Driving Actionable Insights through Interactive Dashboards and Visualizations

In the dynamic landscape of data analytics, data science, business intelligence, and AI projects, the role of Business Analysts (BAs) in delivering actionable insights from complex data has become increasingly pivotal. The convergence of BI and visualization tools, such as Tableau, Power BI, and Qlik, has empowered BAs to create interactive dashboards and compelling visualizations, thereby facilitating the dissemination of data-driven narratives and enhancing stakeholder engagement. This chapter delves into the significance of BI and visualization tools, elucidating their methodologies, capabilities, and transformative impact on the realm of business analysis.

Tableau: Unleashing the Power of Interactive Data Storytelling

Tableau stands as a premier BI and visualization tool, empowering BAs to craft immersive and interactive dashboards that transcend the traditional confines of static reporting. With its intuitive drag-and-drop interface and robust visualization capabilities, Tableau enables BAs to seamlessly connect to diverse datasets, transform raw data into compelling visualizations, and construct dynamic dashboards that facilitate exploratory data analysis and insight dissemination. The seamless integration of Tableau with various data sources, including relational databases, cloud platforms, and big data repositories, empowers BAs to harness the richness of disparate datasets and weave cohesive narratives that resonate with stakeholders.

The interactive nature of Tableau dashboards allows stakeholders to engage with data dynamically, enabling them to drill down into specific data points, filter visualizations based on contextual parameters, and derive actionable insights in real-time. BAs leverage the versatility of Tableau to create a spectrum of visualizations, encompassing bar charts, line graphs, scatter plots, heat maps, and geographic representations, thereby distilling complex data into visually compelling narratives that drive informed decision-making and strategic foresight within organizations.

Power BI: Empowering Data-Driven Decision-Making

Microsoft Power BI stands as a formidable force in the domain of business intelligence and data visualization, equipping BAs with a comprehensive suite of tools to transform raw data into actionable insights. The seamless integration of Power BI with Microsoft Azure and other data sources enables BAs to ingest, transform, and model data, culminating in the creation of impactful reports and dashboards that resonate with stakeholders across organizational hierarchies. Power BI's robust data modeling capabilities, coupled with its rich library of visualizations and AI-powered insights, empowers BAs to uncover patterns, trends, and correlations that underpin informed decision-making and operational optimization.

The extensibility of Power BI through custom visuals and plugins enables BAs to tailor visualizations to the unique requirements of their projects, fostering a culture of data-driven decision-making and stakeholder engagement. Collaborative features, such as shared workspaces and real-time collaboration, facilitate knowledge exchange and interdisciplinary teamwork, enabling BAs to coalesce diverse perspectives into cohesive data narratives that drive organizational excellence.

Qlik: Accelerating Data Discovery and Insights

Qlik, renowned for its associative data model and augmented intelligence, empowers BAs to accelerate data discovery and derive transformative insights from complex datasets. The associative nature of Qlik's data model enables BAs to traverse data relationships dynamically, uncovering hidden associations and correlations that elude traditional query-based approaches. BAs leverage Qlik's associative engine to create interactive visualizations that facilitate exploratory data analysis, enabling stakeholders to navigate data intuitively and derive actionable insights that drive strategic planning and operational efficiency.

Qlik's augmented intelligence capabilities, encompassing AI-powered data preparation, automated insights, and natural language processing, augment the analytical prowess of BAs, enabling them to distill complex data into actionable narratives that resonate with diverse stakeholders. The collaborative nature of Qlik's platform, underpinned by shared apps and interactive dashboards, fosters knowledge exchange and stakeholder engagement, propelling organizations towards data-driven excellence and competitive advantage.

Implications for Business Analysts

The utilization of BI and visualization tools imparts several implications for BAs, reshaping their roles, interactions, and contributions within organizations engaged in data analytics, data science, business intelligence, and AI projects.

Visual Data Storytelling: BAs immersed in the realm of BI and visualization tools must cultivate a deep understanding of visual data storytelling, leveraging the capabilities of Tableau, Power BI, and Qlik to craft immersive narratives that distill complex data into actionable insights. By harnessing the interactive features of these tools, BAs empower stakeholders to engage with data dynamically, enabling them to derive insights that guide informed decision-making and strategic planning.

Stakeholder Engagement: BI and visualization tools engender stakeholder engagement by enabling BAs to create interactive dashboards and visualizations that resonate with diverse audiences. BAs collaborate with stakeholders to understand their informational needs, tailoring visualizations to communicate insights effectively and foster a culture of data-driven decision-making across organizational hierarchies.

Data Exploration and Discovery: The utilization of BI and visualization tools equips BAs to explore and discover hidden patterns, trends, and correlations within complex datasets. BAs leverage the interactive features of Tableau, Power BI, and Qlik to conduct exploratory data analysis, enabling them to uncover actionable insights that drive strategic foresight and operational optimization within organizations.

Operational Excellence: BI and visualization tools enable BAs to drive operational excellence by distilling complex data into actionable narratives that guide informed decision-making. BAs harness the capabilities of Tableau, Power BI, and Qlik to create dashboards and visualizations that illuminate opportunities, mitigate risks, and optimize operational efficiencies, thereby aligning organizational imperatives with strategic objectives.

Integration with Data Science and AI: BI and visualization tools serve as catalysts for interdisciplinary collaboration between BAs, data scientists, and AI practitioners, bridging the realms of business intelligence and predictive analytics. BAs collaborate with data scientists and AI practitioners to integrate visual insights into machine learning models, enabling them to interpret model outputs, validate predictions, and evaluate model performance within the context of business requirements.

Interview, Documentation, and Requirements Gathering Techniques

Interviews, documentation, and requirements gathering are essential components of business analysis, serving as the foundation for capturing and communicating business and system requirements effectively. In this chapter, we will explore the intricacies of structured and unstructured interviews, various documentation techniques, and requirements gathering methods, delving into their significance and the best practices for harnessing their potential in data analytics, data science, business intelligence, and AI projects.

Structured and Unstructured Interviews

Interviews stand as a cornerstone of eliciting information from stakeholders, subject matter experts, and end users, providing business analysts with invaluable insights into business processes, user needs, and system requirements. Structured interviews entail a predefined set of questions, enabling business analysts to gather specific information in a systematic manner. On the other hand, unstructured interviews offer the flexibility to explore diverse perspectives and unearth unanticipated requirements, fostering a holistic understanding of business needs and operational challenges.

Best practices for conducting structured interviews involve meticulous preparation, including the formulation of clear and concise questions, the identification of relevant stakeholders, and the establishment of a conducive environment for the interview. Business analysts should ensure active listening, ask open-ended questions, and employ probing techniques to delve into the intricacies of business processes and user requirements. Documentation of interview findings is paramount, encompassing detailed notes, audio recordings, and visual aids to capture and convey the nuances of stakeholder insights effectively.

Unstructured interviews necessitate adeptness in adapting to dynamic conversations, fostering rapport with stakeholders, and encouraging open dialogue to uncover implicit requirements and tacit knowledge. Business analysts should exercise empathy, empathy, and a keen awareness of nonverbal cues to glean valuable insights from unstructured interviews. Documentation of unstructured interviews demands the synthesis of diverse perspectives and the articulation of emergent requirements, necessitating the adept use of narrative techniques, affinity diagrams, and mind mapping to distill complex insights into actionable requirements.

Documentation Techniques

Documentation serves as the conduit for preserving and communicating business and system requirements, facilitating the alignment of stakeholder expectations with project deliverables. Business analysts employ a myriad of documentation techniques, such as use case diagrams, process flowcharts, data dictionaries, and entity-relationship diagrams, to delineate the functional and non-functional requirements of data analytics, data science, business intelligence, and AI projects.

Use case diagrams encapsulate the interactions between system actors and the system itself, portraying the various scenarios in which the system functions to fulfill user needs and operational objectives. Process flowcharts visualize the sequential flow of activities within a business process, elucidating the dependencies, decision points, and control flows that govern the operational workflow. Data dictionaries catalog the data elements, their attributes, and the relationships between them, providing a comprehensive reference for data management and system integration. Entity-relationship diagrams delineate the entities, attributes, and relationships within a data model, facilitating the design and implementation of database systems and data warehouses.

Best practices for effective documentation entail the use of standardized notations and modeling languages, ensuring clarity, consistency, and comprehensiveness in articulating business and system requirements. Business analysts should engage stakeholders in the review and validation of documentation, fostering a shared understanding and consensus on the depicted requirements. The utilization of documentation tools, such as Microsoft Visio, Enterprise Architect, and draw.io, augments the efficiency and accuracy of requirement documentation, enabling business analysts to create, collaborate, and iterate on requirement artifacts with precision and agility.

Requirements Gathering Methods

Requirements gathering encompasses a spectrum of methods and approaches for eliciting, analyzing, and prioritizing business and system requirements, culminating in the formulation of a comprehensive and coherent requirement specification. Business analysts leverage techniques such as workshops, surveys, observations, and prototyping to capture and validate requirements, aligning stakeholder needs with project objectives and technical constraints.

Workshops congregate stakeholders and subject matter experts in a collaborative setting, fostering the exchange of ideas, perspectives, and requirements through facilitated discussions, brainstorming sessions, and group activities. Surveys solicit feedback and input from a wide array of stakeholders, enabling business analysts to gather diverse perspectives and preferences in a structured and scalable manner. Observations entail firsthand immersion in the operational environment, enabling business analysts to glean insights into user behaviors, system interactions, and contextual factors that influence requirements. Prototyping involves the creation of mock-ups, wireframes, and interactive prototypes to visualize and validate system features, user interfaces, and workflow dynamics.

Best practices for requirements gathering encompass the tailoring of methods to the unique needs and characteristics of the project, ensuring the inclusivity of diverse stakeholders and the mitigation of bias in requirement elicitation. Business analysts should employ a mix of quantitative and qualitative methods to triangulate requirement data, fostering a comprehensive and nuanced understanding of user needs and system functionalities. The iterative and incremental nature of requirements gathering necessitates continuous stakeholder engagement, feedback solicitation, and validation of evolving requirements to adapt to changing business dynamics and technological landscapes.

Implications for Business Analysts

The adept utilization of interview, documentation, and requirements gathering techniques engenders several implications for business analysts, reshaping their roles, interactions, and contributions within organizations engaged in data analytics, data science, business intelligence, and AI projects.

Stakeholder Engagement and Collaboration: Interview, documentation, and requirements gathering techniques foster stakeholder engagement and collaboration, enabling business analysts to harness diverse perspectives, tacit knowledge, and emergent requirements to drive project success. Business analysts facilitate dialogues, bridge communication gaps, and coalesce stakeholder insights into coherent requirement artifacts, fostering a culture of inclusivity, empathy, and shared ownership of project deliverables.

Requirement Clarity and Validation: The adept application of documentation and requirements gathering techniques ensures the clarity, consistency, and validation of business and system requirements, aligning stakeholder expectations with project deliverables. Business analysts curate requirement artifacts, solicit stakeholder feedback, and iterate on requirement documentation to foster a shared understanding and consensus on project scope, objectives, and constraints.

Alignment with Project Objectives: Interview, documentation, and requirements gathering techniques enable business analysts to align stakeholder needs with project objectives, technical constraints, and strategic imperatives. Business analysts discern implicit requirements, prioritize critical functionalities, and synthesize diverse stakeholder perspectives into a coherent requirement specification that guides project planning, design, and implementation.

Adaptive Agility and Continuous Improvement: Interview, documentation, and requirements gathering techniques foster adaptive agility and continuous improvement by enabling business analysts to elicit, analyze, and validate evolving requirements in response to changing business dynamics and technological landscapes. Business analysts foster a culture of responsiveness, flexibility, and iterative refinement of requirements, propelling organizations towards operational excellence and competitive advantage.

Business Process Modeling and BPMN Tools

The realm of business analysis is a multifaceted landscape where the ability to model and analyze business processes plays a pivotal role in driving organizational efficiency and effectiveness. In this chapter, we delve into the intricacies of business process modeling and the tools that facilitate this essential aspect of business analysis. Business Process Model and Notation (BPMN) tools, such as Bizagi Modeler and Lucidchart, provide business analysts with the means to create detailed business process diagrams using standardized symbols, thereby aiding in the visualization and communication of workflows.

Bizagi Modeler: Orchestrating Business Process Excellence

Bizagi Modeler stands as a prominent BPMN tool, offering a comprehensive suite of features that empowers business analysts to model, analyze, and optimize business processes with precision and agility. The intuitive drag-and-drop interface of Bizagi Modeler simplifies the creation of BPMN diagrams, enabling business analysts to capture the intricacies of business processes through a visual representation that aligns with BPMN standards. The modularity and reusability of process components within Bizagi Modeler facilitate the decomposition of complex processes into manageable subprocesses, fostering a granular understanding of business workflows and their interdependencies.

The process simulation capabilities of Bizagi Modeler enable business analysts to assess the performance and efficiency of business processes in a risk-free environment, allowing for the identification of bottlenecks, redundancies, and optimization opportunities. By simulating various scenarios, business analysts can evaluate the impact of process modifications, resource reallocations, and workflow reengineering, thereby fostering a culture of continuous improvement and operational excellence within organizations.

Bizagi Modeler's seamless integration with enterprise architecture frameworks, such as TOGAF and ArchiMate, enables business analysts to align business process modeling with broader architectural principles, fostering coherence and synergy across organizational domains. The collaborative features of Bizagi Modeler, including real-time coauthoring and version control, facilitate interdisciplinary teamwork and knowledge exchange, propelling organizations towards business process excellence and adaptive agility.

Lucidchart: Visualizing Business Processes with Clarity

Lucidchart emerges as a versatile BPMN tool, equipping business analysts with the capability to create visually compelling business process diagrams that foster clarity, comprehension, and communication. The flexibility of Lucidchart's diagramming canvas enables business analysts to construct BPMN diagrams that encapsulate the intricacies of business processes, encompassing activities, gateways, events, and flows, thus providing stakeholders with a comprehensive view of organizational workflows and their interrelationships.

The collaborative nature of Lucidchart facilitates stakeholder engagement and knowledge dissemination, enabling business analysts to coalesce diverse perspectives into coherent process narratives that guide informed decision-making and strategic planning. The integration of Lucidchart with cloud platforms and productivity suites fosters seamless data interchange and accessibility, thereby ensuring the ubiquity of business process diagrams across organizational hierarchies.

Lucidchart's extensibility through integrations with project management tools, such as Jira and Trello, enables business analysts to align business process modeling with project execution, fostering a seamless transition from process design to operational implementation. The interactive features of Lucidchart, including comments, annotations, and real-time collaboration, engender stakeholder engagement and knowledge exchange, propelling organizations towards process-driven excellence and adaptive innovation.

Implications for Business Analysts

The utilization of BPMN tools, exemplified by Bizagi Modeler and Lucidchart, engenders several implications for business analysts, reshaping their roles, interactions, and contributions within organizations engaged in data analytics, data science, business intelligence, and AI projects.

Process Optimization and Efficiency: BPMN tools empower business analysts to model, analyze, and optimize business processes, thereby fostering operational efficiency, resource optimization, and adaptive agility within organizations. Business analysts leverage the capabilities of Bizagi Modeler and Lucidchart to identify bottlenecks, streamline workflows, and orchestrate process improvements that align with strategic objectives and operational imperatives.

Stakeholder Communication: BPMN tools facilitate stakeholder communication by enabling business analysts to create visually compelling business process diagrams that resonate with diverse audiences. Business analysts collaborate with stakeholders to understand their operational needs, tailoring BPMN diagrams to communicate process insights effectively and foster a culture of process-driven decision-making across organizational hierarchies.

Business Process Governance: The utilization of BPMN tools enables business analysts to govern business processes with precision and coherence, aligning process modeling with regulatory requirements, industry standards, and best practices. Business analysts leverage the modularity and reusability of process components within Bizagi Modeler and Lucidchart to ensure compliance, mitigate risks, and foster a culture of process-driven excellence and adaptive innovation.

Adaptive Agility and Continuous Improvement: BPMN tools foster adaptive agility and continuous improvement by enabling business analysts to simulate, analyze, and optimize business processes in a risk-free environment. Business analysts utilize the process simulation capabilities of Bizagi Modeler to evaluate the impact of process modifications, resource reallocations, and workflow reengineering, thereby fostering a culture of adaptive agility and operational excellence within organizations.

Integration with Enterprise Architecture: BPMN tools facilitate the integration of business process modeling with enterprise architecture frameworks, fostering coherence and synergy across organizational domains. Business analysts leverage the seamless integration of Bizagi Modeler with enterprise architecture frameworks to align business process modeling with broader architectural principles, ensuring the harmonization of business processes with organizational strategies and technological landscapes.

Fostering a Data-Centric Culture Within Organizations

In today's data-driven landscape, organizations are increasingly recognizing the transformative potential of fostering a data-centric culture. This session delves into the strategies and initiatives that business analysts (BAs) can undertake to cultivate an organizational environment that values data, promotes data-driven decision-making, encourages innovation, and strives for continuous improvement. Fostering a data-centric culture is not only about leveraging technology and analytics but also about instilling a mindset that embraces the power of data as a strategic asset for organizational success.

Training and Education

One of the fundamental pillars of fostering a data-centric culture within organizations is through investing in the training and education of BAs. Encouraging BAs to pursue training and formal qualifications in areas that bolster their ability to lead data-centric projects effectively is paramount. Training programs could encompass technical skills such as data analysis, data visualization, and statistical modeling, as well as soft skills including communication, stakeholder management, and change leadership. By equipping BAs with a robust skill set, organizations can empower them to drive data-centric initiatives with confidence and proficiency.

Creating a Career Development Plan

Guiding BAs on how to create a personal career development plan that aligns with their goals of leading data-driven projects and fostering a data-centric culture within their organizations is essential. A well-structured career development plan should outline the necessary skills, experiences, and knowledge that BAs need to cultivate to become effective leaders in data-centric environments. This plan should also encompass opportunities for mentorship, exposure to diverse projects, and continuous learning to ensure that BAs are equipped to navigate the complexities of data-driven initiatives and drive meaningful organizational change.

Leadership Commitment and Vision

Fostering a data-centric culture within organizations necessitates strong leadership commitment and a compelling vision that emphasizes the strategic importance of data. Leaders play a pivotal role in setting the tone for embracing data as a core organizational asset and promoting a culture of data-driven decision-making. This involves articulating a clear vision for how data will be leveraged to drive business outcomes, fostering a collaborative environment where data insights are valued, and championing initiatives that prioritize the ethical and responsible use of data. By aligning leadership commitment with a compelling vision, organizations can engender a culture that is inherently data-centric.

Empowering Data Literacy Across the Organization

Empowering individuals across the organization with data literacy is instrumental in fostering a data-centric culture. BAs can advocate for initiatives that promote data literacy, such as conducting training sessions, creating self-service analytics resources, and establishing communities of practice focused on data-related skills and knowledge sharing. By democratizing access to data and fostering a culture of curiosity and inquiry, organizations can cultivate a workforce that is adept at leveraging data to drive informed decision-making and innovation at all levels.

Establishing Data Governance Frameworks

Establishing robust data governance frameworks is pivotal in fostering a data-centric culture, ensuring that data is managed, protected, and utilized effectively. BAs can collaborate with cross-functional teams to define data governance policies, standards, and processes that govern the collection, storage, quality assurance, and access to data. By establishing clear guidelines for data usage, organizations can mitigate risks associated with data misuse, enhance data quality, and build trust in the data assets that underpin critical business decisions and initiatives.

Cultivating a Culture of Experimentation and Innovation

Encouraging a culture of experimentation and innovation is integral to fostering a data-centric environment. BAs can advocate for initiatives that promote agile methodologies, rapid prototyping, and iterative experimentation with data-driven solutions. By creating an environment that values learning from failures, embraces iterative improvement, and rewards innovative approaches to problem-solving, organizations can harness the full potential of data to drive transformative outcomes and stay ahead in a rapidly evolving business landscape.

Measuring and Communicating the Impact of Data

Measuring and communicating the impact of data initiatives is crucial in fostering a data-centric culture. BAs can collaborate with stakeholders to define key performance indicators (KPIs) that align with the strategic objectives of data-centric initiatives. By continuously monitoring and communicating the impact of data-driven projects on business outcomes, organizations can reinforce the value of data, garner support for ongoing initiatives, and demonstrate the tangible benefits of embracing a data-centric culture.

Building Your BA Career in Data Centric Projects

Skill Development

Foundational Knowledge:

To excel in the dynamic fields of data science and AI, business analysts (BAs) need to lay a strong foundation of knowledge. This includes a robust understanding of statistical analysis, programming languages such as Python or R, and a deep comprehension of machine learning algorithms. These skills are fundamental and provide the groundwork for further specialization and expertise in the field. It's essential for BAs to invest time and effort in mastering these foundational skills, as they form the building blocks for more advanced applications in data science and AI projects.

Practical Application:

While theoretical knowledge is crucial, the ability to apply this knowledge in real-world scenarios is equally important for BAs. Engaging in hands-on projects or internships allows BAs to gain practical experience and insight into the complexities of implementing data science and AI solutions. This hands-on experience not only enhances their skill set but also provides a valuable perspective on the challenges and opportunities within the field. By actively participating in practical applications, BAs can bridge the gap between theory and practice, preparing themselves for the demands of data science and AI projects in the real world.

Advancement through Certification

Certification Programs:

Pursuing specialized certification programs in data science and AI can significantly enhance the professional profile of BAs. These programs offer in-depth knowledge and practical skills that are highly valued in the industry. Certifications not only validate the expertise of BAs but also open doors to new career opportunities and often lead to higher earning potential. It's important for BAs to carefully consider reputable certification programs that align with their career goals and provide them with a competitive edge in the rapidly evolving landscape of data science and AI.

Continuous Learning:

The field of data science and AI is characterized by constant innovation and evolution. To stay relevant and competitive, BAs must be committed to continuous learning and professional development. Keeping abreast of the latest technologies, tools, and methodologies through ongoing education and training is essential for career growth. By embracing a mindset of continuous learning, BAs can adapt to emerging trends and advancements in the field, ensuring that their skills remain current and applicable to the ever-changing demands of data science and AI projects.

Exploring Career Paths and Opportunities

Career Stages:

Recognizing and understanding the different stages of a career in data science and AI is crucial for BAs. From establishment to advancement, maintenance, and potential withdrawal, each stage presents unique challenges and opportunities. By identifying the stage they are currently in and the stage they aspire to reach, BAs can create a targeted career development plan that aligns with their professional objectives. Understanding the distinct characteristics of each stage enables BAs to navigate their career trajectory strategically and make informed decisions about skill development, certification, and professional networking.

Diverse Roles:

The fields of data science and AI encompass a diverse range of roles, from Data Analysts and Data Scientists to Machine Learning Engineers and AI Researchers. BAs should explore these various roles to identify the best fit for their interests, skills, and long-term career aspirations. By gaining insight into the responsibilities, requirements, and growth opportunities associated with each role, BAs can make informed decisions about specialization and career progression within the dynamic landscape of data science and AI. Understanding the nuances of these roles empowers BAs to pursue paths that resonate with their professional aspirations and strengths.

Networking and Community Engagement:

Active engagement with the data science and AI community is invaluable for BAs. Participating in forums, attending conferences, and building professional networks within the industry provides access to valuable insights, mentorship opportunities, and potential career paths. Networking allows BAs to stay informed about industry trends, connect with professionals who can offer guidance and support, and explore collaborative opportunities. By actively engaging with the community, BAs can expand their knowledge, establish meaningful connections, and gain exposure to diverse perspectives that can enrich their career journey in data science and AI.

Emerging Trends in Business Analysis and Data Technology

Trends in Business Analysis

As businesses continue to navigate the ever-changing landscape of technology and data-driven decision-making, the role of the business analyst has evolved to become increasingly complex and dynamic. In response to the rapid advancements in data analytics, data science, business intelligence, and AI projects, the traditional responsibilities of business analysts have expanded to incorporate new techniques and methodologies. This chapter will explore the trends in business analysis and how professionals in this field are adapting to the demands of the modern business environment.

One of the most significant trends in business analysis is the integration of data analytics and data science into the traditional business analysis process. With the proliferation of big data and the increasing importance of data-driven insights, business analysts are now tasked with not only understanding business processes and requirements but also with leveraging data to drive strategic decision-making. This shift has led to the emergence of a new breed of business analysts who possess a strong foundation in statistical analysis, machine learning, and predictive modeling, allowing them to uncover valuable insights from complex data sets.

Furthermore, the adoption of agile methodologies has revolutionized the way business analysts approach project management and requirements gathering. Agile practices, such as scrum and kanban, have become widely embraced in the business analysis community due to their emphasis on iterative development, continuous feedback, and collaboration. Business analysts are now expected to work closely with cross-functional teams, engage in frequent stakeholder interactions, and adapt to changing project requirements in real-time. This agile mindset has enabled business analysts to deliver value more efficiently and effectively in today's fast-paced business environment.

In addition to embracing new methodologies, business analysts are also leveraging advanced technologies such as artificial intelligence and machine learning to enhance their analytical capabilities. Through the use of AI-powered tools, business analysts can automate repetitive tasks, identify patterns in data, and generate predictive insights at a scale that was previously unattainable. This has streamlined the analysis process, allowing business analysts to focus on interpreting the results and providing actionable recommendations to stakeholders.

Moreover, the role of the business analyst has expanded beyond traditional project-based work to encompass a strategic advisory function within organizations. As businesses increasingly recognize the importance of leveraging data to gain a competitive advantage, business analysts are being called upon to provide thought leadership and strategic guidance on how to best utilize data assets for business growth. This shift has elevated the status of business analysts within organizations, positioning them as critical contributors to decision-making at both tactical and strategic levels.

Another trend that is shaping the future of business analysis is the increasing emphasis on data governance and regulatory compliance. With the implementation of data privacy regulations such as the GDPR and the CCPA, business analysts are required to ensure that data collection, storage, and usage align with these stringent guidelines. This has led to a growing focus on data quality, data lineage, and metadata management, as business analysts play a pivotal role in ensuring that data is handled ethically and in compliance with regulatory requirements.

Furthermore, the rise of self-service analytics tools has empowered business analysts to explore and visualize data independently, reducing their reliance on IT departments for data access and manipulation. These tools enable business analysts to create interactive dashboards, conduct ad-hoc analysis, and share insights with stakeholders in a more agile and responsive manner. This democratization of data analytics has enabled business analysts to be more self-sufficient and has accelerated the pace at which insights are generated and acted upon.

In conclusion, the evolving role of business analysts in response to technological advancements has led to a paradigm shift in the way business analysis is conducted. From integrating data analytics and data science into the traditional business analysis process to embracing agile methodologies, leveraging advanced technologies, and assuming a strategic advisory function, business analysts are at the forefront of driving data-driven decision-making within organizations. As the business landscape continues to evolve, business analysts will need to remain agile, adaptable, and continuously upskill to meet the demands of the rapidly changing business environment.

Innovations in Data Analytics

As businesses continue to harness the power of data to drive decision-making and gain a competitive edge, the field of data analytics has witnessed a surge in innovations that are reshaping the way organizations extract value from their data assets. In this chapter, we will delve into the cutting-edge tools and practices that are transforming the landscape of data analytics, including predictive analytics, prescriptive analytics, and real-time data processing.

Predictive Analytics:

Predictive analytics has emerged as a powerful tool for organizations seeking to anticipate future trends and outcomes based on historical data and statistical algorithms. By leveraging machine learning models and advanced statistical techniques, predictive analytics enables business analysts to forecast future events, identify potential risks, and optimize business processes. From predicting customer churn and demand forecasting to identifying fraudulent activities, the applications of predictive analytics are far-reaching and continue to evolve with advancements in data science and technology.

One of the key innovations in predictive analytics is the integration of deep learning algorithms, which have shown remarkable success in handling complex and unstructured data to make accurate predictions. Deep learning models, such as neural networks, have demonstrated superior performance in image recognition, natural language processing, and pattern recognition, opening new frontiers for predictive analytics in diverse domains, including healthcare, finance, and e-commerce.

Prescriptive Analytics:

While predictive analytics focuses on forecasting future events, prescriptive analytics goes a step further by recommending actions and strategies to optimize outcomes based on the predicted scenarios. This innovative approach empowers business analysts to not only understand what is likely to happen but also determine the best course of action to achieve desired outcomes. By combining optimization algorithms, simulation modeling, and decision support systems, prescriptive analytics enables organizations to make data-driven decisions that maximize efficiency, minimize risks, and capitalize on opportunities.

Real-Time Data Processing:

In today's fast-paced business environment, the ability to process and analyze data in real time is critical for staying agile and responsive to rapidly changing market conditions. Real-time data processing technologies, such as stream processing and in-memory computing, have revolutionized the way organizations extract insights from high-velocity data streams, enabling them to make instant decisions, detect anomalies, and personalize customer experiences in real time. This innovation has significant implications for industries such as finance, telecommunications, and IoT, where timely insights can drive competitive advantage and operational excellence.

Moreover, the convergence of real-time data processing with edge computing has extended the capabilities of data analytics to the network edge, allowing organizations to analyze data closer to the source, reduce latency, and harness the power of distributed computing for mission-critical applications. This paradigm shift in data processing has paved the way for innovative solutions in areas such as predictive maintenance, autonomous vehicles, and smart infrastructure, where real-time insights are paramount for ensuring safety, efficiency, and reliability.

Ethical Considerations in Data Analytics:

Amidst the rapid advancements in data analytics, it is essential for organizations and business analysts to uphold ethical standards and data privacy principles. As the volume and variety of data continue to grow, ensuring the responsible and ethical use of data has become a pressing concern. Business analysts must be cognizant of the ethical implications of their data analytics practices, including the potential for algorithmic bias, data privacy violations, and the ethical considerations of deploying AI-powered decision-making systems.

Furthermore, the increasing focus on ethical data analytics has led to the development of tools and frameworks that promote transparency, fairness, and accountability in data-driven decision-making. Innovations such as explainable AI, privacy-preserving techniques, and ethical AI frameworks are shaping the future of data analytics by enabling organizations to leverage data responsibly while respecting the rights and interests of individuals and communities.

The Future of Data Analytics:

Looking ahead, the future of data analytics holds immense promise for organizations seeking to harness the power of data to drive innovation and strategic decision-making. As advancements in artificial intelligence, machine learning, and big data technologies continue to unfold, business analysts will be at the forefront of adopting and adapting these innovations to unlock new opportunities, mitigate risks, and drive sustainable growth.

In conclusion, the innovations in data analytics, including predictive analytics, prescriptive analytics, real-time data processing, and ethical considerations, are reshaping the way organizations leverage data to gain actionable insights and create value. By embracing these cutting-edge tools and practices, business analysts can position themselves as strategic partners in driving data-driven decision-making and shaping the future of business analytics in a rapidly evolving digital landscape.

AI Integration in Business Analysis

The landscape of business analysis is evolving at an unprecedented pace, and at the heart of this transformation lies artificial intelligence (AI). As we delve into the integration of AI in business analysis processes, it becomes clear that this technology is not just an adjunct tool but a fundamental game-changer. It revolutionizes automated decision-making, natural language processing, and cognitive computing, thereby reshaping how businesses approach problems and devise solutions.

Imagine a world where decision-making is not merely a product of human judgment but is significantly enhanced by AI. Automated decision-making systems, powered by AI, can analyze vast amounts of data in fractions of a second, making highly informed decisions almost instantaneously. These systems are not constrained by human limitations and can consider a broader range of factors and potential outcomes. But how does this impact businesses?

Consider the financial sector, where AI-driven decision-making can assess credit risk with remarkable precision. By analyzing data points beyond the traditional credit scores, including transaction histories, social media activity, and even typing patterns, AI can predict an applicant's creditworthiness with a depth and accuracy that were previously unattainable. This not only speeds up the decision-making process but also enables more nuanced and personalized decision-making.

Natural language processing (NLP) is another area where AI integration has made significant strides. NLP allows machines to understand, interpret, and respond to human language in a way that is both meaningful and contextually relevant. This capability transforms customer service interactions, enabling automated systems to handle inquiries, complaints, and transactions in a manner that closely mimics human agents.

But the implications extend beyond customer service. NLP is revolutionizing how businesses analyze textual data, extracting insights from customer reviews, social media posts, and even internal documents. For instance, sentiment analysis can gauge public opinion about a product or brand, providing businesses with valuable feedback that can guide marketing strategies and product development.

Cognitive computing, a subset of AI, simulates human thought processes in a computerized model. It involves self-learning systems that use data mining, pattern recognition, and natural language processing to mimic the way the human brain works. This approach enables businesses to tackle complex problems with a level of understanding and analysis previously reserved for human experts.

One particularly compelling application of cognitive computing is in the healthcare sector. By analyzing patient data, including medical histories, genetic information, and lifestyle factors, cognitive systems can assist in diagnosing diseases and recommending personalized treatment plans. This not only enhances patient care but also paves the way for breakthroughs in medical research.

But what does the integration of AI into business analysis mean for the workforce? Does it herald the obsolescence of human analysts? Quite the contrary.

AI systems excel at processing and analyzing data, but they lack the innate human abilities of creativity, empathy, and ethical judgment. Therefore, the future of business analysis is not about replacing human analysts with machines but rather about leveraging AI to augment human capabilities. Analysts equipped with AI tools can achieve insights of greater depth and breadth, enabling more informed decision-making and innovative problem-solving.

Imagine the synergy of human and machine working together. An analyst identifies a complex business problem, formulates hypotheses, and then uses AI to rapidly test these hypotheses against vast datasets. The AI system provides insights and predictions, which the analyst then interprets and contextualizes, considering the nuances of human behavior and societal trends. This collaboration between human and machine unlocks new possibilities, driving businesses forward with strategies that are both data-driven and deeply human-centric.

In conclusion, the integration of AI in business analysis is not just a technological advancement; it is a paradigm shift. It opens new horizons for automated decision-making, natural language processing, and cognitive computing, transforming how businesses understand their customers, markets, and internal processes. But amidst this technological revolution, the human element remains central. The future of business analysis lies in the harmonious integration of AI and human intelligence, a partnership that promises to redefine the boundaries of what is possible.

As we stand at the cusp of this new era, one question looms large: How will we navigate the challenges and opportunities presented by AI in business analysis? The answer lies in embracing change, fostering innovation, and remembering that at the heart of every technological advancement is the pursuit of understanding and improving the human experience.

The journey of translating business strategy into powerful data solutions is both thrilling and daunting. But one thing is clear: the future is bright for those ready to embrace the transformative power of AI in business analysis.

Future Predictions for Business Analysis

The horizon of business analysis is expanding, moving towards a future where data analytics, the Internet of Things (IoT), and machine learning play pivotal roles in defining industry practices and job functions. As we venture into this uncharted territory, the question arises: how will these technological advancements shape the landscape of business analysis?

In the realm of big data, the volume, velocity, and variety of information being generated are staggering. Every click, swipe, and interaction contributes to this ever-expanding sea of data. Herein lies an opportunity for business analysts to dive deep, extracting pearls of insight that can drive strategic decisions and foster innovation. But, to navigate these waters successfully, analysts must adapt, developing skills in data science and analytics that complement their traditional expertise.

Imagine a future where a business analyst, equipped with skills in both traditional analysis and data science, uncovers patterns in customer behavior that were previously invisible. By integrating data from diverse sources—social media posts, sensor data from IoT devices, transaction records—they reveal a comprehensive view of the customer journey. This depth of insight enables businesses to personalize products and services, enhancing customer satisfaction and loyalty.

But what role does the IoT play in this future? The proliferation of connected devices is generating a torrent of real-time data, offering a granular view of how products are used and how services are consumed. Analysts, by leveraging this data, can not only monitor performance but also predict future trends and behaviors. For instance, a manufacturing company could use IoT data to anticipate equipment failures before they occur, minimizing downtime and maintaining productivity. This proactive approach, powered by the insights of business analysts, transforms how companies operate, making them more agile and responsive.

Machine learning, meanwhile, is redefining the boundaries of what's possible in data analysis. By automating the identification of patterns and anomalies, machine learning enables analysts to focus on higher-level tasks—formulating strategic questions, interpreting data in the context of business goals, and crafting narratives that drive action. The synergy between machine learning and human analysis enhances the accuracy and relevance of insights, empowering businesses to make decisions with unprecedented speed and confidence.

But how will these technological shifts impact job roles in business analysis? Far from rendering human analysts obsolete, the future highlights the unique value of human intuition, creativity, and ethical judgment. Analysts will become orchestrators of technology, guiding machine learning algorithms, interpreting their outputs, and ensuring that analyses are aligned with business objectives and ethical standards. This evolution of the analyst role underscores the importance of lifelong learning, adaptability, and cross-disciplinary collaboration.

Consider the ethical implications of automated decision-making. As algorithms play a larger role in business analysis, ensuring fairness, transparency, and accountability becomes paramount. Analysts, therefore, must develop a keen understanding of the ethical dimensions of their work, advocating for practices that respect individual rights and promote social good. This ethical compass will be critical as businesses navigate the complexities of a data-driven world.

The future of business analysis is also marked by collaboration. Analysts, data scientists, IoT experts, and machine learning engineers will form interdisciplinary teams, pooling their knowledge to tackle complex challenges. These collaborations will break down silos, fostering a culture of innovation and continuous improvement. As these teams work together, they will craft solutions that are not only technologically advanced but also deeply attuned to human needs and values.

In conclusion, the future of business analysis is both exciting and challenging. As big data, IoT, and machine learning reshape industry practices, analysts will play a crucial role in guiding businesses through this transformation. By embracing new skills, fostering collaboration, and upholding ethical standards, analysts will ensure that the future of business is not only intelligent but also humane and just.

As we stand on the brink of this new era, one thing is certain: the journey of translating business strategy into powerful data solutions is a journey of continuous learning, adaptation, and innovation. The road ahead is filled with opportunities for those willing to embrace change and harness the power of technology to create a better, smarter future.

Further Reading

Introduction to Business Analysis in Data-Driven Projects

- **BABOK Guide v3.** International Institute of Business Analysis. (2015). A Guide to the Business Analysis Body of Knowledge (BABOK Guide).
- **Ward, J., & Peppard, J.** (2016). The Strategic Management of Information Systems: Building a Digital Strategy. Wiley.

Data Science Fundamentals

- **Provost, F., & Fawcett, T.** (2013). Data Science for Business: What You Need to Know about Data Mining and Data-Analytic Thinking. O'Reilly Media.
- **James, G., Witten, D., Hastie, T., & Tibshirani, R.** (2013). An Introduction to Statistical Learning. Springer.

Data Analytics Essentials

- **Davenport, T.H., & Kim, J.** (2013). Keeping Up with the Quants: Your Guide to Understanding and Using Analytics. Harvard Business Review Press.
- **Few, S.** (2009). Now You See It: Simple Visualization Techniques for Quantitative Analysis. Analytics Press.

Business Intelligence in Modern Business Analysis

- **Loshin, D.** (2012). Business Intelligence: The Savvy Manager's Guide. Morgan Kaufmann.
- **Howson, C., & Levine, B.** (2020). Successful Business Intelligence: Unlock the Value of BI & Big Data. McGraw-Hill Education.

Artificial Intelligence Basics

- **Russell, S., & Norvig, P.** (2016). Artificial Intelligence: A Modern Approach. Pearson.
- **Copeland, M.** (2016). "What's the Difference Between Artificial Intelligence, Machine Learning, and Deep Learning?" NVIDIA Blog.

Agile Business Analysis

- **Cohn, M.** (2004). User Stories Applied: For Agile Software Development. Addison-Wesley Professional.
- **Rubin, K.S.** (2012). Essential Scrum: A Practical Guide to the Most Popular Agile Process. Addison-Wesley Professional.

Data Governance and Compliance

- **Otto, B.** (2016). "The Importance of Data Governance in Healthcare." Journal of AHIMA.
- **Tallon, P.** (2019). "Data Governance: How to Approach It and How to Make It Work." Journal of

Information Technology.

Emerging Trends in Business Analysis and Data Technology

- **Davenport, T.H.** (2018). "The AI Advantage: How to Put the Artificial Intelligence Revolution to Work." MIT Press.
- **Marr, B.** (2020). Tech Trends in Practice: The 25 Technologies That Are Driving the 4th Industrial Revolution. Wiley.

Introduction to Business Analysis in Data-Driven Projects

- **Lapão, L. V.** (2019). "Digital Transformation in Healthcare: A Contribution to a Systematic Review." *Technology and Health Care*, 27(S1), 101-112. https://pubmed.ncbi.nlm.nih.gov/30909185/
- **Reinsel, D., Gantz, J., & Rydning, J.** (2020). *The Digitization of the World from Edge to Core*. IDC. https://www.seagate.com/files/www-content/our-story/trends/files/idc-seagate-dataage-whitepaper.pdf

Data Science Fundamentals

- **Breiman, L.** (2001). "Statistical Modeling: The Two Cultures." *Statistical Science*, 16(3), 199-231. https://projecteuclid.org/euclid.ss/1009213726
- **Blei, D. M., & Smyth, P.** (2017). "Science and Data Science." *Proceedings of the National Academy of Sciences*, 114(33), 8689-8692. https://www.pnas.org/content/114/33/8689

Data Analytics Essentials

- **Davenport, T.H.** (2013). "Analytics 3.0." *Harvard Business Review*. https://hbr.org/2013/12/analytics-30
- **KDNuggets**. "Data Visualization in Analytics." https://www.kdnuggets.com/data-visualization

Business Intelligence in Modern Business Analysis

- **Gartner Magic Quadrant for Analytics and Business Intelligence Platforms**. (2021). https://www.gartner.com/en/documents/3994102
- **Eckerson, W. W.** (2020). "The Rise of Self-Service Business Intelligence." *Eckerson Group*. https://www.eckerson.com/articles/the-rise-of-self-service-business-intelligence

Artificial Intelligence Basics

- **Ng, A.** (2016). "What Artificial Intelligence Can and Can't Do Right Now." *Harvard Business Review*. https://hbr.org/2016/11/what-artificial-intelligence-can-and-cant-do-right-now
- **Tegmark, M.** (2018). "Life 3.0: Being Human in the Age of Artificial Intelligence." Knopf.

Agile Business Analysis

- **VersionOne 14th Annual State of Agile Report**. (2020). https://stateofagile.versionone.com/
- **Leffingwell, D.** (2011). "Agile Software Requirements: Lean Requirements Practices for Teams, Programs, and the Enterprise." Addison-Wesley Professional.

Data Governance and Compliance

- **Data Governance Institute**. "What is Data Governance?" https://www.datagovernance.com/adg_data_governance_definition/
- **Kelleher, J.D., & Tierney, B.** (2018). "Data Science." MIT Press. (Chapter on Data Ethics and Privacy)

Emerging Trends in Business Analysis and Data Technology

- **Forbes Technology Council**. (2021). "15 Top Tech Trends That Will Shape The Business World In 2021 And Beyond." Forbes. https://www.forbes.com/sites/forbestechcouncil/2021/01/04/15-top-tech-trends-that-will-shape-the-business-world-in-2021-and-beyond/
- **Morgan, B.** (2019). "Top 10 Digital Transformation Trends For 2021." Forbes. https://www.forbes.com/sites/blakemorgan/2020/10/25/top-10-digital-transformation-trends-for-2021/

About the Author

Ikwe Gideon, a distinguished expert in data analytics and technology, boasts over two decades of experience across various sectors. Holding a Master's in Data Science from Cardiff University and certifications such as Microsoft's Power BI Data Analyst Associate, he excels at converting complex data sets into actionable strategic insights. Gideon has led BI strategies, fraud detection, and risk management projects for prominent organizations including Shop City Marketplace, Airtel Africa, Mcel Mozambique, and MCCI Iran. As a published author, he imparts wisdom on data-driven decision-making, the application of AI/ML, and adhering to ethical data practices for enhancing business performance. A visionary thought leader, Gideon is dedicated to equipping professionals with the transformative potential of analytics.

www.ingramcontent.com/pod-product-compliance
Lightning Source LLC
Chambersburg PA
CBHW062102220526
45471CB00010B/3575